Spatial Analytics with ArcGIS

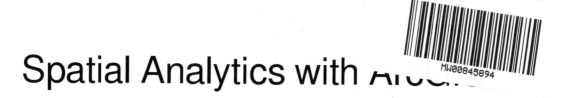

Use the spatial statistics tools provided by ArcGIS and build your own to perform complex geographic analysis

Eric Pimpler

BIRMINGHAM - MUMBAI

Spatial Analytics with ArcGIS

First published: April 2017

Production reference: 1200417

Published by Packt Publishing Ltd.
Livery Place
35 Livery Street
Birmingham
B3 2PB, UK.

ISBN 978-1-78712-258-1

www.packtpub.com

Credits

Author
Eric Pimpler

Reviewer
Ken Doman

Commissioning Editor
Aaron Lazar

Acquisition Editor
Vinay Argekar

Content Development Editor
Zeeyan Pinheiro

Technical Editor
Vibhuti Gawde

Copy Editor
Pranjali Chury

Project Coordinator
Vaidehi Sawant

Proofreader
Safis Editing

Indexer
Mariammal Chettiyar

Graphics
Abhinash Sahu

Production Coordinator
Aparna Bhagat

About the Author

Eric Pimpler is the founder and owner of GeoSpatial Training Services (`geospatialtraining.com`) and has over 20 years of, experience implementing and teaching GIS solutions using open source technology, ESRI and Google Earth/Maps. Currently, he focuses on ArcGIS scripting with Python and the development of custom ArcGIS Server web and mobile applications using JavaScript.

Eric has a bachelor's degree in geography from Texas A&M University and a master's degree in applied geography with a concentration in GIS from Texas State University.

Eric is the author of *Programming ArcGIS with Python Cookbook* (`https://www.packtpub.com/application-development/programming-arcgis-python-cookbook-second-edition`), first and second edition, *Building Web* (`https://www.packtpub.com/application-development/building-web-and-mobile-arcgis-server-applications-javascript`) and *Mobile ArcGIS Server Applications with JavaScript*, and *ArcGIS Blueprints* (`https://www.packtpub.com/application-development/arcgis-blueprints`), all by Packt Publishing.

About the Reviewer

Ken Doman is a senior frontend engineer at GEO Jobe, a software development company and ESRI business partner that helps public sector organizations and private sector businesses get the most out of geospatial solutions. Ken has worked with web and geospatial solutions for local and county government, and private industry for over 9 years.

Ken is the author of *Mastering ArcGIS Server Development with JavaScript*. He has also reviewed several books for Packt Publishing, including *Building Web and Mobile ArcGIS Server Applications with JavaScript* by Eric Pimpler and *ArcGIS for Desktop Cookbook* by Daniela Christiana Docan.

I'd like to thank my wife for putting up with the late nights while I reviewed books and videos. I would also like to thank GEO Jobe and all my previous employers, Bruce Harris and Associates, City of Plantation, Florida, and the City of Jacksonville, Texas. You all gave me opportunities to learn and work in a career that I enjoy. I would like to thank Packt Publishing, who found me when I was a simple blogger and social media junkie, and let me have a place to make a positive impact in GIS. Finally, I would like to thank the one from whom all blessings flow.

www.PacktPub.com

For support files and downloads related to your book, please visit www.PacktPub.com.

Did you know that Packt offers eBook versions of every book published, with PDF and ePub files available? You can upgrade to the eBook version at www.PacktPub.com and as a print book customer, you are entitled to a discount on the eBook copy. Get in touch with us at service@packtpub.com for more details.

At www.PacktPub.com, you can also read a collection of free technical articles, sign up for a range of free newsletters and receive exclusive discounts and offers on Packt books and eBooks.

https://www.packtpub.com/mapt

Get the most in-demand software skills with Mapt. Mapt gives you full access to all Packt books and video courses, as well as industry-leading tools to help you plan your personal development and advance your career.

Why subscribe?

- Fully searchable across every book published by Packt
- Copy and paste, print, and bookmark content
- On demand and accessible via a web browser

Customer Feedback

Thanks for purchasing this Packt book. At Packt, quality is at the heart of our editorial process. To help us improve, please leave us an honest review on this book's Amazon page at `https://www.amazon.com/dp/https://www.amazon.com/dp/1787123081`.

If you'd like to join our team of regular reviewers, you can e-mail us at `customerreviews@packtpub.com`. We award our regular reviewers with free eBooks and videos in exchange for their valuable feedback. Help us be relentless in improving our products!

Table of Contents

Preface

The Spatial Statistics toolbox in ArcGIS contains a set of tools for analyzing spatial distributions, patterns, processes, and relationships. While similar to traditional statistics, spatial statistics are a unique set of analyses that incorporate geography. These tools can be used with all license levels of ArcGIS Desktop and are a unique way of exploring the spatial relationships inherent in your data. In addition to using ArcBridge, the R programming language can now be used with ArcGIS Desktop to provide customized statistical analysis and tools.

Spatial Analytics in ArcGIS begins with an introduction to the field of spatial statistics. After this brief introduction ,we'll examine increasingly complex spatial statistics tools. We'll start by covering the tools found in the Measuring Geographic Distributions toolset, which provide descriptive spatial statistical information. Next, the Analyzing Patterns toolset will teach the reader how to evaluate datasets for clustering, dispersion, or random patterns. As we move on, you will also be introduced to much more advanced and interesting spatial statistical analysis, including hot spot analysis, similarity search, and least squares regression among others.

After an exhaustive look at the Spatial Statistics Tools toolbox, you will be introduced to the R programming language and you'll learn how to use ArcGIS Bridge to create custom R tools in ArcGIS Desktop.

In the final two chapters of the book, you'll apply the new skills you've learned in the book to solve case studies. The first case study will apply spatial statistics tools and the R programming language to the analysis of crime data. The final chapter of the book will introduce you to the application of spatial statistics to the analysis of real estate data.

What this book covers

Chapter 1, *Introduction to Spatial Statistics in ArcGIS and R*, contains an introduction to spatial statistics, an overview to the Spatial Statistics Tools toolbox in ArcGIS, and an introduction to R and the R-ArcGIS Bridge.

Chapter 2, *Measuring Geographic Distributions with ArcGIs Tools*, covers the basic descriptive spatial statistics tools available through the Spatial Statistics Tools toolset, including the Mean and Median Feature, Central Feature, Linear Directional Distribution, Standard Distribution, and Directional Distribution tools.

Chapter 3, *Analyzing Patterns with ArcGIS Tools*, covers tools that evaluate whether features or the values associated with features form clustered, dispersed, or random spatial patterns. They also define the degree of clustering. These are inferential statistics that define the probability of how confident we are that the pattern is dispersed or clustered. The output is a single result for the entire dataset. Tools covered in this chapter include Average Nearest Neighbor, High/Low Clustering, Spatial Autocorrelation, Multi-Distance Spatial Cluster Analysis, and Spatial Autocorrelation.

Chapter 4, *Mapping Clusters with ArcGIS Tools*, covers the use of various clustering tools. Clustering tools are used to answer not only the question of *Is there clustering?* and *Where is the clustering?* but also *Is the Clustering Statistically Significant?* Tools covered in this chapter include Cluster and Outlier Analysis, Grouping Analysis, Hot Spot Analysis, Optimized Hot Spot Analysis, and Similarity Search.

Chapter 5, *Modeling Spatial Relationships with ArcGIS Tools*, shows how beyond analyzing spatial patterns, GIS analysis can be used to examine or quantify relationships among features. The Modeling Spatial Relationships tools construct spatial weights matrices or model spatial relationships using regression analyses. Tools covered in this chapter include Ordinary Least Squares (OLS), Geographically Weighted Regression, and Exploratory Regression.

Chapter 6, *Working with the Utilities Toolset*, covers the utility scripts that perform a variety of data conversion tasks. These tools can be used in conjunction with other tools in the Spatial Statistics Tools toolbox. Tools covered in this chapter include Calculate Areas, Calculate Distance Band from Neighbor Count, Collect Events, and Export Feature Attribute to ASCI.

Chapter 7, *Introduction to the R Programming Language*, covers the basics of the R programming language for performing spatial statistical programming. You will learn how to create variables and assign data to variables, create and use functions, work with data types and data classes, read and write data, load spatial data, and create basic plots.

Chapter 8, *Creating Custom ArcGIS Tools with the ArcGIS Bridge and R*, covers the R-ArcGIS Bridge, which is a free, open source package that connects ArcGIS and R. Using the Bridge allows developers to create custom tools and toolboxes in ArcGIS that integrate R with ArcGIS to build spatial statistical tools. In this chapter, you will learn how to install the R-ArcGIS Bridge and build custom ArcGIS Tools using R.

Chapter 9, *Application of Spatial Statistics to Crime Analysis*, shows you how to apply the Spatial Statistics tools and R programming language to the analysis of crime data. After finding and downloading a crime dataset for a major U.S. city, you will perform a variety of spatial analysis techniques using ArcGIS and R.

Chapter 10, *Application of Spatial Statistics to Real Estate Analysis,* teaches you how to apply the Spatial Statistics tools and R programming language to the analysis of real estate data. After downloading a real estate dataset for a major U.S. city, you will perform a variety of spatial analysis techniques.

What you need for this book

To complete the exercises in this book, you will need to have installed ArcGIS for Desktop 10.2 or higher with the Basic, Standard, or Advanced license level. We recommend that you use ArcGIS Desktop 10.4 or 10.5. In addition to this, you will also need to install R. Instructions for installing R are provided in Chapter 7, *Introduction to the R Programming Language.*

Who this book is for

Spatial Analytics with ArcGIS is written for intermediate to advanced level GIS professionals who want to use spatial statistics to resolve complex geographic questions.

Conventions

In this book, you will find a number of text styles that distinguish between different kinds of information. Here are some examples of these styles and an explanation of their meaning.

Code words in text, database table names, folder names, filenames, file extensions, pathnames, dummy URLs, user input, and Twitter handles are shown as follows: "Use the **Select by Attributes...** tool to select all records where the OFFENSE_CATEGORY_ID ='burglary' method, as shown in the following screenshot."

A block of code is set as follows:

```
ozone.file = system.file("extdata",
"ca_ozone_pts.shp", package="arcgisbinding")
d = arc.open(ozone.file)
cat('all fields: ', names(d@fields, fill = TRUE)
#print all fields
```

New terms and **important words** are shown in bold. Words that you see on the screen, for example, in menus or dialog boxes, appear in the text like this: "In the **Table Of Contents** pane, right-click on the `Crime` layer and select **Properties....**"

Warnings or important notes appear in a box like this.

Tips and tricks appear like this.

Reader feedback

Feedback from our readers is always welcome. Let us know what you think about this book-what you liked or disliked. Reader feedback is important for us as it helps us develop titles that you will really get the most out of.

To send us general feedback, simply e-mail `feedback@packtpub.com`, and mention the book's title in the subject of your message.

If there is a topic that you have expertise in and you are interested in either writing or contributing to a book, see our author guide at `www.packtpub.com/authors`.

Customer support

Now that you are the proud owner of a Packt book, we have a number of things to help you to get the most from your purchase.

Downloading the example code

You can download the example code files for this book from your account at `http://www.packtpub.com`. If you purchased this book elsewhere, you can visit `http://www.packtpub.com/support` and register to have the files e-mailed directly to you.

You can download the code files by following these steps:

1. Log in or register to our website using your e-mail address and password.
2. Hover the mouse pointer on the **SUPPORT** tab at the top.
3. Click on **Code Downloads & Errata**.

4. Enter the name of the book in the **Search** box.
5. Select the book for which you're looking to download the code files.
6. Choose from the drop-down menu where you purchased this book from.
7. Click on **Code Download**.

Once the file is downloaded, please make sure that you unzip or extract the folder using the latest version of:

- WinRAR / 7-Zip for Windows
- Zipeg / iZip / UnRarX for Mac
- 7-Zip / PeaZip for Linux

The code bundle for the book is also hosted on GitHub at `https://github.com/PacktPubl ishing/Spatial-Analytics-with-ArcGIS`. We also have other code bundles from our rich catalog of books and videos available at `https://github.com/PacktPublishing/`. Check them out!

Downloading the color images of this book

We also provide you with a PDF file that has color images of the screenshots/diagrams used in this book. The color images will help you better understand the changes in the output. You can download this file from `http://www.packtpub.com/sites/default/files/downl oads/SpatialAnalyticswithArcGIS_ColorImages.pdf`.

Errata

Although we have taken every care to ensure the accuracy of our content, mistakes do happen. If you find a mistake in one of our books-maybe a mistake in the text or the code-we would be grateful if you could report this to us. By doing so, you can save other readers from frustration and help us improve subsequent versions of this book. If you find any errata, please report them by visiting `http://www.packtpub.com/submit-errata`, selecting your book, clicking on the **Errata Submission Form** link, and entering the details of your errata. Once your errata are verified, your submission will be accepted and the errata will be uploaded to our website or added to any list of existing errata under the Errata section of that title.

To view the previously submitted errata, go to `https://www.packtpub.com/books/conten t/support` and enter the name of the book in the search field. The required information will appear under the **Errata** section.

Piracy

Piracy of copyrighted material on the Internet is an ongoing problem across all media. At Packt, we take the protection of our copyright and licenses very seriously. If you come across any illegal copies of our works in any form on the Internet, please provide us with the location address or website name immediately so that we can pursue a remedy.

Please contact us at copyright@packtpub.com with a link to the suspected pirated material.

We appreciate your help in protecting our authors and our ability to bring you valuable content.

Questions

If you have a problem with any aspect of this book, you can contact us at questions@packtpub.com, and we will do our best to address the problem.

1
Introduction to Spatial Statistics in ArcGIS and R

Spatial statistics are a set of exploratory techniques for describing and modeling spatial distributions, patterns, processes, and relationships. Although spatial statistics are similar to traditional statistics, they also integrate spatial relationships into the calculations. In spatial statistics, proximity is important. Things that are closer together are more related.

ArcGIS includes the **Spatial Statistics Tools** toolbox available for all license levels of its desktop software. Included with this toolbox are a number of toolsets that help analyze spatial distributions, patterns, clustering, and relationships in GIS datasets. This book will cover each of the toolsets provided with the Spatial Statistics Tools toolbox in ArcGIS to provide a comprehensive survey of the spatial statistics tools available to ArcGIS users.

The R platform for data analysis is a programming language and software platform for statistical computing and graphics, and it is supported by the R Foundation for Statistical Computing. The R language is widely used among statisticians and data analysts for developing statistical software and data analysis. In addition, R can be used for spatial statistical analysis and can also be integrated with ArcGIS through the R-ArcGIS Bridge.

This book also contains an introductory chapter for the R programming language as well as a chapter that covers the installation of the R-ArcGIS Bridge and the creation of custom ArcGIS script tools written with R.

In this chapter, we will cover the following topics:

- Introduction to spatial statistics
- An overview of the Spatial Statistics Tools toolbox in ArcGIS
- An overview of the integration between R and ArcGIS

Introduction to spatial statistics

Let's start with a definition of spatial statistics. The GIS dictionary (`http://gisgeography.com/gis-dictionary-definition-glossary/`) defines spatial statistics as the field of study concerning statistical methods that use space and spatial relationships (such as distance, area, volume, length, height, orientation, centrality, and/or other spatial characteristics of data) directly in their mathematical computations. Spatial statistics are used for a variety of different types of analyses, including pattern analysis, shape analysis, surface modeling and surface prediction, spatial regression, statistical comparisons of spatial datasets, statistical modeling and prediction of spatial interaction, and more. The many types of spatial statistics include descriptive, inferential, exploratory, geostatistical, and econometric statistics.

Spatial statistics are applicable across a wide range of environmental disciplines, including agriculture, geology, soil science, hydrology, ecology, oceanography, forestry, meteorology, and climatology, among others. Many socio-economic disciplines including epidemiology, crime analysis, real estate, planning, and others also benefit from spatial statistical analysis.

Spatial statistics can give answers to the following questions:

- How are the features distributed?
- What is the pattern created by the features?
- Which are the clusters?
- How do patterns and clusters of different variables compare to one another?
- What is the relationship between sets of features or values?

An overview of the Spatial Statistics Tools toolbox in ArcGIS

The ArcGIS Spatial Statistics Tools toolbox is available for all license levels of ArcGIS Desktop, including basic, standard, and advanced. The toolbox includes a number of toolsets, which are as follows:

- The **Analyzing Patterns** toolset
- The **Mapping Clusters** toolset
- The **Measuring Geographic Distributions** toolset
- The **Modeling Spatial Relationships** toolset

The Measuring Geographic Distributions toolset

The **Measuring Geographic Distributions** toolset in the **Spatial Statistics Tools** toolbox contains a set of tools that provide descriptive geographic statistics, including the **Central Feature**, **Directional Distribution**, **Linear Directional Mean**, **Mean Center**, **Median Center**, and **Standard Distance** tools. Together, this toolset provides a set of basic statistical exploration tools. These basic descriptive statistics are used only as a starting point in the analysis process. The following screenshot displays the output from the **Directional Distribution** tool for an analysis of crime data:

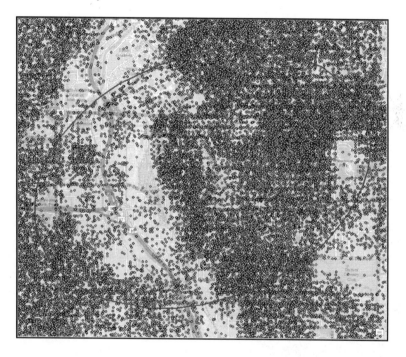

The **Central Feature**, **Mean Center**, and **Median Center** tools all provide similar functionality. Each creates a feature class containing a single feature that represents the centrality of a geographic dataset.

The **Linear Directional Mean** tool identifies the mean direction, length, and geographic center for a set of lines. The output of this tool is a feature class with a single linear feature.

The **Standard Distance** and **Directional Distribution** tools are similar, in that they both measure the degree to which features are concentrated or dispersed around the geometric center, but the **Directional Distribution** tool, also known as the **Standard Deviational Ellipse**, is superior as it also provides a measure of directionality in the dataset.

The Analyzing Patterns toolset

The **Analyzing Patterns** toolset in the **Spatial Statistics Tools** toolbox contains a series of tools that help evaluate whether features or the values associated with features form a clustered, dispersed, or random spatial pattern. These tools generate a single result for the entire dataset in question. In addition, the result does not take the form of a map, but rather statistical output, as shown in the following screenshot:

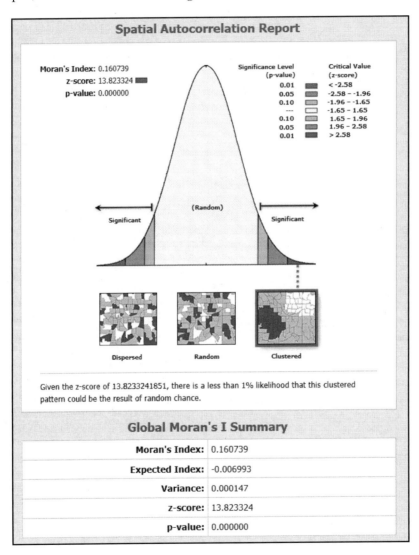

Tools in this category generate what is known as inferential statistics or the probability of how confident we are that the pattern is either dispersed or clustered. Let's examine the following tools found in the **Analyzing Patterns** toolset:

- **Average Nearest Neighbor**: This tool calculates the nearest neighbor index based on the average distance from each feature to its nearest neighboring feature. For each feature in a dataset, the distance to its nearest neighbor is computed. An average distance is then computed. The average distance is compared to the expected average distance. In doing so, an ANN ratio is created, which in simple terms is the observed/expected. If the ratio is less than 1, we can say that the data exhibits a clustered patterns, whereas a value greater than 1 indicates a dispersed pattern in our data.

- **Spatial Autocorrelation**: This tool measures spatial autocorrelation by simultaneously measuring feature locations and attribute values. If features that are close together have similar values, then that is said to be clustering. However, if features that are close together have dissimilar values then they form a dispersed pattern. This tool outputs a Moran's I index value along with a z-score and a p-value.

- **Spatial Autocorrelation (Morans I)**: This tool is similar to the previous tools, but it measures spatial autocorrelation for a series of distances and can create an optional line graph of those distances along with their corresponding z-scores. This tool is similar to the new **Optimized Hot Spot** tool and isn't used as frequently anymore as a result. This tool is often used as a distance aid for other tools such as **Hot Spot Analysis** or **Point Density**.

- **High/Low Clustering (Getis-Ord General G)**: This looks for high value clusters and low value clusters. It is used to measure the concentration of high or low values for a given study area and return the Observed General G, Expected General G, z-score, and p-value. It is most appropriate when there is a fairly even distribution of values.

- **Multi-Distance Spatial Cluster Analysis (Ripleys K Function)**: This determines whether feature locations show significant clustering or dispersion. However, unlike the other spatial pattern tools that we've examined in this section, it does not take the value at a location into account. It only determines clustering by the location of the features. This tool is often used in fields such as environmental studies, health care, and crime where you are attempting to determine whether one feature attracts another feature.

The Mapping Clusters toolset

The **Mapping Clusters** toolset is probably the most well-known and commonly used toolset in the **Spatial Statistics Tools** toolbox, and for a good reason. The output from these tools is highly visual and beneficial in the analysis of clustering phenomena. There are many examples of clustering: housing, businesses, trees, crimes, and many others. The degree of this clustering is also important. The tools in the **Mapping Clusters** toolset don't just answer the question *Is there clustering?*, but they also take on the question of *Where is the clustering?*

Tools in the **Mapping Clusters** toolset are among the most commonly used in the **Spatial Statistics Tools** toolbox:

- **Hot Spot Analysis**: This tool is probably the most popular tool in the Spatial Statistics Tools toolbox, and given a set of weighted features, it will identify statistically hot and cold spots using the `Getis-Ord Gi*` statistics, as shown in the output of real estate sales activity in the following screenshot:

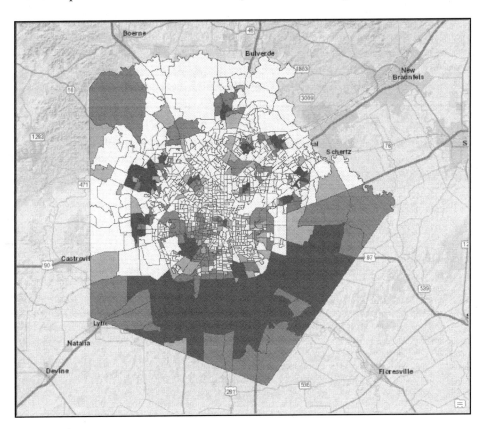

- **Similarity Search**: This tool is used to identify candidate features that are most similar or most dissimilar to one or more input features by the attributes of a feature. Dissimilarity searches can be equally as important as similarity searches. For example, a community development organization, in its attempts to attract new businesses, might show that their city is dissimilar to other competing cities when comparing crimes.

- **Grouping Analysis**: This tool groups features based on feature attributes, as well as optional spatial/temporal constraints. The output of this tool is the creation of distinct groups of data where the features that are part of the group are as similar as possible and between groups are as dissimilar as possible. An example is displayed in the following screenshot. The tool is capable of multivariate analysis and the output is a map and a report. The output map can have either contiguous groups or non-contiguous groups:

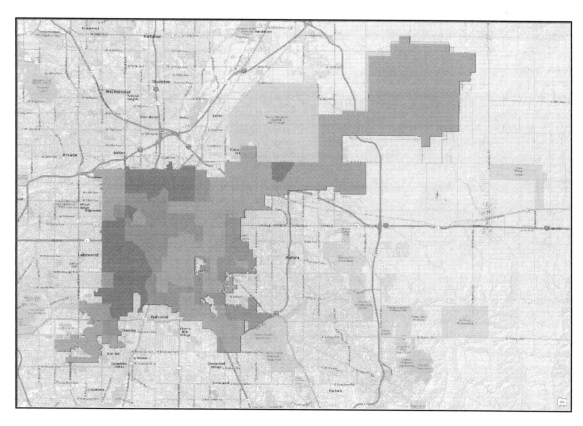

- **Cluster and Outlier Analysis**: The final tool in the **Mapping Clusters** toolset is the **Cluster and Outlier Analysis** tool. This tool, in addition to performing hot spot analysis, identifies outliers in your data. Outliers are extremely relevant to many types of analyses. The tool starts by separating features and neighborhoods from the study area. Each feature is examined against every other feature to see whether it is significantly different from the other features. Likewise, each neighborhood is examined in relationship to all other neighborhoods to see whether it is statistically different than other neighborhoods. An example of the output from the **Cluster and Outlier Analysis** tool is provided in the following screenshot:

The Modeling Spatial Relationships toolset

The **Modeling Spatial Relationships** toolset contains a number of regression analysis tools that help you examine and/or quantify the relationships between features. They help measure how features in a dataset relate to each other in space.

The regression tools provided in the **Spatial Statistics Tools** toolbox model relationships among data variables associated with geographic features, allowing you to make predictions for unknown values or to better understand key factors influencing a variable you are trying to model. Regression methods allow you to verify relationships and to measure how strong those relationships are. The **Exploratory Regression** tool allows you to examine a large number of **Ordinary Least Squares** models quickly, summarize variable relationships, and determine whether any combination of candidate explanatory variables satisfy all of the requirements of the OLS method.

There are two regression analysis tools in ArcGIS which are as follows:

- **Ordinary Least Squares**: This tool is a linear regression tool used to generate predictions or model a dependent variable in terms of its relationships to a set of explanatory variables. OLS is the best-known regression technique and provides a good starting point for spatial regression analysis. This tool provides a global model of a variable or process you are trying to understand or predict. The result is a single regression equation that depicts a positive or negative linear relationship. The following screenshot depicts partial output from the OLS tool:

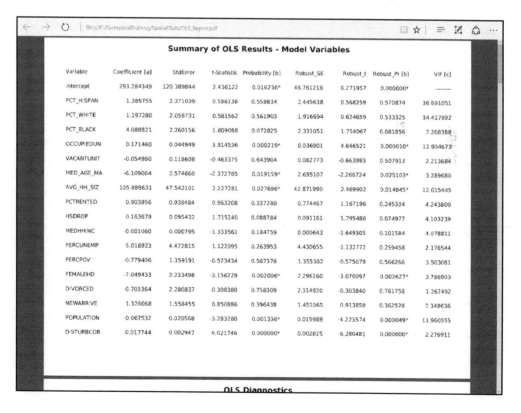

Variable	Coefficient [a]	StdError	t-Statistic	Probability [b]	Robust_SE	Robust_t	Robust_Pr [b]	VIF [c]
Intercept	293.284349	120.389844	2.436122	0.016236*	46.761216	6.271957	0.000000*	-------
PCT_HISPAN	1.389755	2.371039	0.586138	0.558834	2.445638	0.568259	0.570874	36.691051
PCT_WHITE	1.197280	2.058731	0.581562	0.561903	1.916694	0.624659	0.533325	34.417892
PCT_BLACK	4.088821	2.260156	1.809088	0.072825	2.331051	1.754067	0.081856	7.208388
OCCUPIEDUN	0.171460	0.044949	3.814536	0.000219*	0.036901	4.646521	0.000010*	12.904671
VACANTUNIT	-0.054960	0.118608	-0.463375	0.643904	0.082773	-0.663983	0.507913	2.213684
MED_AGE_MA	-6.109064	2.574660	-2.372765	0.019159*	2.695107	-2.266724	0.025103*	3.289680
AVG_HH_SIZ	105.889631	47.542101	2.227281	0.027696*	42.871990	2.469902	0.014845*	12.015445
PCTRENTED	0.903956	0.938484	0.963208	0.337280	0.774467	1.167196	0.245334	4.243800
HSDROP	0.163679	0.095432	1.715140	0.088784	0.091161	1.795488	0.074977	4.103239
MEDHHINC	-0.001060	0.000795	-1.333561	0.184759	0.000643	-1.649305	0.101584	4.078811
PERCUNEMP	5.018923	4.472815	1.122095	0.263953	4.430655	1.132772	0.259458	2.176544
PERCPOV	-0.779406	1.359191	-0.573434	0.567376	1.355302	-0.575079	0.566266	3.503081
FEMALEHD	-7.049433	2.233498	-3.156229	0.002006*	2.296160	-3.070097	0.002627*	3.786903
DIVORCED	-0.703364	2.280837	-0.308380	0.758309	2.314920	-0.303840	0.761758	1.267492
NEWARRIVE	1.326068	1.558455	0.850886	0.396438	1.451065	0.913858	0.362528	2.348636
POPULATION	-0.067532	0.020568	-3.283280	0.001336*	0.015989	-4.223574	0.000049*	11.960555
DISTURBCOR	-0.017744	0.002947	-6.021746	0.000000*	0.002825	-6.280481	0.000000*	2.276911

Summary of OLS Results - Model Variables

OLS Diagnostics

- **Geographically Weighted Regression**: **Geographically Weighted Regression** or GWR is a local form of linear regression for modeling spatially varying relationships. Note that this tool does require an Advanced ArcGIS license. GWR constructs a separate equation for each feature and is most appropriate when you have several hundred features. GWR creates an output feature class (shown in the following screenshot) and table. The output table contains a summary of the tool execution. When running GWR, you should use the same explanatory variables that you specified in your OLS model:

  The **Modeling Spatial Relationships** toolset also includes the **Exploratory Regression** tool.

- **Exploratory Regression**: This tool can be used to evaluate combinations of exploratory variables for OLS models that best explain the dependent variable. This data-mining tool does a lot of the work for you for finding variables that are well suited and can save you a lot of time finding the right combination of variables. The results of this tool are written to the progress dialog, result window, and an optional report file. An example of the output from the **Exploratory Regression** tool can been seen in the following screenshot:

Exploratory Regression

Completed

[x]

Close

<< Details

☐ Close this dialog when completed successfully

```
Executing: ExploratoryRegression Denver_Census_Tracts_Burglary NormBurg
PCT_HISPAN;PCT_WHITE;PCT_BLACK;OCCUPIEDUN;VACANTUNIT;MED_AGE_MA;AVG_HH_SIZ;PctRented;HSDrop;MedHHInc;Per
cUnemp;PercPov;FemaleHd;Divorced;NewArrive;POPULATION;DistUrbCor # C:\GeospatialTraining\SpatialStats
\ExploratoryRegression.txt # 5 1 0.5 0.05 7.5 0.1 0.1
Start Time: Sun Dec 04 20:24:32 2016
Running script ExploratoryRegression...
******************************************************************************
Choose 1 of 17 Summary
     Highest Adjusted R-Squared Results
AdjR2   AICc    JB K(BP)  VIF   SA   Model
 0.34 1835.75 0.01  0.01 1.00 0.00  -DISTURBCOR***
 0.29 1845.87 0.23  0.00 1.00 0.00  +PCTRENTED***
 0.13 1876.66 0.06  0.00 1.00 0.00  +NEWARRIVE***
     Passing Models
AdjR2 AICc JB K(BP) VIF SA  Model


******************************************************************************
Choose 2 of 17 Summary
          Highest Adjusted R-Squared Results
AdjR2    AICc   JB K(BP)  VIF   SA   Model
 0.43 1816.31 0.06  0.01 1.30 0.00  +PCTRENTED***   -DISTURBCOR***
 0.41 1820.54 0.01  0.00 1.00 0.00  -MEDHHINC***   -DISTURBCOR***
 0.40 1824.16 0.00  0.46 1.00 0.00  +OCCUPIEDUN***  -DISTURBCOR***
     Passing Models
AdjR2 AICc JB K(BP) VIF SA  Model


******************************************************************************
Choose 3 of 17 Summary
               Highest Adjusted R-Squared Results
AdjR2    AICc   JB K(BP)  VIF   SA   Model
 0.47 1807.36 0.00  0.06 1.00 0.00  +OCCUPIEDUN***  -MEDHHINC***   -DISTURBCOR***
 0.46 1809.47 0.02  0.08 1.36 0.00  +OCCUPIEDUN***  +PCTRENTED***  -DISTURBCOR***
 0.45 1811.49 0.02  0.08 1.20 0.00  -MEDHHINC***   -FEMALEHD***   -DISTURBCOR***
     Passing Models
AdjR2 AICc JB K(BP) VIF SA  Model


******************************************************************************
Choose 4 of 17 Summary
               Highest Adjusted R-Squared Results
AdjR2    AICc   JB K(BP)  VIF   SA   Model
 0.48 1804.47 0.04  0.26 1.37 0.00  +PCTRENTED***  +HSDROP***  -FEMALEHD***   -DISTURBCOR***
 0.48 1804.82 0.00  0.19 1.38 0.00  +OCCUPIEDUN***  -MEDHHINC***  -FEMALEHD**   -DISTURBCOR***
 0.48 1805.18 0.01  0.05 2.00 0.00  +OCCUPIEDUN***  +PCTRENTED**  -MEDHHINC***  -DISTURBCOR***
     Passing Models
AdjR2 AICc JB K(BP) VIF SA  Model


******************************************************************************
Choose 5 of 17 Summary
               Highest Adjusted R-Squared Results
AdjR2    AICc   JB K(BP)  VIF   SA   Model
```

Integrating R with ArcGIS

The R Project for Statistical Computing, or simply referred to as R, is a free software environment for statistical computing and graphics. It is also a programming language that is widely used among statisticians and data miners for developing statistical software and data analysis.

Although there are other programming languages for handling statistics, R has become the de facto language of statistical routines, offering a package repository with over 6,400 problem solving packages. It offers versatile and powerful plotting. It also has the advantage of treating tabular and multidimensional data as a labeled, indexed series of observations.

The R-ArcGIS Bridge is a free, open source R package that connects ArcGIS and R. It was released together with an R ArcGIS community website on GitHub, encouraging collaboration between the two communities. The package serves the following three purposes:

- ArcGIS developers can now create custom tools and toolboxes that integrate ArcGIS and R
- ArcGIS users can access R code through geoprocessing scripts
- R users can access GIS data managed in traditional GIS ways

This book incudes an introductory chapter on the R language along with a chapter detailing the installation of the RÂArcGIS Bridge and the creation of custom ArcGIS script tools using R. Using R with ArcGIS Bridge enables the creation of custom ArcGIS tools that will connect GIS data sources, such as feature classes to create statistical output from the R programming language, as shown in the following screenshot:

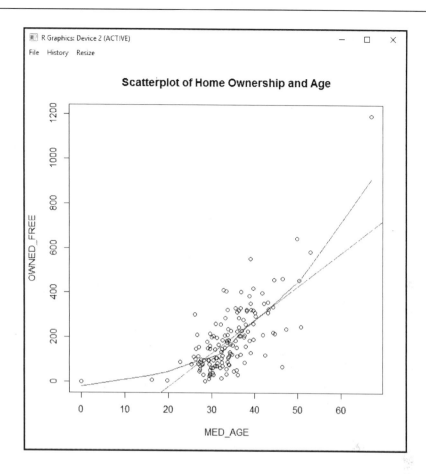

Summary

In this chapter, we introduced the topic of spatial statistics and described its basic characteristics. We also briefly reviewed the spatial statistics tools provided by ArcGIS Desktop. In later chapters, we will dive into these tools for a deeper understanding of the functionality they provide. In the next chapter, we'll examine the tools provided by the **Measuring Geographic Distributions** toolbox.

2

Measuring Geographic Distributions with ArcGIS Tools

Obtaining basic spatial statistics about a dataset is often the first step in the analysis of geographic data. The **Measuring Geographic Distributions** toolset in the ArcGIS **Spatial Statistics Tools** toolbox contains a set of tools that provide descriptive geographic statistics including the **Central Feature**, **Directional Distribution**, **Linear Directional Mean**, **Mean Center**, **Median Center**, and **Standard Distance**. Together, this toolset provides a set of basic statistical exploration tools.

In this chapter, you will learn how to use many of these tools to obtain basic spatial statistical information about a dataset, including the following topics:

- Measuring geographic centrality with the **Central Feature**, **Mean Center**, and **Median Center** tools
- Measuring the degree to which features are concentrated or dispersed around the geometric mean center with the **Standard Distance** tool
- Summarizing spatial characteristics of geographic features, including central tendency, dispersion, and directional trends, with the directional distribution or standard deviational ellipse tool

Measuring geographic centrality

In this exercise, all three tools will be used to obtain descriptive spatial statistics about crime data for the city of Denver.

Preparation

Let's get prepared for obtaining spatial statistical information about a dataset using ArcGIS, as follows:

1. In **ArcMap**, open the
   `C:\GeospatialTraining\SpatialStats\DenverCrime.mxd` file. You should see a point feature class called `Crime`, as shown in the following screenshot:

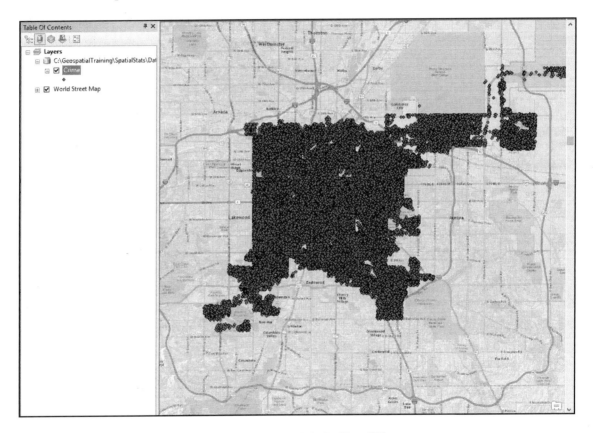

Point locations for all crimes for the city of Denver 2013

2. The `Crime` feature class contains point locations for all crimes for the city of Denver in 2013. The first thing we need to do is isolate a type of crime for our analysis. Open the attribute table for the crime feature class.

3. Use the **Select by Attributes...** tool to select all records where the
   `OFFENSE_CATEGORY_ID ='burglary'` method, as shown in the following
   screenshot. This will select 25,743 burglaries from the dataset. These are
   burglaries within the city limits of Denver in 2013:

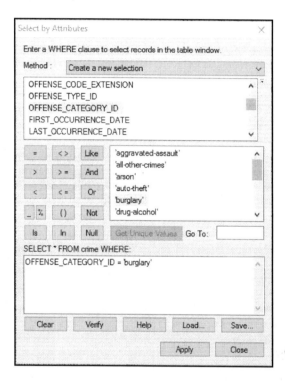

4. Close the attribute table. In the **Table Of Contents** pane, right-click on the `Crime`
   layer and select **Properties....** Go to the **Source** tab and note that the value of
   Geographic Coordinate System is `GCS_WGS_1984`. Data is often stored in this
   WGS84 Web Mercator coordinate system for display purposes on the Web.

> The WGS84 Web Mercator coordinate system, which is so popular today
> for online mapping applications, is not suitable for use with the spatial
> statistics tools. These tools require accurate distance measurements that
> aren't possible with WGS84 Web Mercator. So, it's important to project
> your datasets to a coordinate system that supports accurate distance
> measurements. The Web Mercator coordinate system supports accurate
> directions, but this analysis requires accurate distance measurements.

Take a look at the following screenshot:

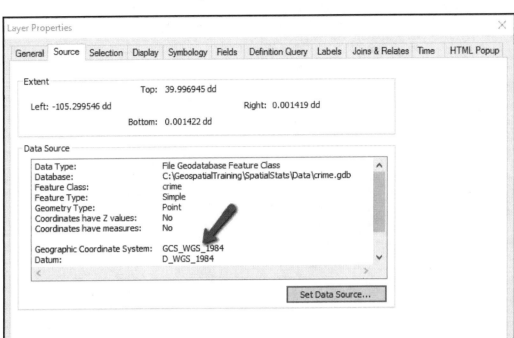

5. Close this dialog by clicking on the **Cancel** button. Now, right-click on the **Layers** data frame and select **Properties...** and then **Coordinate System**. The current coordinate system of the data frame should be set to NAD_1983_UTM_Zone_13N, which is acceptable for our analysis.

6. With the records from the crime layer still selected, right-click on the layer and navigate to **Data | Export Data....** The next dialog is very important. Click on **the data frame** as the coordinate system, as shown in the following screenshot. Name the layer Burglary and export it to the crime geodatabase in C:\GeospatialTraining\SpatialStats\Data\crime.gdb and then click on the **OK** button.

7. The new burglary layer will be added to the **Layers** data frame. Rename the layer to `Denver Burglary`:

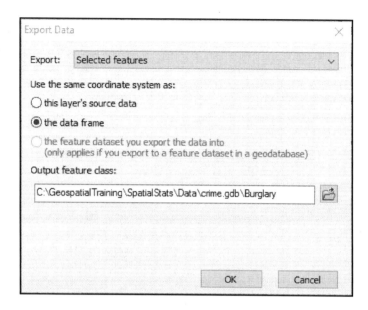

8. You can now remove the `Crime` layer.
9. Save your map document file.

Running the Central Feature tool

The **Central Feature** tool identifies the most centrally located feature from a point, line, or polygon feature class. It sums the distances from each feature to every other feature. The one with the shortest distance is the central feature.

This tool creates an output feature class containing a single feature that represents the most centrally located feature. For example, if you have a feature class of burglaries, the **Central Feature** tool will identify the crime location that is the central most location from the group and it will create a new feature class with a single point feature that represents this location.

Let's take a look at the following steps to learn to run the **Central Feature** tool:

1. If necessary, open **ArcToolbox** and find the **Spatial Statistics Tools** toolbox. Open the toolbox and expand the **Measuring Geographic Distributions** toolset. Double-click on **Central Feature** to display the tool, as shown in the following screenshot:

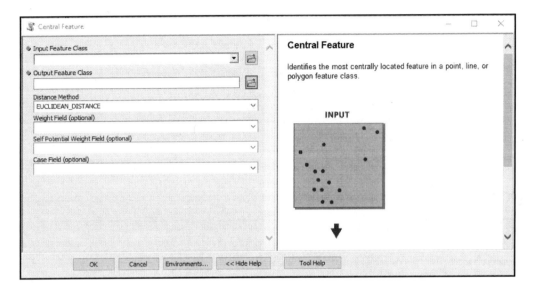

2. Select Denver Burglary as the **Input Feature Class**, C:\GeospatialTraining\SpatialStats\Data\crime.gdb\Burglary_Cent ralFeature as the **Output Feature Class**, and EUCLIDEAN_DISTANCE as the **Distance Method**. Euclidean distance is a straight-line distance between two points. The other distance method is Manhattan distance, which is the distance between two points, measured along axes at right angles and it is calculated by summing the difference between the x and y coordinates.

3. There are three optional parameters for the **Central Feature** tool, which are **Weight Field (optional)**, **Self Potential Weight Field (optional)**, and **Case Field (optional)**. We won't use any of these optional parameters for this analysis, but they do warrant an explanation:

    • **Weight Field (optional)**: This parameter is a numeric field used to weight distances in the origin-destination matrix. For example, if you had a dataset containing real estate sales information, each point might contain a sales price. The sales price could be used to weight the output of the Central Feature tool.

- **Self Potential Weight Field (optional)**: This is a field representing self-potential or the distance or weight between a feature and itself.
- **Case Field (optional):** This parameter is a field used to group features for separate central feature computations. This field can be an integer, data, or string.

4. Click on the **OK** button.

5. The most centrally located burglary will be displayed as shown in the following screenshot. The output is a single point feature:

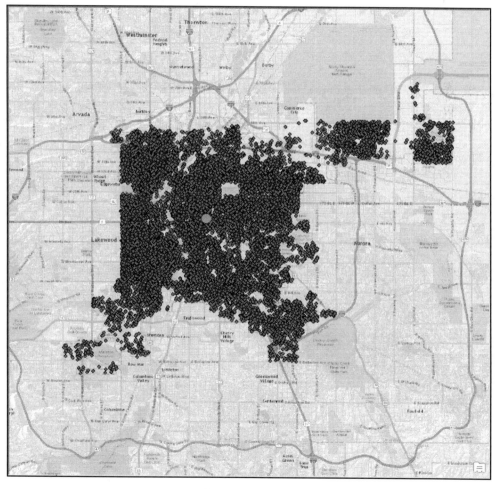

Most centrally located burglary

Running the Mean Center tool

The **Mean Center** tool calculates the geographic center for a set of features and it can also be weighted by a numeric field. One thing to keep in mind when using this tool is that outliers can dramatically alter the mean. So if your data contains outliers, you might be better off using the **Median Center** tool discussed in the *Running the Median Center tool* section.

Let's take a look at the following steps, which will help you to run the **Mean Center** tool:

1. If necessary, open **ArcToolbox** and find the **Spatial Statistics Tools** toolbox. Open the toolbox and expand the **Measuring Geographic Distributions** toolset. Double-click on **Mean Center** to display the tool, as shown in the following screenshot:

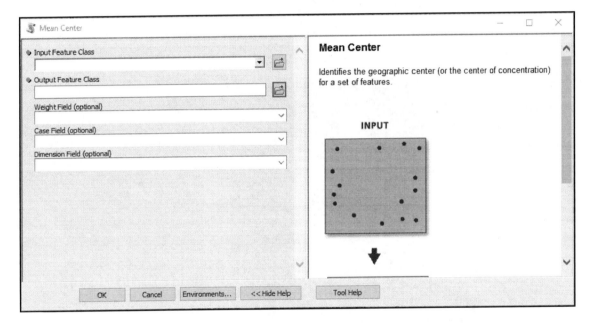

2. Select Denver Burglary as the **Input Feature Class** and C:\GeospatialTraining\SpatialStats\Data\crime.gdb\Burglary_Mean Center as the **Output Feature Class**. Click on the **OK** button. The output feature class will contain a single point location, as shown in the following screenshot. In this case, the point generated by the **Central Feature** tool is also displayed so that you can see the difference:

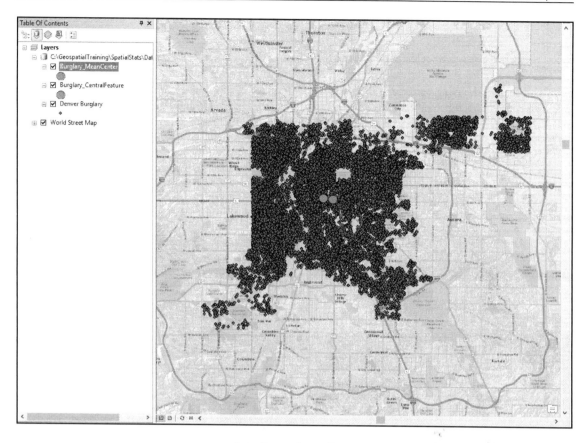

Geographic centers for a set of features

Running the Median Center tool

The **Median Center** tool identifies the location from a feature class that minimizes the overall Euclidean distance to the features in a dataset. Unlike the **Mean Center** tool, the **Median Center** tool is not as affected by outliers.

Let's take a look at the following steps to run the **Median Center** tool:

1. If necessary, open **ArcToolbox** and look for the **Spatial Statistics Tools** toolbox. Open the toolbox and expand the **Measuring Geographic Distributions** toolset. Double-click on **Median Center** to display the tool, as shown in the following screenshot:

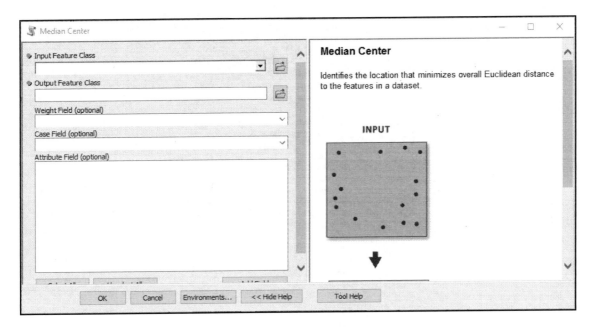

2. Select `Denver Burglary` as the **Input Feature Class** and `C:\GeospatialTraining\SpatialStats\Data\crime.gdb\Burglary_Medi anCenter` as the **Output Feature Class**. Click on the **OK** button. The output feature class will contain a single point location, as shown in the following screenshot. In this case, we have continued to display the points generated by the **Central Feature** and **Mean Center** tools that we ran in the last section so that you can see the difference. In this case, the **Median Center** tool is almost exactly the same as the **Central Feature** tool:

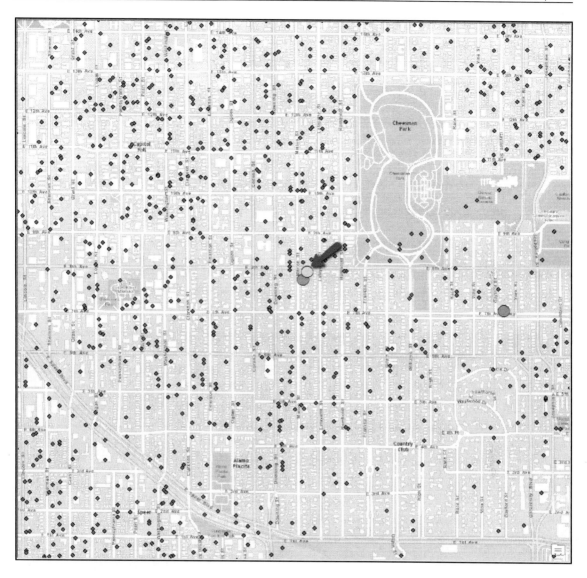

3. Save the map document file before exiting **ArcMap**.

The Standard Distance and Directional Distribution tools

The **Standard Distance** tool measures the degree to which features are concentrated or dispersed around the geometric mean center. It shows the concentration or dispersal of data. The output circle created by this tool is defined by standard deviation and can include one, two, or three standard deviations. In general, the larger the circle, the more dispersed the data.

The **Directional Distribution (Standard Deviational Ellipse)** tool creates standard deviation ellipses to summarize the spatial characteristics of geographic features, including central tendency, dispersion, and directional trends. The ellipses are centered on the mean center. This tool calculates directionality, centrality, and dispersion.

In this exercise, you'll learn how to use both tools.

Preparation

In **ArcMap**, open the C:\GeospatialTraing\SpatialStats\DenverCrime.mxd file. You should see a point feature class called Denver Burglary, as shown in the following screenshot. These are burglaries within the city limits of Denver in 2013. You should also see the point feature classes for the **Central Feature**, **Mean Center**, and **Median Center** tools that we generated in the last exercise:

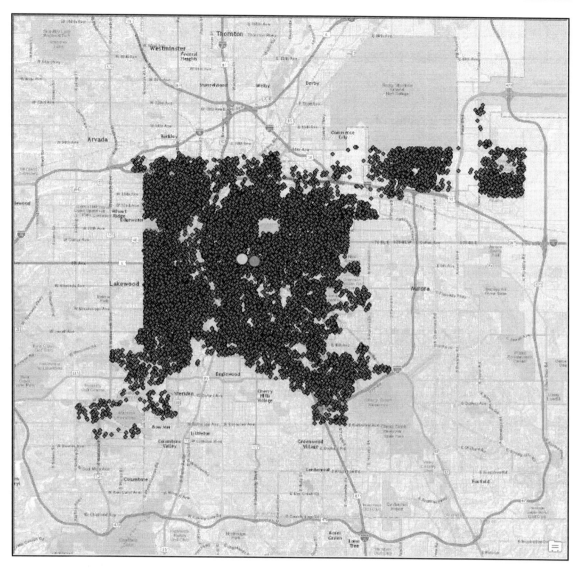

Burglaries in the city of Denver

Running the Standard Distance tool

Let's take a look at the following steps to run the **Standard Distance** tool:

1. If necessary, open **ArcToolbox** and look for the **Spatial Statistics Tools** toolbox. Open the toolbox and expand the **Measuring Geographic Distributions** toolset. Double-click on **Standard Distance** to display the tool.

2. Select `Denver Burglary` as the **Input Feature Class**, `C:\GeospatialTraining\SpatialStats\Data\crime.gdb\Burglary_Stan dardDeviation` as the **Output Standard Distance Feature Class**, and a **Circle Size** of `1_STANDARD_DEVIATION`. Click on the **OK** button to execute the tool.

3. **Weight Field (optional)** and **Case Field (optional)** are optional parameters that we will not use in this instance. These fields were described in the *Running the Central Feature tool* section. Take a look at the following screenshot:

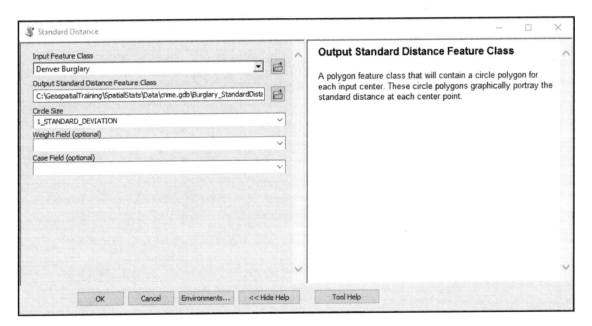

4. A new feature class will be created with a single circular polygon, as shown in the following screenshot. This circle represents the extent of data that falls within one standard deviations of the mean:

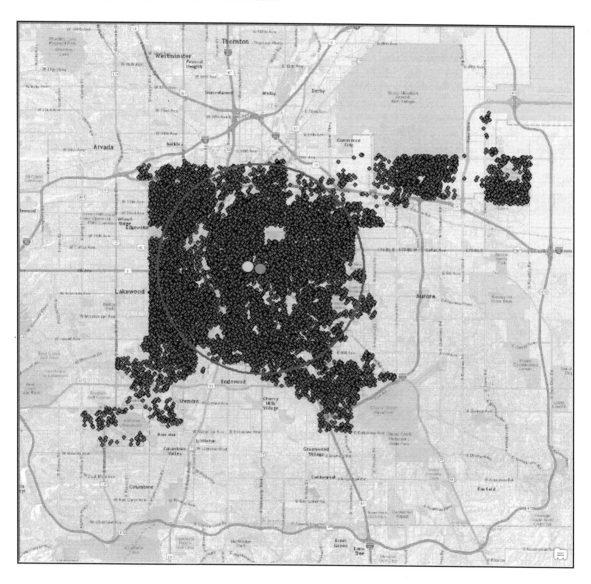

5. Let's see how many features the circle contains-it should be around 68%. Open the **Select by Location...** tool by navigating to **Selection | Select by Location...** on the **ArcMap** menu. Check `Denver Burglary` under **Target layer(s)** and select `Burglary_StandardDistance` as the **Source layer**, as shown in the following screenshot:

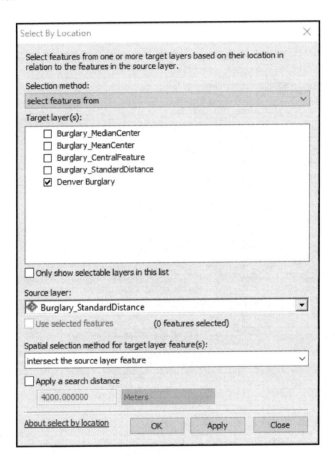

6. Click on the **OK** button to execute the tool. The number of features selected should be 18,220. There are 25,743 features in the layer. This is roughly 70% of the features, which is close to the 68% expected for a single standard deviation. This is quite a large circle for the study area involved, so we can generally say that our data is widely dispersed.

7. Run the **Standard Distance** tool again, but this time use 2 Standard Deviations. The result should be a circle that contains roughly 95% of the features.

Running the Directional Distribution tool

The **Directional Distribution** tool is an improvement over the **Standard Distance** tool because it creates an ellipse that measures the directional trend in the data along with the central tendency and dispersion.

Take a look at the following steps to run the **Directional Distribution** tool:

1. Open the **Directional Distribution (Standard Deviational Ellipse)** tool and define `Denver Burglary` as the **Input Feature Class**, `C:\GeospatialTraining\SpatialStats\Data\crime.gdb\Burglary_Dire ctionalDistribution` as the **Output Ellipse Feature Class**, and `1_STANDARD_DEVIATION` as **Ellipse Size**. Click on the **OK** button to execute the tool, as shown in the following screenshot:

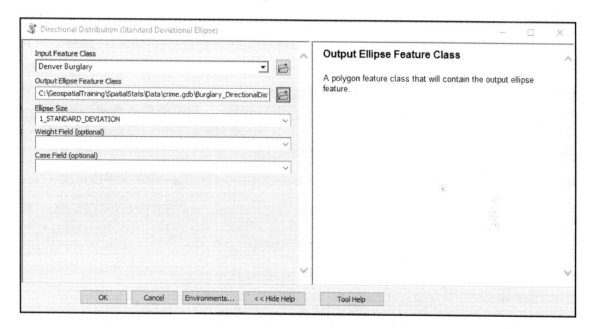

2. The output ellipse will appear as shown in the following screenshot. Note how the elliptical shape of the output gives us a sense of directionality. The data is still widely dispersed, but it gives us some indication of a southwest to northeast directionality.

3. Save your map document file when done:

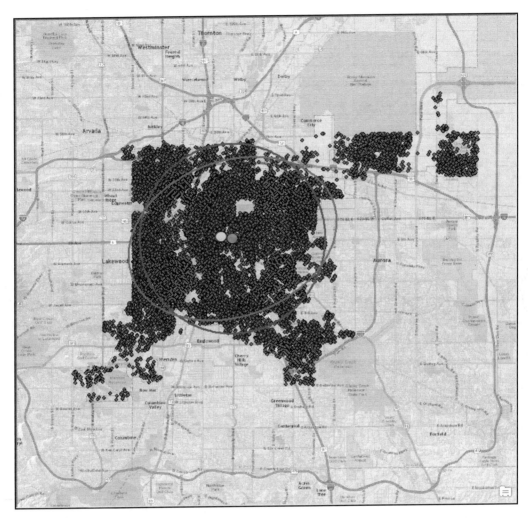

Summary

This chapter covered the use of a set of descriptive spatial statistics tools found in the **Measuring Geographic Distributions** toolset. These tools, including **Central Feature**, **Mean Center**, **Median Center**, **Standard Distance**, and **Directional Distribution**, return basic spatial statistical information about a dataset. The next chapter covers tools that analyze patterns in geographic datasets.

3
Analyzing Patterns with ArcGIS Tools

The **Analyzing Patterns** toolset in the **Spatial Statistics Tools** toolbox contains a series of tools that help evaluate if features or the values associated with features form a clustered, dispersed, or random spatial pattern. These tools generate a single result for the entire dataset in question. Tools in this category generate what is known as *inferential statistics* or the probability of how confident we are that the pattern is either dispersed or clustered.

In this chapter, you will learn how to use many of these tools to determine if a dataset is dispersed or clustered, including the following:

- Using the **Average Nearest Neighbor** tool
- Using the **Spatial Autocorrelation** tool to analyze patterns
- Using the **Multi-Distance Spatial Cluster Analysis** tool

The Analyzing Patterns toolset

The **Analyzing Patterns** toolset, found in the **Spatial Statistics Tools** toolbox and shown in the following screenshot, contains a set of tools that perform pattern analysis against a dataset. Each of these tools returns statistical information about the entire dataset. The output of these tools is not a map, but rather statistical information that helps determine if a dataset is clustered, dispersed, or has a random pattern.

To help interpret the results of these tools, this section will provide information about the null hypothesis, p-values, z-scores, and standard deviations.

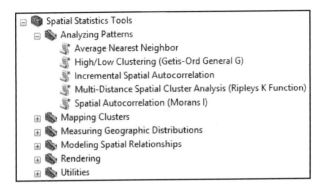

Understanding the null hypothesis

All the pattern analysis tools that we examine in this chapter work on the premise that our features or the values associated with those features are randomly distributed. This is known as **Complete Spatial Randomness (CSR)**. This is the null hypothesis used with all the ArcGIS spatial statistics tools.

The pattern analysis tools return z-scores and p-values. These scores tell us if we can reject the null hypothesis of CSR. If we're able to reject the null hypothesis, then we can say that our data is either clustered or dispersed in a statistically significant pattern, and this is an indicator of some sort of significant underlying process at work that has caused this pattern.

P-values

Let's first examine p-values. A p-value is a measure of probability that a random process created the observed spatial pattern. Small p-values are an indicator that the spatial pattern is not random. P-values range from 0 to 1 with a lower p-value indicating that the spatial value is not random. A confidence value can be assigned to various p-values, as shown in the following table:

P-value (Probability)	Confidence Level
< 0.10	90%
< 0.05	95%
< 0.01	99%

Z-scores and standard deviation

Z-scores are standard deviations, which are a measure of how many standard deviations away an element is from the mean. A z-score of **0** represents an element equal to the mean, while a score of **+2.5** would indicate that the element is **2.5** standard deviations away. These scores can be positive or negative. We can also associate z-scores with confidence levels just like we saw with p-values. A z-score of less than **-1.65** or greater than **+1.65** equates to a **90%** confidence level. A z-score of less than **-1.96** or greater than **+1.96** gives a confidence level of **95%**, and a z-score of less than **-2.58** or greater than **+2.58** gives a confidence level of **99%**:

Z-score (Standard Deviation)	Confidence Level
< -1.65 or > + 1.65	90%
< -1.96 or > + 1.96	95%
< -2.58 or > + 2.58	99%

Typically, the z-scores and p-values are analyzed together. In general, very high or low z-scores plus small p-values will allow us to consider rejecting the null hypothesis:

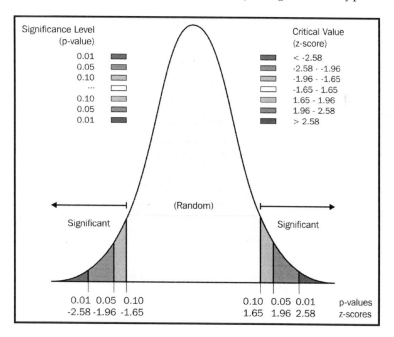

Rejecting the null hypothesis requires a subject judgment. You must determine what degree of risk you are willing to accept for being wrong. Before the pattern analysis tool is run, you will want to select a confidence value and not reject the null hypothesis unless the output matches or exceeds the confidence value. Typical confidence values include **90%**, **95%**, and **99%** with **99%** being the most conservative. In other words, if you selected a **99%** confidence level, you would not reject the null hypothesis unless the probability that the pattern was created by random chance is less than **1%**.

Using the Average Nearest Neighbor tool

The **Average Nearest Neighbor** tool calculates a nearest neighbor index based on the average distance from each feature to its nearest neighboring feature. For each feature in a dataset, the distance to its nearest neighbor is computed. An average distance is then computed.

The average distance is compared to the expected average distance. In doing so, an **Average Nearest Neighbor (ANN)** ratio is created which in simple terms is the ratio of observed/expected. If the ratio is less than 1, we can say that the data exhibits a clustered pattern, whereas a value greater than 1 indicates a dispersed pattern in our data.

The ANN ratio created as a result of dividing the observed distance by the expected distance creates a value between 0 and 1. If the ratio is less than 1, we can say that the data exhibits a clustered pattern, whereas a value greater than 1 indicates a dispersed pattern in our data.

Preparation

If necessary, open **ArcMap** with the `C:\GeospatialTraining\SpatialStats\DenverCrime.mxd` file. You should see a point feature class called `Denver Burglary` as shown in the following screenshot along with a number of other layers you've created in past exercises. You may want to turn these additional layers off at this time:

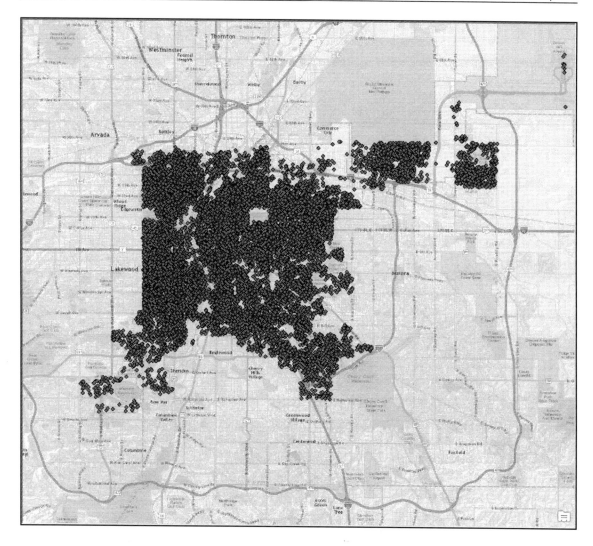

Running the Average Nearest Neighbor tool

Take a look at the following steps to run the **Average Nearest Neighbor** tool:

1. If necessary, open **ArcToolbox** and navigate to the **Spatial Statistics Tools** toolbox and the **Analyzing Patterns** toolset. Double-click on the **Average Nearest Neighbor** tool to display the dialog as shown in the following screenshot. Select `Denver Burglary` in the **Input Feature Class** field and make sure that you check the checkbox for **Generate Report (optional)**, as shown in the following screenshot:

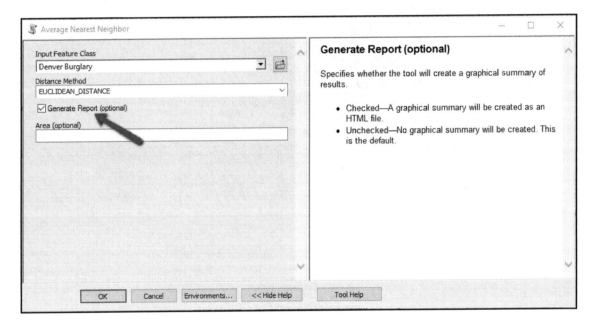

2. Click on the **OK** button to execute the tool.

3. The progress dialog will output the results of the tool, as shown in the following screenshot, along with an HTML report. Let's discuss what the results mean. The distance measurements reported are in meters, as we can see here:

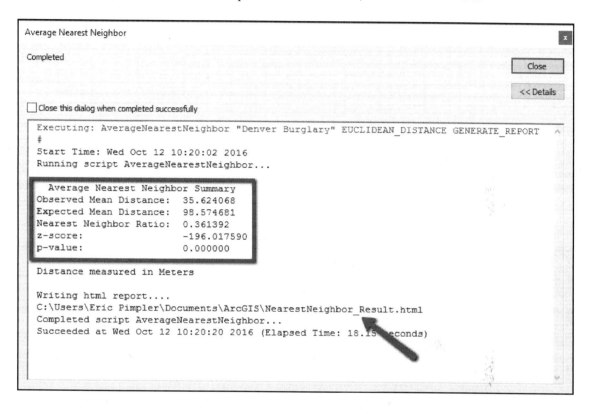

4. We'll start with `Observed Mean Distance`. This is the average distance between features in meters. For each feature in the study area, the distance to its nearest neighbor is calculated. The sum of all feature distances is then divided by the number of features to arrive at `Observed Mean Distance`. In this case, the value is `35.624068` meters.

5. Next is `Expected Mean Distance`. This is the expected mean distance for the dataset. In this case, the value is `98.574681` meters.

6. The ANN ratio, also called `Nearest Neighbor Ratio` is `Observed Mean Distance` divided by `Expected Mean Distance`. In this case, the ANN ratio is `0.361392`. When the value is less than 1.0, we say that the data is clustered. Values beyond 1.0 are said to be dispersed. In this particular case, our value is a lot less than 1.0, so we can generally state that our data is clustered. However, the z-score and p-value give us additional information about the result.

7. The z-score reported for this dataset is `-196.017590` and the p-value is `0.000000`. When you examine the preceding tables for z-score and p-values, you'll see that both scores in this case put us in the **99%** confidence level. In other words, what we can say about our Burglary dataset is that it exhibits a clustered pattern, and based on the z-score and p-values, we can say with 99% confidence that this pattern is not random. However, it doesn't tell us why the clustering occurred.

Examining the HTML report

Let's examine the HTML report by performing the following steps:

1. The HTML report is nice because it gives us a graphic display of the results. The progress dialog will tell you where the file has been stored. Open the file now in a web browser and we'll examine the contents.

2. The values we examined in the last section are also in the HTML file along with a visual representation of where the data fell along a normal bell curve of standard deviations. You'll also notice that it provides us with a description of the outcome:

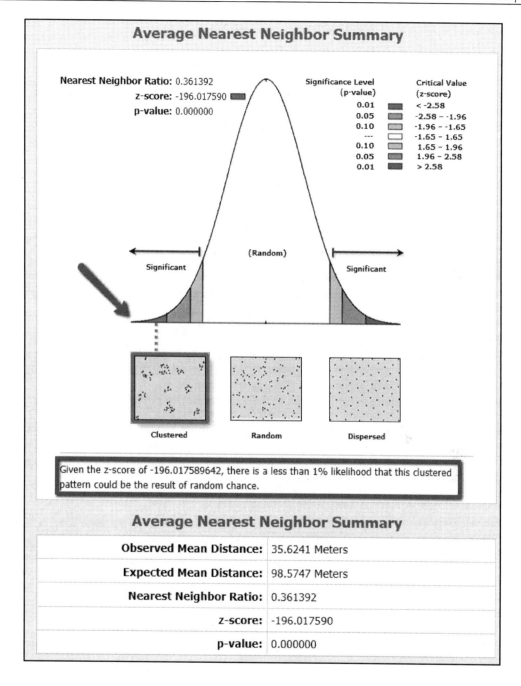

Average Nearest Neighbor Summary

Nearest Neighbor Ratio: 0.361392
z-score: -196.017590
p-value: 0.000000

Significance Level (p-value)		Critical Value (z-score)
0.01		< -2.58
0.05		-2.58 – -1.96
0.10		-1.96 – -1.65
---		-1.65 – 1.65
0.10		1.65 – 1.96
0.05		1.96 – 2.58
0.01		> 2.58

(Random)

Significant   Significant

Clustered   Random   Dispersed

Given the z-score of -196.017589642, there is a less than 1% likelihood that this clustered pattern could be the result of random chance.

Average Nearest Neighbor Summary

Observed Mean Distance:	35.6241 Meters
Expected Mean Distance:	98.5747 Meters
Nearest Neighbor Ratio:	0.361392
z-score:	-196.017590
p-value:	0.000000

Using Spatial Autocorrelation to analyze patterns

The **Spatial Autocorrelation** tool measures spatial autocorrelation by simultaneously measuring feature locations and attribute values. If features that are close together have similar values, then that is said to be clustering. However, if features that are close together have dissimilar values, then they are said to be dispersed. This tool outputs a Moran's I index value along with a z-score, and a p-value.

In this exercise, you'll use the **Spatial Autocorrelation** tool to analyze home sales by census tract.

Preparation

Let's get prepared by performing the following steps for using the **Spatial Autocorrelation** tool to analyze patterns:

1. Open **ArcMap** with the
   `C:\GeospatialTraining\SpatialStats\SeattleNeighborhoodBurglary.`
   `mxd` file. You should see a polygon feature class called `Seattle Neighborhood Burglary`, as shown in the following screenshot:

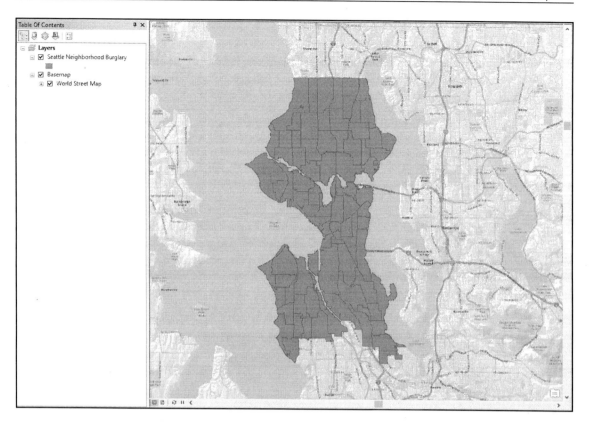

2. We'll first symbolize the data, so we have an idea about the contents of the data
   we'll be examining in this exercise. For this exercise we're going to use the
   `Count_` field attached to this layer. This field contains the number of burglaries in
   a recent year for each neighborhood.

3. Double-click the `Seattle Neighborhood Burglary` layer to display the properties dialog box. If necessary, click the **Symbology** tab and then click on **Quantities**. Select **Graduated colors** and then `Count_` as the field. You can accept the default colors and click on the **OK** button. Refer to the following screenshot if you need assistance:

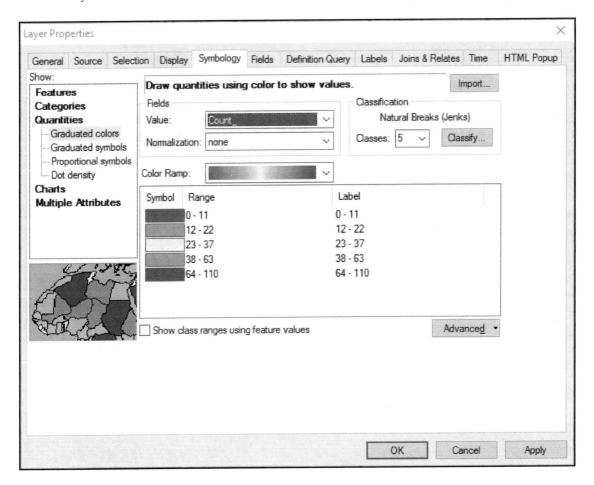

4. After applying the symbology, you should see something similar to this:

Running the Spatial Autocorrelation tool

Let's take a look at the following steps to run the Spatial Autocorrelation tool:

1. If necessary, open **ArcToolbox** and navigate to the **Spatial Statistics Tools** toolbox and the **Analyzing Patterns** toolset. Double-click on the **Spatial Autocorrelation (Morans I)** tool to display the following dialog. Select Seattle Neighborhood Boundary as input feature class, Count_ as input field, FIXED_DISTANCE_BAND as conceptualization of spatial relationships, and make sure that you check the checkbox for general report:

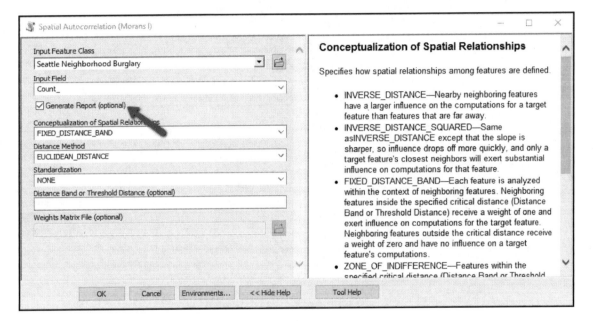

2. Click on the **OK** button to execute the tool.
3. The progress dialog will output the results of the tool, as shown in the following screenshot, along with an HTML report. Let's discuss what the results mean. The distance measurements reported are in meters:

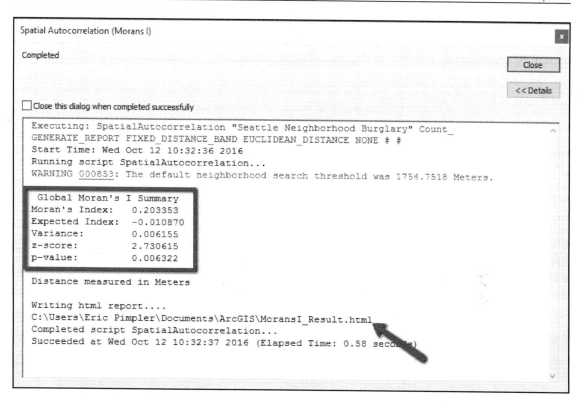

4. You can also view the output of this tool (and any other tool) from the **Results** window. In **ArcMap**, navigate to **Geoprocessing | Results**. Open the current session and you should see an entry for the tool. This displays the Moran's **Index** as **0.203353**, **ZScore** as **2.730615**, **PValue** as **0.006322**, and you can also double-click on the output HTML report file: MoransI:

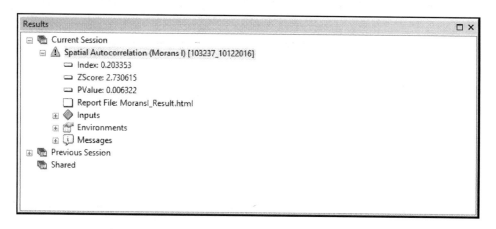

Examining the HTML report

Let's examine the HTML report by performing the following steps:

1. If you haven't already done so, open the HTML report in a web browser.
2. The **Moran's Index** will usually fall somewhere between -1.0 and +1.0. A value of 0 indicates a random spatial pattern. In this particular case, the value is **0.203353**, but we can't examine this index in isolation. We need to look at the p-value and z-score in the following screenshot for more information:

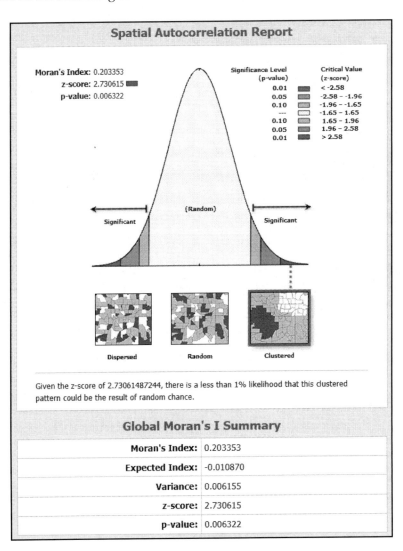

3. The p-value of **0.006322** is quite low, indicating that we can be confident at the 99% level that the pattern we're seeing is not the result of random spatial processes.

4. The z-score is positive and high indicating clustering.

5. Again, these are global statistics, so any conclusions we make are about the dataset as a whole rather than the individual features within the dataset. However, in general, we can reject the null hypothesis of spatial randomness. There is clear evidence of clustering for burglary in the neighborhoods of Seattle.

Using the Multi-Distance Spatial Cluster Analysis tool to determine clustering or dispersion

Multi-Distance Spatial Cluster Analysis (Ripleys K Function) determines whether feature locations show significant clustering or dispersion. However, unlike the other spatial pattern tools that we've examined in this section, it does not take the value at a location into account. It only determines clustering by the location of the features. This tool is often used in fields like environmental studies, health care, and crime, where you are attempting to determine if one feature attracts another feature. Also, keep in mind that a dataset can be both clustered and dispersed as seen in the line graph on this slide. We'll examine what this means in more detail on the next slide.

In this exercise, you'll use the **Multi-Distance Spatial Cluster Analysis** tool to analyze the clustering or dispersion of burglaries.

Preparation

Let's get prepared by performing the following steps to learn to use the **Multi-Distance Spatial Cluster Analysis** tool to determine clustering or dispersion:

1. Open **ArcMap** with the
   `C:\GeospatialTraining\SpatialStats\DenverCrime.mxd` map document
   file. You'll be using the `Denver Burglary` layer in this exercise, so you may
   want to turn off the other layers, if necessary:

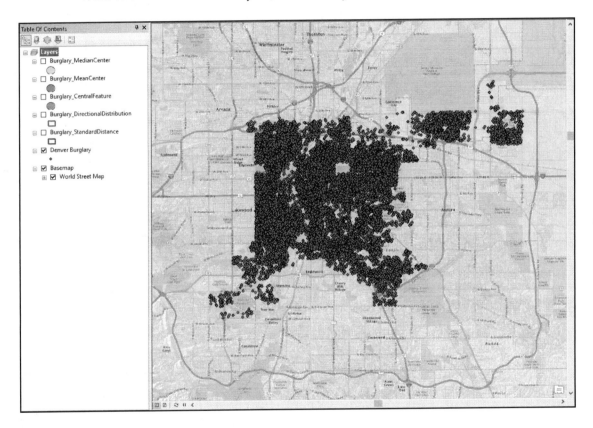

2. The Multi-Distance Spatial Cluster Analysis tool is a computationally intensive
   function that can take an extended time to execute with large datasets. There are
   approximately 25,000 records in the `Denver Burglary` layer, so for this exercise
   we will use only a subset of these records.

3. In **ArcMap**, click on the **File** menu and then click on the **Add Data** button and navigate to `C:\GeospatialTraining\SpatialStats\Data\crime.gdb` and add the `Denver_Census_Tracts` feature class.

4. Use the **Selection** tool in **ArcMap** to select a handful of census tracts similar to what you can see in the following screenshot. The census tracts you select do not have to be identical to the screenshot:

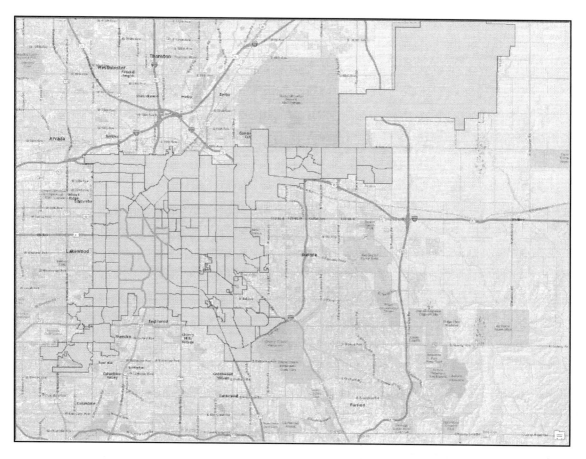

5. Use the **Select by Location...** tool to select features from the `Denver Burglary` layer that intersect the selection set of census tracts that you just created.

6. Export the selected set from `Denver Burglary` as `Denver_Burglary_Tracts` in the crime geodatabase. The exported layer contains approximately 2,400 records. Your record count will probably not be exactly the same:

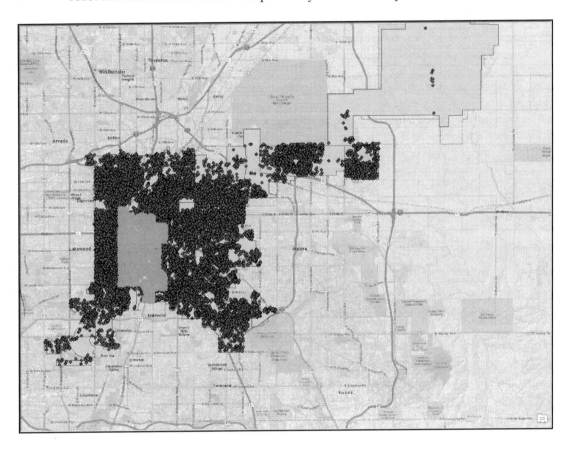

Running the Multi-Distance Spatial Cluster Analysis tool

Let's run the **Multi-Distance Spatial Cluster Analysis** tool by performing the following steps:

1. If necessary, open **ArcToolbox** and navigate to the **Spatial Statistics Tools** toolbox and the **Analyzing Patterns** toolset. Double-click on the **Multi-Distance Spatial Cluster Analysis (Ripleys K Function)** tool to display the following dialog:

2. Select `Denver_Burglary_Tracts_Prj` in the **Input Feature Class**, `Denver_Burglary_Tracts_Multi` in the **Output Table**, **10** in the **Number of Distance Bands**, and `9_PERMUTATIONS` in the **Compute Confidence Envelope (optional)**. Also, check the checkbox for **Display Results Graphically (optional)**. We will not use the **Weight Field (optional)** parameter in this case. Weight fields are normally used in situations where a number of incidents or counts for a location are involved. That's not the case in this situation:

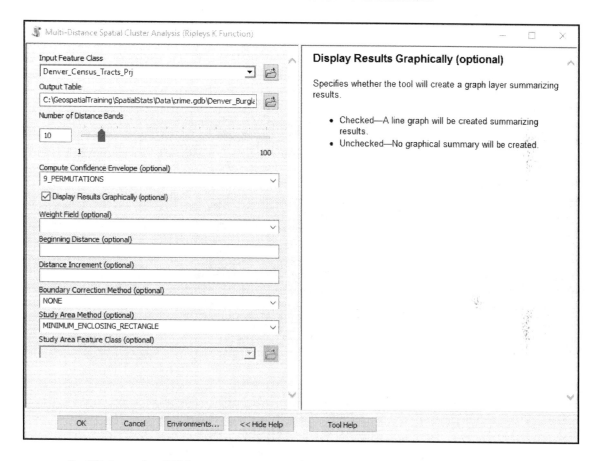

3. Click on the **OK** button to execute the tool.

Examining the output

Let's examine the output by performing the following steps:

1. The tool will write the output to the progress dialog, create the output table, and display a graph:

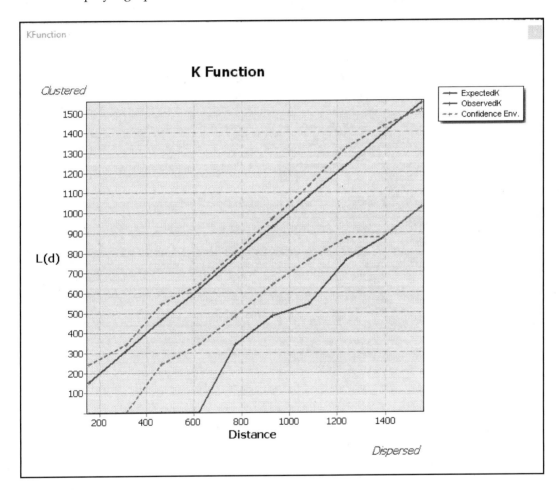

2. The table is probably the best way to interpret the results. Take a look at the following screenshot and we'll discuss the results. Note the following output information:

- There are 10 records, one for each distance band.
- In an unweighted interpretation, we will examine the ObservedK field versus the ExpectedK field. For the 10 records generated in this case, the ObservedK field is greater than the ExpectedK field in all cases. This indicates a clustered pattern. However, we must examine this in relation to the HiConfEnv field for statistical significance.
- If the ObservedK field is greater than the HiConfEnv field, it indicates statistically significant clustering. And again in all 10 cases, our ObservedK field is higher than the HiConfEnv field, indicating that we have statistically significant clustering for burglaries in the Denver area. This indicates that there is some underlying spatial process that causes burglaries to cluster at all distances observed in this example:

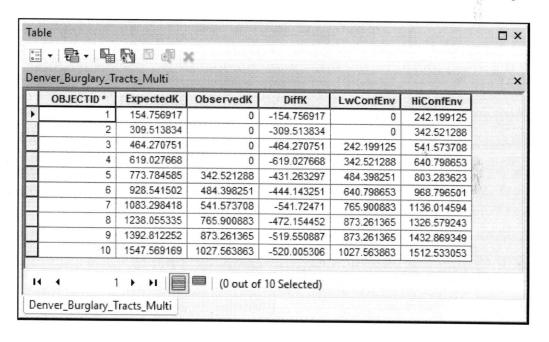

Table

Denver_Burglary_Tracts_Multi

OBJECTID *	ExpectedK	ObservedK	DiffK	LwConfEnv	HiConfEnv
1	154.756917	0	-154.756917	0	242.199125
2	309.513834	0	-309.513834	0	342.521288
3	464.270751	0	-464.270751	242.199125	541.573708
4	619.027668	0	-619.027668	342.521288	640.798653
5	773.784585	342.521288	-431.263297	484.398251	803.283623
6	928.541502	484.398251	-444.143251	640.798653	968.796501
7	1083.298418	541.573708	-541.72471	765.900883	1136.014594
8	1238.055335	765.900883	-472.154452	873.261365	1326.579243
9	1392.812252	873.261365	-519.550887	873.261365	1432.869349
10	1547.569169	1027.563863	-520.005306	1027.563863	1512.533053

1 ▸ ▸| (0 out of 10 Selected)

Denver_Burglary_Tracts_Multi

Summary

This chapter covered the use of a number of tools found in the **Analyzing Patterns** toolset that can be used to generate a single statistic for an entire dataset that indicates whether the data exhibits a clustered, dispersed, or random spatial pattern. In the next chapter, you'll learn how to use the clustering tools found in the **Spatial Statistics Tools** toolbox.

4
Mapping Clusters with ArcGIS Tools

Many things in life naturally tend to cluster. Housing, businesses, trees, and crimes are all examples of clustering. The degree of this clustering is important. The tools in the Mapping Clusters toolset don't just answer the question "*Is there clustering?*", but they also answer the question "*Where is the clustering?*"

The Mapping Clusters tools are helpful in identifying statistically significant hot and cold spots, spatial outliers, as well as locating similar features, and grouping features. This toolset can also be used to define actions that should take place based on the location of clusters. For example, the Mapping Clusters tools can be used to identify areas of high crime activity (burglaries, for example) that can be useful in allocating police officers to deal with this activity in those areas. While these clusters don't typically identify *why* a phenomena is occurring, they can often provide clues.

The tools in this toolset allow us to visualize the patterns of clustering in our datasets. This is unlike the tools we examined in Chapter 3, *Analyzing Patterns with ArcGIS Tools*, that gave us a simple *Yes* or *No* as an answer to the question of whether our dataset was clustered or dispersed.

In this chapter, you will learn how to use many of these tools, including the following ones, to determine various cluster analyses :

- The **Similarity Search** tool
- The **Grouping Analysis** tool
- The **Hot Spot Analysis** tool
- The **Optimized Hot Spot Analysis** tool
- The **Cluster and Outlier Analysis** tool

Using the Similarity Search tool

The **Similarity Search** tool is used to identify candidate features that are mot similar or most dissimilar to one or more input features by on the attributes of a feature. For input, you select either a layer or a selected subset of a layer. The tool can be used to select *most similar*, *least similar*, or *both*. Dissimilar searches can be equally as important as similarity searches. For example, a community development organization, in its attempts to attract new businesses, might show that their city is dissimilar to other competing cities when comparing crimes.

Here is an example of when using the **Similarity Search** tool would be appropriate. The following screenshot displays a successful store location along with several potential new store locations. This current successful location has a number of attached attributes, including `Average Income`, `Population Density`, and `Distance to Competitor`. A number of possible candidate features are displayed as green points. This layer also includes the same attributes. Using the **Similarity Search** tool, we can define which of those potential candidate locations is most similar to the successful store location and create a ranking of the potential stores:

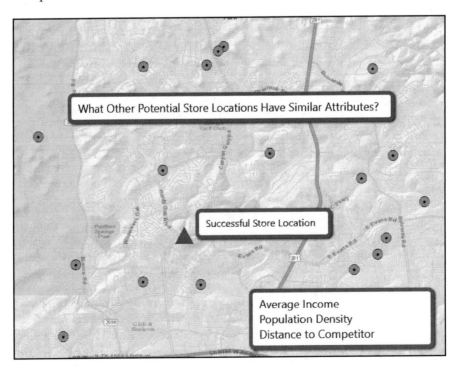

So what does it mean to be similar? How does the tool actually work? The first thing that needs to be done is a standardization of the attributes. Since we're most often working with several attributes in the analysis, we don't want one attribute to overwhelm the others. For example, if you were using population, percent uninsured, and distance to store as the primary attributes, population could easily overwhelm the other attributes because of the size of the numbers. Population numbers tend to be really large, whereas a percentage of uninsured will be less than 1.0. The scale of the numbers is very different. So the tool uses a process called **Z-transform** to create new values for population, percent uninsured, and distance. The calculation for **Z-transform** is to subtract the mean from the value and then divide by the standard deviation. This is illustrated in the following screenshot:

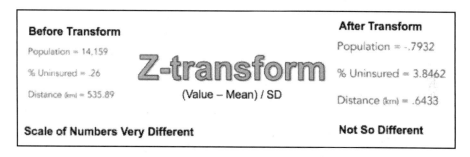

Once the **Z-transform** has been performed to standardize the attribute, the tool subtracts the candidate values from the target and squares the differences. The differences are squared because we don't want higher or lower values to matter. We just want the actual distance in data space. Finally, the sum of the squares for each of the attributes is calculated and the shortest distance in data space is defined as the most similar:

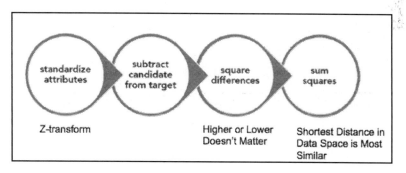

In this exercise, you'll learn how to use the **Similarity Search** tool on various demographic attributes.

Preparation

Let's get prepared before we use the **Similarity Search** tool by performing the following steps:

1. In the **ArcMap** window, open the
   `C:\GeospatialTraing\SpatialStats\DenverDemographics.mxd` file. You should see a polygon feature class called `Denver_Census_Tracts_Prj`, which is a census tracts layer projected to `NAD 83 UTM Zone 13` and a layer called `DenverTractHispanicHigh`. This layer has already been projected for you, but keep in mind that when you start using your own datasets for analysis, you'll need to project the data into a coordinate system that accurately represents distances. The `DenverTractHispanicHigh` feature class contains a single polygon feature that represents the census tract in Denver with the highest percentage of Hispanic population (84.78%):

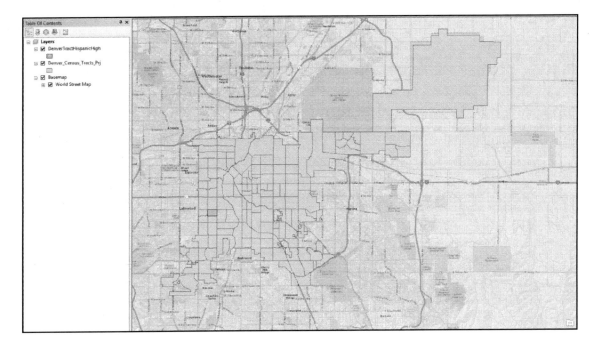

2. Open the attribute table for `Denver_Census_Tracts_Prj` and examine some of the many attribute values. In this exercise, we will use the `PCT_HISPAN` and `RENTED` fields to find census tracts that are similar to that provided in the single feature found in the `DenverTractHispanicHigh` layer in terms of the Hispanic population that rents a home.

Running the Similarity Search tool

Let's run the **Similarity Search** tool by performing the following steps:

1. If necessary, open the **ArcToolbox** toolbox and find the **Spatial Statistics Tools** toolbox. Open the toolbox and expand the **Mapping Clusters** toolset. Double-click on the **Similarity Search** tool to display the tool. Select the following input parameters:

   - **Input Features to Match**: `DenverTractHispanicHigh`
   - **Candidate Features**: `Denver_Census_Tracts_Prj`
   - **Output Features**:
     `C:\Users\<user>\Documents\ArcGIS\Default.gdb\DenverTrac tHispanicHigh_Simi`
   - **Most or Least Similar**: `MOST_SIMILAR`
   - **Match Method**: `ATTRIBUTE_VALUES`
   - **Attributes Of Interest**: Check `PCT_HISPAN` and `PctRented`

- **Additional Options: Fields To Append To Output (optional):** Check
  `PCT_HISPAN` and `PctRented`

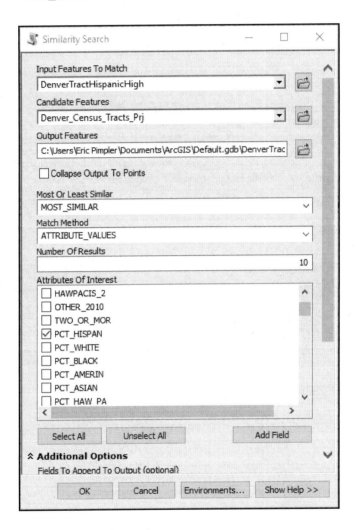

2. Click on **OK** to execute the tool.

Interpreting the results

This tool will create a new feature class containing the features most like the input features to match along with a table of results printed to the progress dialog. The progress dialog information can be seen in the following screenshot. Take a look at the results and then we'll discuss what they mean:

```
          Summary of Attributes of Interest
Attribute     Min      Max      SD     Mean    Input
PCT_HISPAN 0.0000  84.7800  24.6647  30.0395  84.7800
PCTRENTED  0.0000  91.1392  20.8561  41.9986  55.2215


10 Most Similar Locations (Values)
OID SIMRANK SIMINDEX
 84       1   0.0000
 82       2   0.0705
 30       3   0.1129
 50       4   0.1270
 28       5   0.2136
 85       6   0.2270
 83       7   0.2614
 87       8   0.3564
  7       9   0.3681
132      10   0.4885
             2.2254
```

The first table is just a summary of the attributes of interest, including PCT_HISPAN and PCTRENTED. This includes the minimum and maximum values found for the attributes along with the standard deviation, mean, and input feature value.

The second table has the 10 most similar locations from the candidate features. This table lists the OID, SIMRANK, and SIMINDEX values. The SIMRANK value is a ranking of the features that most closely match the input. The SIMINDEX value quantifies how similar each solution match is to the target feature.

A new layer containing the most similar features will also be created and added to the ArcMap **Table Of Contents** pane. You can see the features symbolized in light green in the following screenshot:

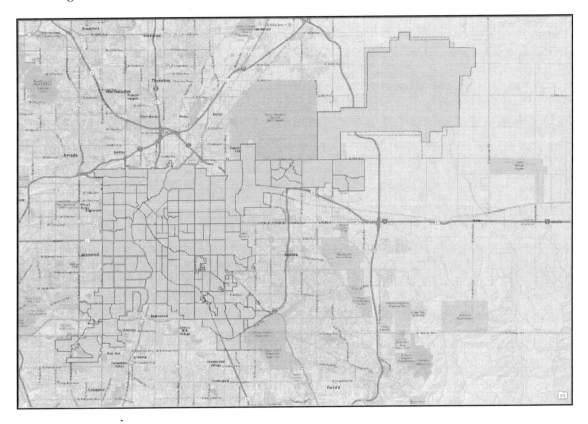

Using the Grouping Analysis tool

The **Grouping Analysis** tool groups features based on feature attributes as well as optional spatial/temporal constraints. The output of this tool is the creation of distinct groups of data where the features that are part of the group are as similar as possible and between groups are as dissimilar as possible. The tool is capable of multivariate analysis and the output is a map and a report. The output map can have either contiguous groups or non-contiguous groups. With contiguous groups, there is an added spatial component that can limit the effectiveness of the results. The creation of sales territories would be an example of a contiguous group. When groups are created in a non-contiguous manner, we allow the data to speak for itself without the introduction of a spatial limiter.

The output from the **Grouping Analysis** tool consists of a map along with a box plot, as shown in the following screenshot. By itself, the map doesn't tell you a whole lot. Obviously, you can see the groups, but the statistical analysis of the data is best seen in the resulting box plot. This tool uses a combination of K means testing along with clustering. This is what looks for the groups in the data. If you've selected non-contiguous, then it allows the data to speak for itself without the introduction of a spatial limiter. The resulting box plot enables you to examine how each variable in the analysis compares between groups:

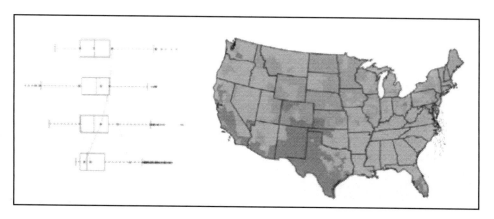

Box plots are excellent for illustrating several basic descriptive statistics of a dataset in a visual manner. The whiskers of the plot show the spread of the variable with the left whisker being the lowest value and the right whisker being the highest value. The range of the dataset would the highest value minus the lowest value. In our example on this slide, the lowest value is 8 and the highest is 50, and that gives a range of 42. The vertical line inside the box represents the median of the dataset. So in this case, that would be 21. What this means is that half the values are between 8 and 21 and the other half are between 21 and 50. The beginning of the box plot also represents the median of the lower half of the data and the ending of the box represents the median of the upper half of the data.

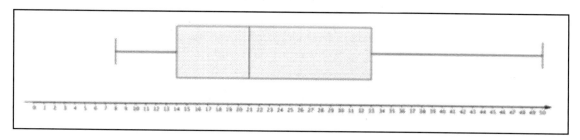

The combination of the whiskers and box combine to break the data into quartiles. The **1st Quartile** starts with the minimum value of **8** up to the beginning of the box, which is **14**. The **2nd Quartile** begins at value **14** up to the median of the dataset, which is **21**. The **3rd Quartile** begins at value **21** and ends at **33**. The **4th Quartile** extends from value **33** to **50**:

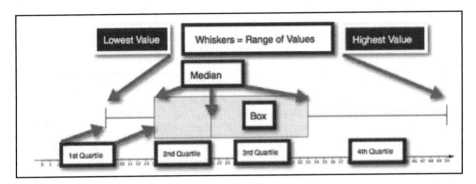

In this exercise, you'll learn how to use the **Grouping Analysis** tool on various demographic attributes.

Preparation

Let's get prepared before using the Grouping Analysis tool by performing the following steps:

1. In ArcMap, open the
   `C:\GeospatialTraing\SpatialStats\DenverDemographics.mxd` file. You should see a polygon feature class called `Denver_Census_Tracts_Prj`, which is a census tracts layer projected to `NAD 83 UTM Zone 13` and a layer called `DenverTractHispanicHigh`. These layers have already been projected for you, but keep in mind that when you start using your own datasets for analysis, you'll need to project the data into a coordinate system that accurate represents distances. The `DenverTractHispanicHigh` contains a single polygon feature that represents the census tract in Denver with the high percent of Hispanic population (84.78%). We won't use this dataset in the analysis, so feel free to turn the visibility off:

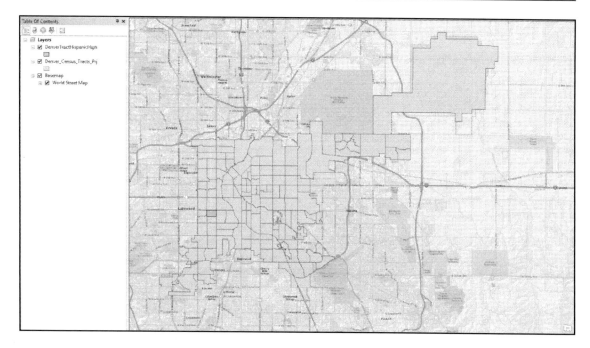

2. Open the attribute table for `Denver_Census_Tracts_Prj` and examine some of the many attribute values. In this exercise, we will use the `PCT_HISPAN` and `PctRented` fields to group census tracts that are similar in terms of the percentage of Hispanic population and percentage of residents that are renters.

Running the Grouping Analysis tool

Let's run the **Grouping Analysis** tool by performing the following steps:

1. If necessary, open the **ArcToolbox** toolbox and find the **Spatial Statistics Tools** toolbox. Open the toolbox and expand the **Mapping Clusters** toolset. Double-click on **Grouping Analysis** to display the tool. Select the following input parameters:
   - **Input Features**: `Denver_Census_Tracts_Prj`
   - **Unique ID Field**: `TractID`
   - **Output Feature Class**: `C:\Users\<user>\Documents\ArcGIS\Default.gdb\Denver_Census_Tracts_Groups`
   - **Number of Groups**: 4

- **Analysis Fields**: `PCT_HISPAN` and `PCTRented`
- **Spatial Constraints**: `NO_SPATIAL_CONSTRAINT`
- **Distance Method**: `EUCLIDEAN`
- **Output Report File**:
  `C:\GeospatialTraining\SpatialStats\GroupingAnalysis.pdf`

Leave the default for all other input parameters.

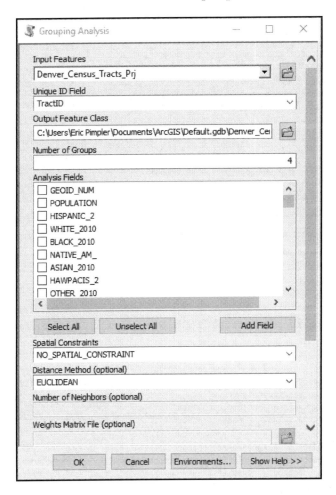

2. Click on **OK** to execute the tool.

Interpreting the results

This tool will create a new feature class containing the groups that have been defined. You can see this feature class in the following screenshot:

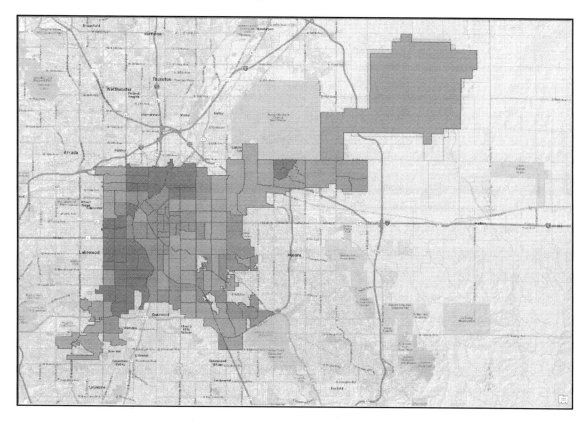

You may also want to remove the outline from the boundaries of the polygons to see the groups better:

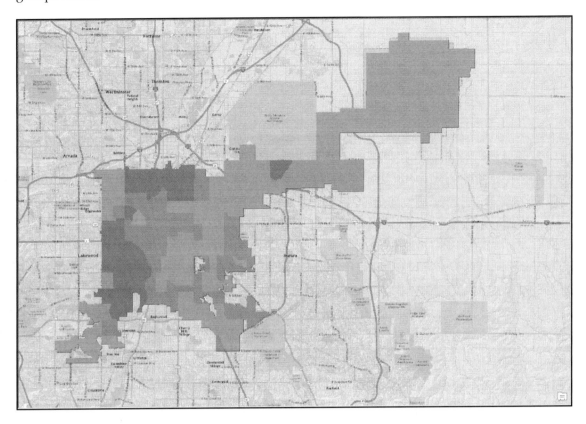

The tool will also create an output PDF file containing tables and box plots. Open that file now. It will be located at
`C:\GeospatialTraining\SpatialStats\GroupingAnalysis.pdf` or wherever you defined in the input parameters.

The first section in the report is `Group-Wise Summary`. This section contains tables and box plots for each group that describes the various groups. Initially, the report presents information for the entire dataset, as shown in the following screenshot. Each table will have descriptive statistics including the variable name, mean, standard deviation, min, max, and share of the total:

Overall Variable Statistics: Count = 144, Std. Distance = 32.0686, SSD = 63.6830						
Variable	Mean	Std. Dev.	Min	Max	R2	
PCT_HISPAN	29.6594	24.3232	0.0000	84.7800	0.8078	
PCTRENTED	41.9068	20.8992	0.0000	91.1392	0.7500	

Let's take a look at the following various groups:

- **Group 1 (blue group)**: Based on the information provided in this section, this group has a very high percentage of Hispanic population but only an average amount of renters in relation to the entire study area:

Group 1: Count = 53, Std. Distance = 16.4579, SSD = 28.2231						
Variable	Mean	Std. Dev.	Min	Max	Share	
PCT_HISPAN	18.9951	12.0928	6.3400	53.8700	0.5606	
PCTRENTED	61.5603	11.1636	42.6446	91.1392	0.5321	

- **Group 2 (red group)**: This group has a roughly average percentage of Hispanic residents but a high percentage of renters:

Group 2: Count = 32, Std. Distance = 15.1172, SSD = 14.6322						
Variable	Mean	Std. Dev.	Min	Max	Share	
PCT_HISPAN	67.5328	10.4922	49.0200	84.7800	0.4218	
PCTRENTED	44.9108	10.8832	24.9833	70.9888	0.5048	

- **Group 3 (green group)**: This group also has a roughly average percentage of Hispanic residents but a low percentage of renters relative to the study area as a whole:

Group 3: Count = 10, Std. Distance = 13.7583, SSD = 3.5051						
Variable	Mean	Std. Dev.	Min	Max	Share	
PCT_HISPAN	47.2270	11.7600	30.6400	63.0000	0.3817	
PCTRENTED	3.3596	7.1410	0.0000	22.2046	0.2436	

- **Group 4 (orange group)**: This group has a slightly lower percentage of Hispanic residents and a slightly lower percentage of renters relative to the study area as a whole:

Group 4: Count = 49, Std. Distance = 13.2012, SSD = 17.3227						
Variable	Mean	Std. Dev.	Min	Max	Share	
PCT_HISPAN	12.8753	8.7114	0.0000	37.3700	0.4408	
PCTRENTED	26.5538	9.9189	0.0000	44.8955	0.4926	

The next section of the report is `Variable-Wise Summary`. This presents a table for each variable with descriptive statistics and box plots. It makes it easier to compare the variables between groups. For example, you can clearly see that `Group 2` has a much higher percentage of renters and that `Group 3` has a much lower percentage of renters. In the second table containing the percentage of Hispanic residents, the high percentage of Hispanic residents in `Group 1` is very obvious:

PCT_HISPAN: R2 = 0.81						
Group	Mean	Std. Dev.	Min	Max	Share	
1	18.9951	12.0928	6.3400	53.8700	0.5606	
2	67.5328	10.4922	49.0200	84.7800	0.4218	
3	47.2270	11.7600	30.6400	63.0000	0.3817	
4	12.8753	8.7114	0.0000	37.3700	0.4408	
Total	29.6594	24.3232	0.0000	84.7800	1.0000	
PCTRENTED: R2 = 0.75						
Group	Mean	Std. Dev.	Min	Max	Share	
1	61.5603	11.1636	42.6446	91.1392	0.5321	
2	44.9108	10.8832	24.9833	70.9888	0.5048	
3	3.3596	7.1410	0.0000	22.2046	0.2436	
4	26.5538	9.9189	0.0000	44.8955	0.4926	
Total	41.9068	20.8992	0.0000	91.1392	1.0000	

The final section in the report is `Parallel Box Plot`. This contains the same data but with lines drawn between the variables:

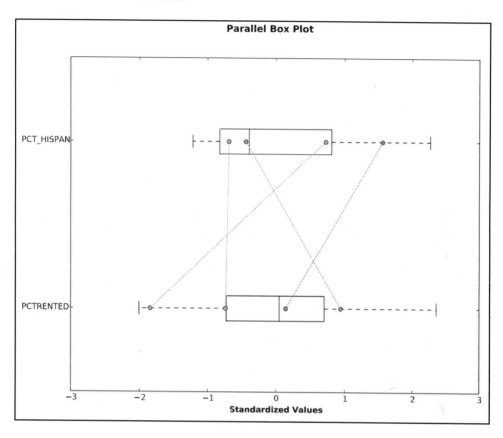

Analysing real estate sales with the Hot Spot Analysis tool

The **Hot Spot Analysis** tool examines features and their attributes to identify statistically significant hot spots and cold spots using the `Getis-Ord Gi*` statistics. It provides a visual clustering of high, low, and not significant values. Each feature is assigned as a hot spot, cold spot, or not significant. To perform the analysis, a neighborhood is defined for each feature. How a neighborhood is defined is critical to the output of the tool as it is the neighborhood that is examined in relation to the study area for assignment of each feature.

Explanation

At a high level, let's examine what occurs during the hot spot analysis process. Each feature in the dataset has an attribute value that is being measured in the analysis. A neighborhood is assigned to each feature. This neighborhood is critical to the analysis. You must decide how the neighborhood is to be defined as part of the input parameters of the tool. If you don't have a good idea of what the neighborhood should be, then you should consider using the **Optimized Hot Spot Analysis** tool instead. After the neighborhood has been defined, it is the neighborhood that is compared to the entire study area. If the neighborhood values are significantly higher than the study area, the feature will be marked as a hot spot. Conversely, if the neighborhood value is significantly lower than the study area, the feature is marked as a cold spot. If neither is the case, then the feature is marked as not significant.

To further illustrate, let's look at a specific example. In this exercise, we'll examine the number of residential real estate sales by census block group. The number of sales for each census block group has been determined via a spatial join. Furthermore, to remove the inherent bias associated with larger census block groups, we have normalized the counts by the area of each block group. Each feature in the study area (shown in the following screenshot) has both a geographic definition as well as an attribute value that represents the number of sales normalized by area:

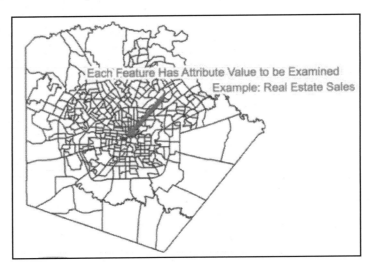

Each feature has a neighborhood. The neighborhood is defined as the features nearest to the feature being examined. How the neighborhood is defined is critical and there are different ways the neighborhood can be defined. We'll examine these methods later in the exercise:

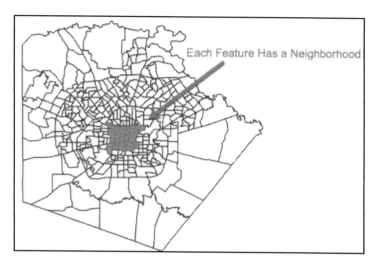

After the neighborhood has been defined, the tool compares the neighborhood to the entire study area. The study area defines the entire set of features to be examined:

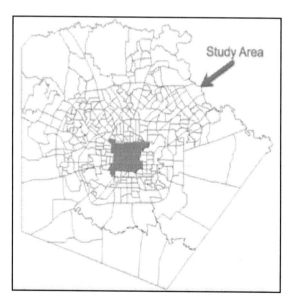

If the neighborhood values are significantly higher than the study area, the feature will be marked as a hot spot. Conversely, if the neighborhood value is significantly lower than the study area, the feature is marked as a cold spot. If neither is the case, then the feature is marked as not significant:

In hot spot analysis, the question we are attempting to answer is this: *Is the neighborhood significantly different than the study area?* If the neighborhood is significantly different than the study area, then the feature is marked as either a hot spot or a cold spot depending upon the some factors that we'll study later. If the neighborhood is not significantly different than the study area, then a feature is marked as not significant.

Preparation

Let's get prepared before using the **Hot Spot Analysis** tool to analyze the real estate sales by performing the following steps:

1. If necessary, open **ArcMap** with the
   `C:\GeospatialTraining\SpatialStats\SanAntonioRealEstate.mxd` file.
   You should see a point feature class called `ResidentialSales` and a polygon feature class called `BexarCountyCensusBlockGroups` as shown in the following screenshot:

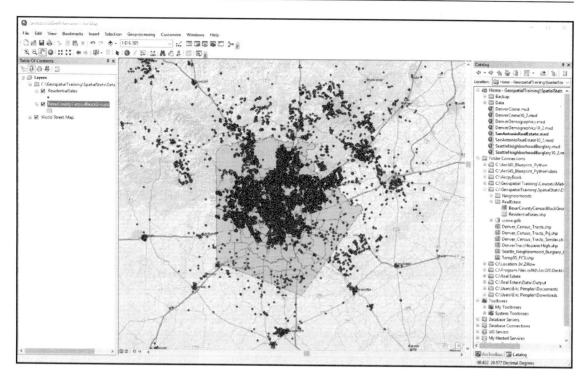

2. The `ResidentialSales` feature class contains one point feature for each residential property sale in the San Antonio area over the span of 1 year. In this step, you'll get a count of the number of sales by census block group by performing a spatial join operation. Right-click on the `BexarCountyCensusBlockGroups` layer and navigate to **Joins and Relates** | **Join**. In the **Join Data** dialog, define the parameters as follows:

   - **What do you want to join to this layer: Join data from another layer based on spatial location**
   - **Choose the layer to join to this layer, or load spatial data from disk:** `ResidentialSales`
   - Leave the defaults for item 2

- **The result of the join will be saved into a new layer**: `C:\GeospatialTraining\SpatialStats\Data\RealEstate\Bexa rCountyCensusBlockGroupsJoined.shp`:

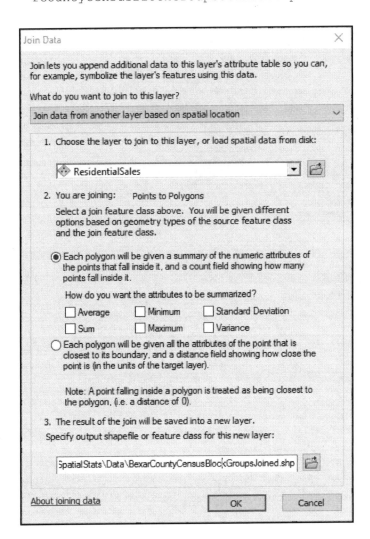

3. Click on **OK**
4. The output shapefile will be added to the ArcMap **Table Of Contents** pane. Open the attribute table by right-clicking on the layer and selecting **Open Attribute Table**. A `Count_` field has been added to the end of the attribute table. This field contains a count of the number of sales in each census block group:

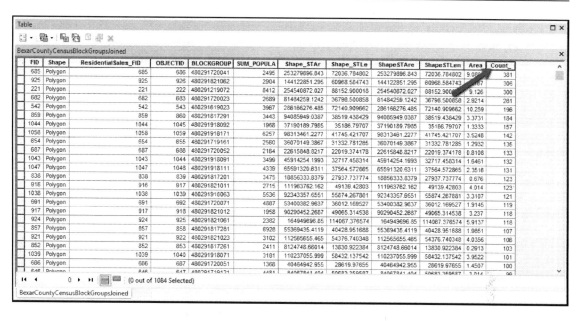

5. The size of census block groups varies widely, so we need to normalize the counts by the area of each block group to minimize the differences in value based on the size of each block group. The attribute table contains a field called `Area`, which is the area of each census block group in square miles. We'll use this field to normalize the counts. Add a new field to the attribute table called `NormCount`. It should be defined as a `Float` data type with a precision of `10` and scale of `6`, as shown in the following screenshot:

6. Right-click on the new `NormCount` field and select **Field Calculator**. Set the field equal to the `Count_` divided by the `Area` as shown in the following screenshot and click on **OK**. The values should range from `0-353.58`:

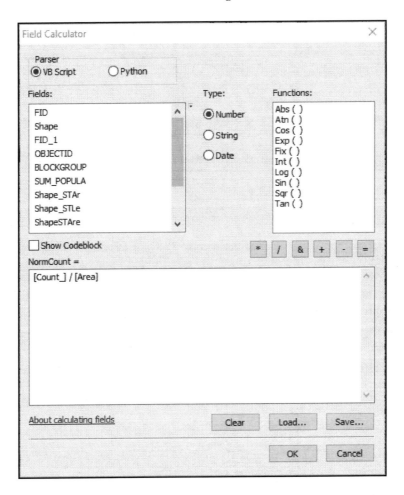

7. Before running the Hot Spot Analysis tool, we'll create a thematic map of the census block group data. Right-click on the `BexarCountyCensusBlockGroupsJoined` layer and select **Properties...**.

8. Navigate to **Symbology | Quantities | Graduated colors**. Under **Fields**, in the **Value** section, select `NumCount`, as shown in the following screenshot, and click on **OK**:

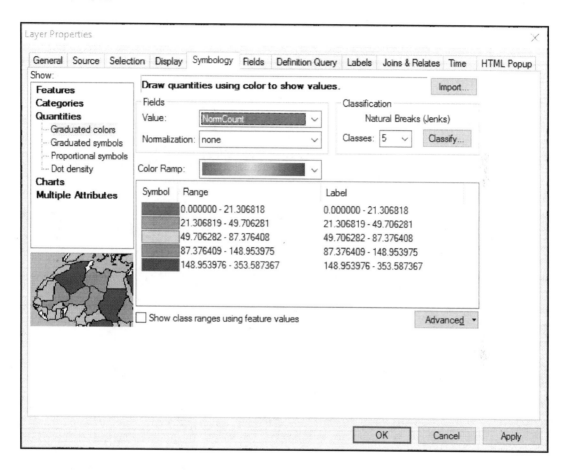

9. The resulting color-coded map gives us some indication of areas where sales have been strong. In the next step, we'll apply spatial statistics in the form of the Hot Spot Analysis tool to get a more accurate view of areas that are both hot and cold from a sales perspective:

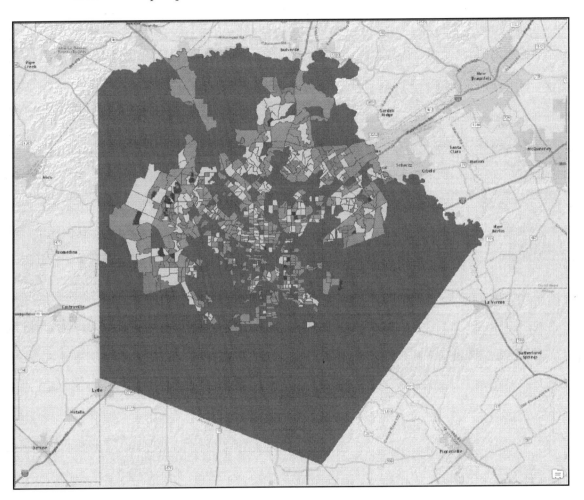

Running the Hot Spot Analysis tool

The **Hot Spot Analysis** tool identifies statistically significant hot spots and cold spots using the `Getis-Ord Gi*` statistic using a set of weighted features. The weighting is based on the numeric attribute field selected from the layer being analyzed. In this exercise, the weighting will be the normalized count of residential sales for census block groups.

As I mentioned in the explanation section of this exercise, the neighborhood of each feature is compared to the study area to determine a value for each feature. The way that the neighborhood is determined is critical in deriving the output. The **Hot Spot Analysis** tool provides a number of ways that the neighborhood can be determined, including **Fixed Distance Band**, **Inverse Distance**, **Inverse Distance Squared**, **Zone of Indifference**, **Contiguity Edges Only**, and **Contiguity Edges and Corners**. I will briefly describe each of the methods used to determine the neighborhood here:

- `Fixed Distance Band`: Using this method of creating a neighborhood, each feature is analyzed within the context of its neighboring features. A band is drawn around the target feature. Features that are within the band receive a weight of 1 and exert influence on the target feature. Features that are outside the band receive a weight of 0 and have no influence on the target feature.

- `Inverse Distance`: There are two inverse distance methods for calculating neighborhoods: Inverse Distance and Inverse Distance Squared. They are essentially the same except that with the squared method, the slope is sharper and the influence based on distance drops off more quickly. Only the target feature's closest neighbors will exercise substantial influence on the target feature. The basic idea of both is that nearby neighbor features will have a larger influence on the target feature than features that are further away.

- `Zone of Indifference`: With this, features within a specific distance of the target feature receive a weight of 1 and have the most influence on the target feature. It weighs and influence then gradually diminish with greater distances.

- `Contiguity (Edges Only and Edges and Corner)`: The contiguity method includes edges only and edges and corner. With edges only, neighboring polygon features that share a boundary or overlap will influence the computations for the target polygon features. For edges and corner, polygon features that share a boundary, node, or overlap will influence computations for the target feature.

The method you select for determining the neighborhood requires a good understanding of your data. You want to make sure that the spatial relationship you select for determining the neighborhood is appropriate for your study. For example, a study of county-level infant mortality in California would require a different neighborhood size than a study of residential real estate sales by census block group for Austin, TX.

Let's run the **Hot Spot Analysis** tool by performing the following steps:

1. In the **ArcToolbox** toolbox, find the **Spatial Statistics Tools** toolbox and then the **Mapping Clusters** toolset. Open this toolset and find the **Hot Spot Analysis (Getis-Ord Gi*)** tool. Double-click on the tool to display the dialog shown in the following screenshot:

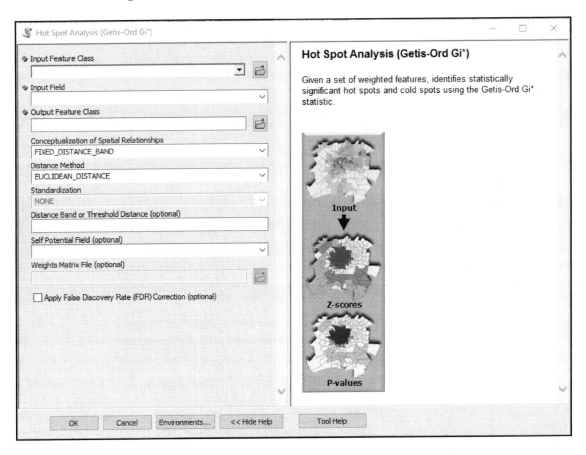

2. There are three required parameters including the input feature class, input field, and output feature class. The tool also requires a conceptualization of spatial relationships and a distance method. Both parameters provide default values if you don't specify a particular parameter value. We're going to run this tool multiple times to see how changes in the **Conceptualization of Spatial Relationships** parameter can dramatically affect the output. This is the parameter that defines the neighborhood that we discussed earlier. We'll start by specifying CONTIGUITY_EDGES_CORNERS. This method will define the neighborhood as any

feature that shares a boundary or shares an edge with another polygon. This is a reasonable way of determining the neighborhood for this particular study, though it may or may not be the best. Specify the parameters with the given values:

- **Input Feature Class**: `BexarCountyCensusBlockGroupsJoined`
- **Input Field**: `NormCount` (this is the count of the number of sales normalized by the area of the census block group)
- **Output Feature Class**: `C:\Users\<user>\Documents\ArcGIS\Default.gdb\BexarCountyCBG_HS_CEC.shp`
- **Conceptualization of Spatial Relationships**: `CONTIGUITY_EDGES_CORNERS`

3. Click on the **OK** button.

4. The output shapefile will be symbolized according to confidence levels between **90%** and **99%** in addition to any features determined to be not statistically significant. The new layer will be added to the **Table Of Contents** pane and should appear as shown in the following screenshot:

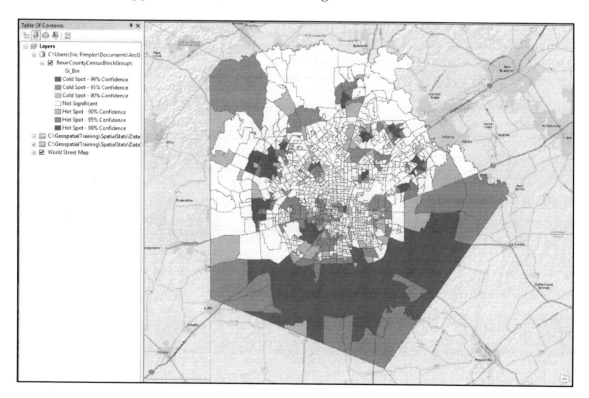

5. Run the tool again but with the following differences:

- **Output Feature Class**:
  `C:\Users\<user>\Documents\ArcGIS\Default.gdb\BexarCount`
  `yCBG_HS_ZID.shp`.

- **Conceptualization of Spatial Relationships**:
  `ZONE_OF_INDIFFERENCE`.

- **Distance Method**: `EUCLIDEAN_DISTANCE`.

- **Distance Band or Threshold Distance (optional)**: Specify a value of `8046` (meters). This is 5 miles. For Zone of Indifference, the influence of features outside the given distance is reduced with increasing distance. Those features inside the distance threshold are equally considered.

The output should appear as shown here:

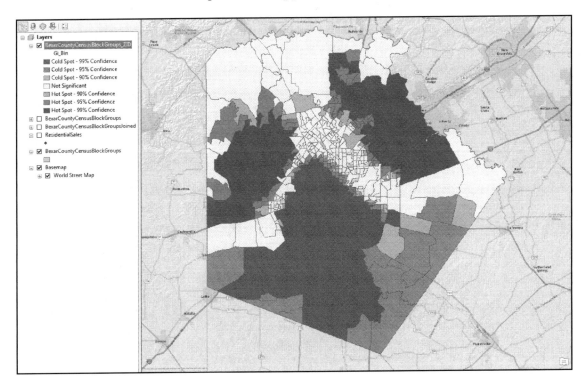

6. Run the tool again but with the following differences:

- **Output Feature Class**:
  `C:\Users\<user>\Documents\ArcGIS\Default.gdb\BexarCount
  yCBG_HS_ID.shp`

- **Conceptualization of Spatial Relationships**: `INVERSE_DISTANCE`

- **Distance Band or Threshold Distance**: We'll leave this value blank. This will allow the tool to apply a default threshold value to be computed and applied. The default value in this case is the Euclidean distance, which ensures that every feature has at least one neighbor.

7. Click on **OK** to execute the tool again. The output should appear as shown in the following screenshot:

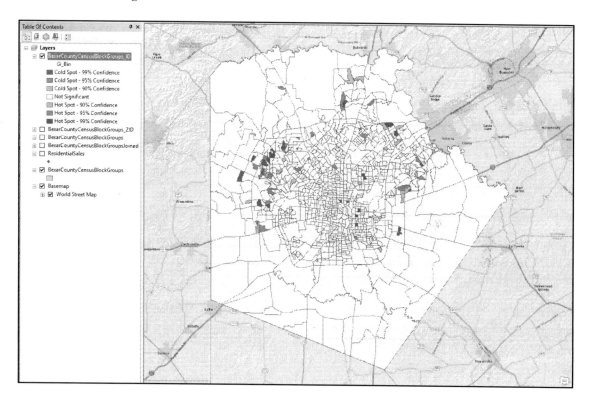

8. You can run the tool again with other parameters if you'd like to see additional results. In particular, you may want to run the tool using FIXED_DISTANCE under **Conceptualization of Spatial Relationships** since it is the default parameter used when running the **Optimized Hot Spot Analysis** tool that we'll examine in the next section.

9. As you've seen with the three results we've generated so far, it is certainly possible to obtain different results by selecting different parameters for how the neighborhood is generated. Before you run this tool, you should attempt to understand your data well enough to answer the question, *What is an appropriate neighborhood for this dataset?* In the case of residential real estate sales, a fairly small neighborhood tends to work well. That's why using CONTIGUITY_EDGES_CORNERS is likely the most appropriate spatial relationship in this case. The number of sales can vary widely over a relatively small distance.

10. Close the **ArcMap** window and save the map document.

Using the Optimized Hot Spot Analysis tool in real estate sales

Many analysts have difficulty in defining the neighborhood for their analysis. The neighborhood you define should match the question you are asking. For example, a study of obesity in California counties would need a large neighborhood due to the size of counties. However, a study of real estate sales for a metro area would need a much smaller neighborhood. If you are unsure of the distance to use for the neighborhood calculation, the **Optimized Hot Spot Analysis** tool will calculate the optimized neighborhood along with simplifying and optimizing some of the other input parameters. For example, it tosses out outliers. However, keep in mind that it automatically uses FIXED_DISTANCE as its conceptualization of spatial relationship, and this may not be appropriate in your particular study. In this exercise, you'll learn how to use the **Optimized Hot Spot Analysis** tool to determine hot and cold spots of residential real estate sales activity.

Preparation

Let's get prepared before using the **Optimized Hot Spot Analysis** tool in real estate sales:

1. In ArcMap, open the
   `C:\GeospatialTraining\SpatialStats\SanAntonioRealEstate.mxd` file.
   You should see a number of layers that were created in the last exercise. To
   reduce clutter, you may want to turn off the visibility of many of these layers.
2. Leave the `BexarCountyCensusBlockGroupsJoined`, `ResidentialSales`, and
   `basemap` layers turned on.

In the last exercise, we aggregated real estate sales to census block groups and then
normalized the data by the area of each census block group to create a new attribute field
called `NormCount`, which is available on the
`BexarCountyCensusBlockGroupsJoined.shp` shapefile. We'll use this field again in this
exercise.

Running the Optimized Hot Spot Analysis tool

Let's run the **Optimized Hot Spot Analysis** tool by performing the following steps:

1. If necessary, open the **ArcToolbox** toolbox and find the **Spatial Statistics Tools**
   toolbox. Open the toolbox and expand the **Mapping Clusters** toolset. Double-
   click on **Optimized Hot Spot Analysis** to display the tool. The **Optimized Hot
   Spot Analysis** tool will automatically use the `FIXED_DISTANCE` parameter for
   determining the neighborhood of each feature. Keep in mind that this may or
   may not be suitable for the dataset you are analyzing. If you have a good
   understanding of your data and how neighborhoods should be defined, then you
   should in most cases use the Hot Spot Analysis tool instead. Select the following
   input parameters:
   - **Input Features**: `BexarCountyCensusBlockGroupsJoined`

- **Output Features**: Save the feature class as
  `C:\Users\<user>\Documents\ArcGIS\Default.gdb\Residentia lSalesOptimizedHotSpots`
- **Analysis Field**: `NormCount`

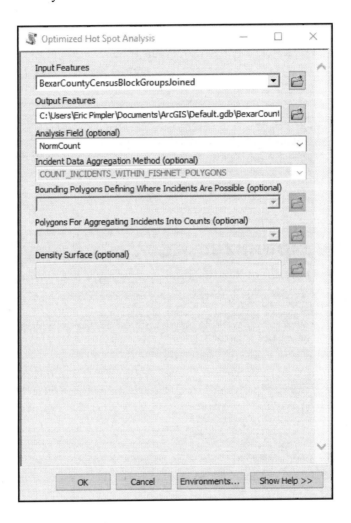

2. Click on OK to execute the tool.

The progress dialog will display information about the tool and results as it is running. This is illustrated in the following screenshot:

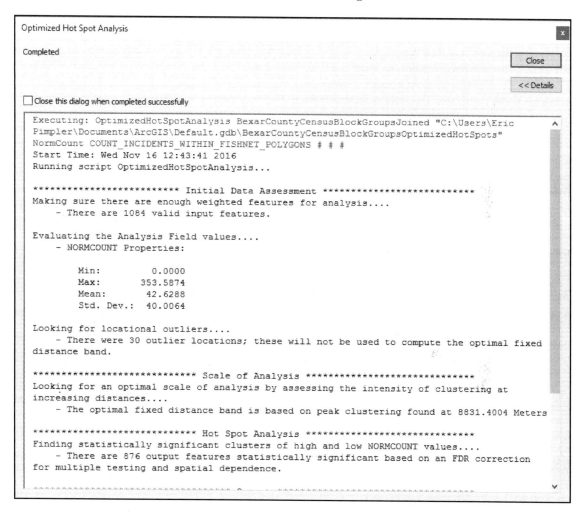

Interpreting the results

The primary output of the **Optimized Hot Spot Analysis** tool as a new feature class symbolized with hot spots, cold spots, and areas of no statistical significance. In this case, the results indicate statistically significant hot spots in the western and northern portions of the county. When we color coded the data in a prior step, we noted this pattern as well, but there was no statistical significance to the results nor did the pattern stand out like it did with the hot spot analysis. The cold spots, as expected, are centrally located in the county near the downtown area:

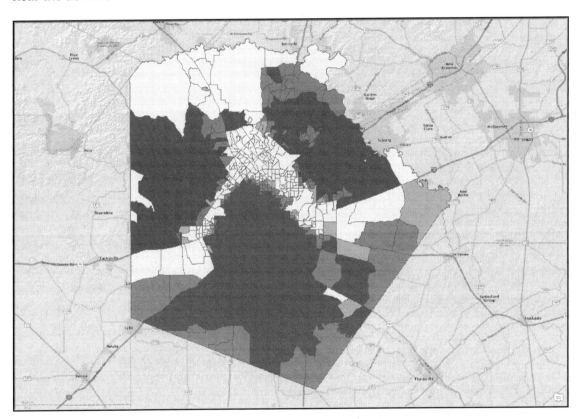

If we apply a transparency to the layer (40% in this case), we can get a better idea of the boundaries of our hot and cold spots, as shown in the following screenshot. The hot spots are largely outside the outer loop of San Antonio (TX 1604 Loop) and the cold spots are largely inside the inner loop (Loop 410):

Let's briefly return to the information displayed in the progress dialog. The tool displays the number of valid input features (1084 in this case), basic descriptive statistics (min, max, mean, and standard deviation), outlier locations that won't be used in the computation (30 in this case), defines an optimal fixed distance band based on peak clustering (7230 meters), displays the number of features that are statistically significant (626), and displays the output.

The optimal fixed distance band is of particular interest because the appeal of using this **Optimized Hot Spot Analysis** tool instead of the regular **Hot Spot Analysis** tool is that it determines this fixed distance band for you. Many analysts don't know what distance to use for the neighborhood, so often it is easier, though not necessarily better, to let the tool determine this value for you:

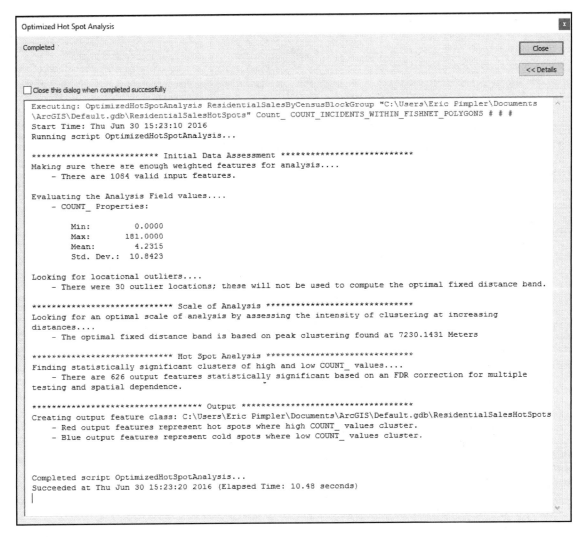

Now you can save your map document file.

Creating Hot Spot maps from point data using the Optimized Hot Spot Analysis tool

The **Hot Spot Analysis** and **Optimized Hot Spot Analysis** tools are traditionally used with polygon data. However, there may be times when your source data is represented by point locations. These locations may or may not have applicable attribute information.

There are two ways to handle this situation. If you have a suitable boundary layer such as census tracts or blocks, ZIP codes, or other political boundaries, you can aggregate the point data to the boundaries and then perform the hot spot analysis. You've already seen some examples of this. But there may be times when you don't have a suitable boundary layer to aggregate the points or simply want to use the point layer instead. In these situations, you can use the **Optimized Hot Spot Analysis** tool to create a fishnet of rectangular features to use as the aggregation layer. In this exercise, you'll learn how to use this tool with point features to generate a hot spot layer.

Preparation

Let's get prepared before hot spot maps from point data using the Optimized Hot Spot Analysis tool:

1. In ArcMap, open the `C:\GeospatialTraining\SpatialStats\SanAntonioRealEstate.mxd` file. You should see a number of layers that were created in the last two exercises.
2. To reduce clutter, you may want to turn off the visibility of many of these layers. Leave the `BexarCountyCensusBlockGroupsJoined`, `ResidentialSales`, and `Basemap` layers turned on.
3. In this exercise, we'll use the `ResidentialSales` point layer as the input to the **Optimized Hot Spot Analysis** tool to create a new hot spot layer.

Running the Optimized Hot Spot Analysis tool

1. If necessary, open the **ArcToolbox** toolbox and find the **Spatial Statistics Tools** toolbox. Open the toolbox and expand the **Mapping Clusters** toolset. Double-click on **Optimized Hot Spot Analysis** to display the tool. Select the following input parameters:
    - **Input Features**: `ResidentialSales`

- **Output Features**: Save the feature class as
  `C:\Users\<user>\Documents\ArcGIS\Default.gdb\Residentia`
  `lSalesHS`
- **Incident Data Aggregation Method**:
  `COUNT_INCIDENTS_WITHIN_FISHNET_POLYGONS`
- **Bounding Polygons Defining Where Incidents Are Possible
  (optional)**: `BexarCountyCensusBlockGroupsJoined`

2. The **Bounding Polygons Defining Where Incidents Are Possible (optional)**
   parameter is important when calculating a hot spot layer from a point layer. This
   polygon layer defines the limits of the analysis and will discard outlier points that
   are outside the boundary of this layer. Outliers can greatly affect the results of a
   hot spot map created from points:

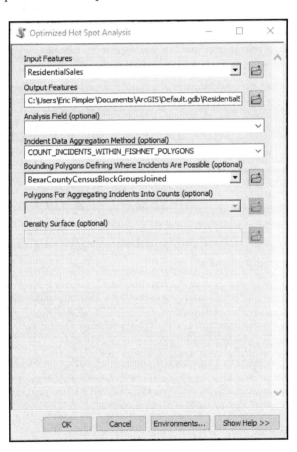

3. Click on **OK** to execute the tool.

4. The progress dialog will report information as the tool is running. You should see something similar to the following screenshot. Note that the tool identified 174 outlier locations that will not be used in the output. These are the points that fell outside the bounding polygon. The tool also reports the polygon cell size of the fishnet layer as 666.00 meters:

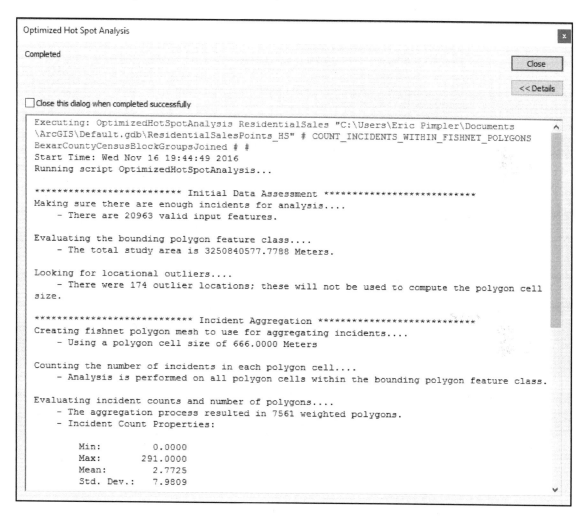

Optimized Hot Spot Analysis

Completed

Close

<< Details

☐ Close this dialog when completed successfully

```
Executing: OptimizedHotSpotAnalysis ResidentialSales "C:\Users\Eric Pimpler\Documents
\ArcGIS\Default.gdb\ResidentialSalesPoints_HS" # COUNT_INCIDENTS_WITHIN_FISHNET_POLYGONS
BexarCountyCensusBlockGroupsJoined # #
Start Time: Wed Nov 16 19:44:49 2016
Running script OptimizedHotSpotAnalysis...

************************* Initial Data Assessment ***************************
Making sure there are enough incidents for analysis....
    - There are 20963 valid input features.

Evaluating the bounding polygon feature class....
    - The total study area is 3250840577.7788 Meters.

Looking for locational outliers....
    - There were 174 outlier locations; these will not be used to compute the polygon cell
size.

*************************** Incident Aggregation ****************************
Creating fishnet polygon mesh to use for aggregating incidents....
    - Using a polygon cell size of 666.0000 Meters

Counting the number of incidents in each polygon cell....
    - Analysis is performed on all polygon cells within the bounding polygon feature class.

Evaluating incident counts and number of polygons....
    - The aggregation process resulted in 7561 weighted polygons.
    - Incident Count Properties:

        Min:        0.0000
        Max:      291.0000
        Mean:       2.7725
        Std. Dev.:  7.9809
```

5. The output layer should appear as seen in the following screenshot. Note that the output is restricted to the boundaries of the county census block groups:

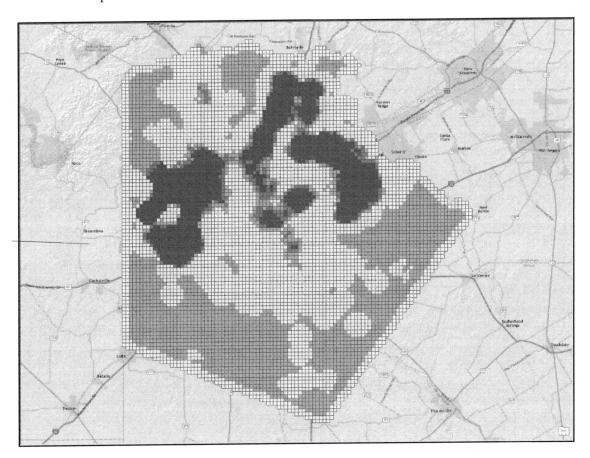

6. Run the tool again, but this time leave the **Bounding Polygons Defining Where Incidents Are Possible** parameter empty so that you can see how outliers affect the result. You should see an output that is similar to the screenshot. You'll recall from the previous execution of this tool that there were 174 outliers not included in the results. Since a bounding polygon was not defined in this case, a fishnet rectangle feature will be created for each area where there is at least one feature.

7. Some of the features fell well outside the boundaries of Bexar County, TX, but they are still included in the analysis. Note the dramatic effect on the results. You'll also notice large gaps between some of the output fishnet features. This is another effect of not specifying a bounding polygon. Even though it's possible to have an event in these areas, a fishnet feature does not represent them. When possible, you should include a bounding polygon to remove outliers and fill in the inevitable gaps in the output layer:

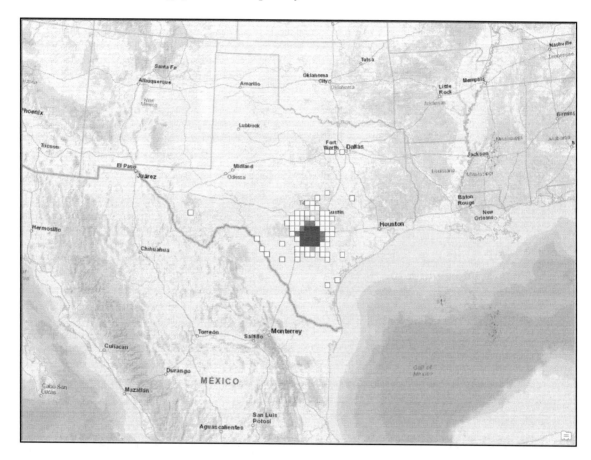

Finding outliers in real estate sales activity using the Cluster and Outlier Analysis tool

The next tool we'll examine is the **Cluster and Outlier Analysis** tool. This tool, in addition to performing hot spot analysis, identifies outliers in your data. Outliers are extremely relevant to many types of analysis. The tool starts by separating features and neighborhoods from the study area. Each feature is examined against every other feature to see if it is significantly different from the other features. Likewise, each neighborhood is examined in relationship to all other neighborhoods to see if it is statistically different than other neighborhoods. In this exercise, you'll learn how to use the **Cluster and Outlier Analysis** tool to find outliers (hot spots located in areas of cold spots and cold spots located in areas of hot spots).

Preparation

Let's get prepared before using the **Cluster and Outlier Analysis** tool for finding outliers in real estates sales activity by performing the following steps:

1. In ArcMap, open the
   `C:\GeospatialTraining\SpatialStats\SanAntonioRealEstate.mxd` file.
   You should see a number of layers that were created in the last few exercises.
2. To reduce clutter, you may want to turn off the visibility of many of these layers.
   Leave `BexarCountyCensusBlockGroupsJoined`, `ResidentialSales`, and the
   `Basemap` turned on. We're going to use the
   `BexarCountyCensusBlockGroupsJoined` layer with the **Cluster and Outlier
   Analysis** tool.
3. You'll remember from the last exercise that this layer has a `NormCount` field with
   the number of residential sales for each census block group.

Running the Cluster and Outlier Analysis tool

Let's run the **Cluster and Outlier Analysis** tool by performing the following steps:

1. If necessary, open the **ArcToolbox** toolbox and find the **Spatial Statistics Tools**
   toolbox. Open the toolbox and expand the **Mapping Clusters** toolset. Double-
   click on the **Cluster and Outlier Analysis** tool to display the tool. Select the
   following input parameters:
   - **Input Features**: `BexarCountyCensusBlockGroupsJoined`

- **Input Field**: NormCount
- **Output Features**: Save the feature class as
  C:\Users\<user>\Documents\ArcGIS\Default.gdb\Residentia
  lSalesOutlierAnalysis
- **Conceptualization of Spatial Relationships -**
  CONTIGUITY_EDGES_CORNERS

Leave the defaults for the remainder of the input parameters.

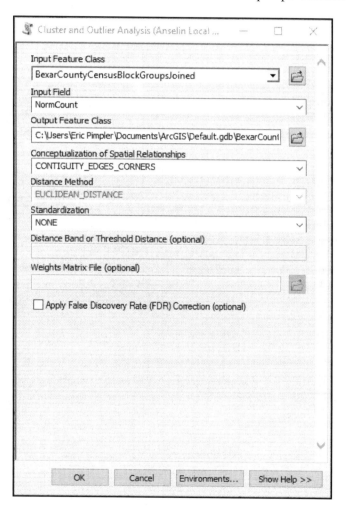

2. Click on **OK** to execute the tool

Interpreting the results

This is one of my favorite tools in the **Spatial Statistics Tools** toolbox because it uncovers information about your dataset that wouldn't otherwise be obvious. Take a look at the output feature class in the following screenshot:

The hot spots (pink) and cold spots (light blue) are still readily apparent. However, the dark blue and dark red areas indicate outliers:

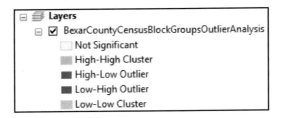

First, we'll examine the dark blue features. These fall in the Low-High (LH) category of outlier. What this means is that the feature itself is low but the neighborhood is high. In our case, dark blue features represent census block groups where sales are low but the surrounding neighborhood sales are high or not statistically significant. Keep in mind that the **Hot Spot Analysis** and **Optimized Hot Spot Analysis** tools did not pick this up. The reason is that each feature was identified as high, low, or not significant based on the results of the neighborhood of that feature in relation to the study area rather than the feature itself:

The tool also found several High-Low (HL) outliers. For the HL outliers, these are census block groups where sales activity is high but the surrounding neighborhood has low or not statistically significant sales activity. These are area doing unexpectedly well in terms of sales activity:

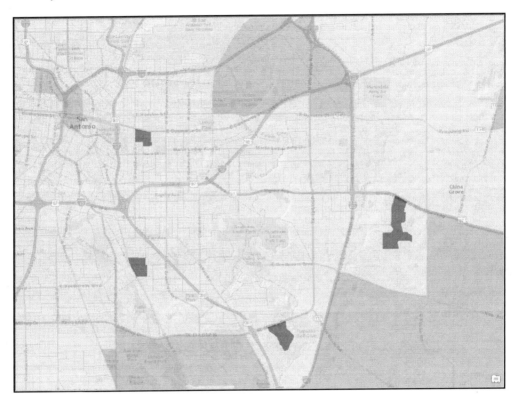

Summary

The tools found in the **Mapping Clusters** toolset are among the most valuable and frequently used tools in the **Spatial Statistics Tools** toolbox. The **Hot Spot Analysis**, **Optimized Hot Spot Analysis**, and **Cluster and Outlier Analysis** tools are used to create visualizations of hot and cold spots as well as features that can be defined as outliers from the common pattern in a dataset. The **Similarity Search** tool is used to find features that are either similar or dissimilar to an input feature, and the **Grouping Analysis** tools is used to group features that are most alike. All of these tools are valuable to many types of cluster analysis across many disciplines. In the next chapter, we'll examine how you can model various types of spatial relationships.

5
Modeling Spatial Relationships with ArcGIS Tools

In previous chapters, we examined tools that help us answer *where* questions. For example, where do burglaries cluster in a particular city? However, you may have noticed that they didn't address the logical progression of the problem such as *why* are the burglaries occurring in the first place? What are the factors that determine why burglaries are prevalent in a particular area? Answering these types of questions helps us model the relationships in our data. The **Measuring Spatial Relationships** toolset contains a number of regression analysis tools that help you examine and/or quantify the relationships among features. They help measure how features in a dataset relate to each other in space.

In this chapter, you will learn how to use many of these tools to gain an understanding of a phenomenon, create predictive models of a phenomenon, and explore hypotheses. The following tools will be used to model the relationships between various spatial and attribute data:

- The basics of Regression Analysis
- Using the **Ordinary Least Squares** tool
- Using the **Exploratory Regression** tool
- Using the **Geographically Weighted Regression** tool

The basics of Regression Analysis

Up until this section of the course, we examined tools that help us answer the *where* questions. Where are crimes occurring? Where do wildfires cluster? Where are the hot spots for real estate sales? However, you may have noticed that these tools don't help determine the *why* questions. The regression tools found in the **Modeling Spatial Relationships** toolset help with the logical progression of obtaining a deeper understanding of our problem. Tools such as **Ordinary Least Squares** and **Exploratory Regression** help us determine the variables that explain why an observed pattern is present. These explanatory variables can lead to the development of models that can predict the occurrence of these patterns in other places.

Why use Regression Analysis?

There are essentially three reasons to use Regression Analysis. The first is to gain an understanding of a phenomenon and effect policy or make decisions about appropriate actions to take. The next is to create predictive models of a phenomenon that can be applied to other areas, and finally, to explore hypotheses. Can you think of some examples that would apply to each of these?

Regression Analysis terms and concepts

Before we examine the regression tools that are available to you, it's important to have an understanding of the terms that will be used in this section. In particular, you need to become familiar with the regression equation illustrated in the following screenshot. These include a dependent variable, coefficients, explanatory variables, a random error/residual, p-values, and r-squared:

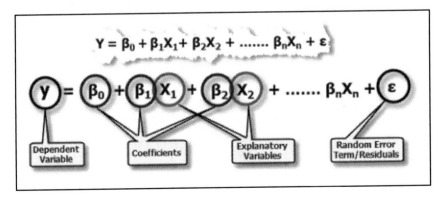

Let's begin by discussing the most obvious parts of the regression equation. The dependent variable or **Y** is the phenomenon you are trying to understand or predict whether that be burglaries, sales, foreclosures, wildfires, or something else. These are also known as the Y, or observed values. It is possible to use regression to predict this variable, but you always start with a set of known y-values and use these to construct the regression model that can be used in predictive analysis for other areas.

The explanatory or independent variables, represented by **X** in the equation, are used to model or predict the dependent variable. For example, if you were interested in predicting the location of a successful retail store, you might include explanatory variables such as the number of potential customers within a 5 miles radius, average annual income, distance to a competitor, and others.

The regression coefficient is a value for each explanatory variable that is computed by the regression tool. Its value represents the strength and type of relationship whether that is positive or negative.

Other terms you'll frequently encounter when working with the regression equation include p-values, r-squared, and residuals. These p-values are a measure of probability. Each coefficient is assigned a p-value. Small p-values indicate small probabilities that suggest that a coefficient is important to your model. For example, a p-value of 0.01 for a particular coefficient indicates that there is a 99% probability that the coefficient is important for your model.

The r-squared part of regression equation is used to quantify model performance and ranges in value between 0 and 100. The higher the value, the better your dependent variables are explained by your independent variables. If your model were a perfect fit, an r-squared value of 1.0 would be generated. In practice though, this never occurs unless you've done something incorrectly. Obviously though, the closer the value is to 1.0, the better the model fit. Finally, a residual or random error is the unexplained portion of the dependent variable.

Linear regression with the Ordinary Least Squares (OLS) tool

The **Ordinary Least Squares** tool or OLS is a linear regression tool used to generate predictions or model a dependent variable in terms of its relationships to a set of explanatory variables. OLS is the best known regression technique and provides a good starting point for spatial regression analysis. This tool provides a global model of a variable or process you are trying to understand or predict. The result is a single regression equation that depicts a positive or negative linear relationship.

OLS is almost always an iterative process, so don't expect to simply run this tool once and be done. It's very challenging, especially in the social sciences, to find the correct explanatory variables for a dependent variable. In addition to spending many hours of research in identifying potential explanatory variables, you will, in most cases, need to run the OLS tool many times, examine the results, and perform your checks. At some point, you will arrive at a model that is properly defined and without bias.

When running the OLS tool, you will need to provide several required input parameters including an input feature class along with a unique ID field, a variable, and explanatory variables. The unique ID, dependent variable, and explanatory variables should all be fields from the input feature class. An output feature class also needs to be defined. Optional parameters include an output report file, a coefficient output table, and a diagnostic output table. These parameters can be seen in the following screenshot:

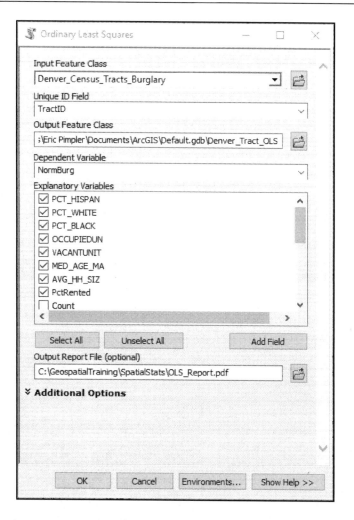

When defining the input parameters for the OLS tool, you will need to define the explanatory variables that you think will explain the dependent variables. You may be wondering how to determine the explanatory variables. You will need to do research beforehand, consult existing literature and theory in the field, talk to experts, and use common sense. It should also be noted that you will probably have to rerun this tool multiple times with different combinations of explanatory variables before you develop a workable model. The information for the explanatory variables should be found in the attribute fields of the input feature class, so you may need to do some pre-preparation of your dataset before you ever run the OLS tool.

The output of the OLS tool includes an output feature class, a message window report containing statistical results, an optional PDF report file, an optional table of explanatory variable coefficients, and an optional table of regression diagnostics.

In this section, we'll use the OLS tool to gain an understanding of burglary incidents in Denver, CO. Specifically, we want to understand the variables that lead to high burglary rates. In this case, the dependent variable is burglary rate by census tract. A number of potential explanatory variables will be used in the analysis. These will be described in the next section.

Running the Ordinary Least Squares tool

Let's see how to run the **Ordinary Least Squares** tool by performing the following steps:

1. If necessary, open **ArcMap** with the
   `C:\GeospatialTraining\SpatialStats\DenverCrimeModel.mxd` file. You should see a feature class called `Denver_Census_Tracts_Burglary`, as shown in the following screenshot, along with an American Community Survey layer and metadata table that we'll use later in the exercise:

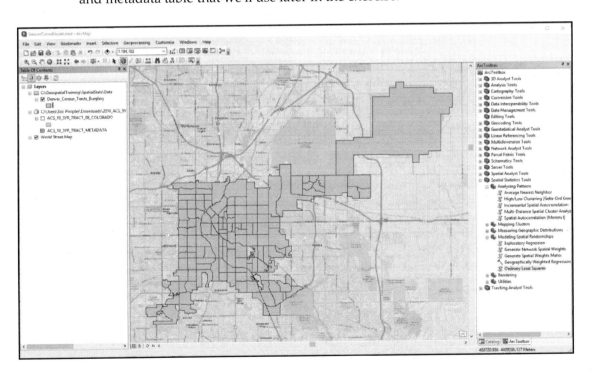

2. The amount of preparation depends on a number of factors including the study topic, variables used in the study, accessibility of the variables, and others. Open the attribute table for the `Denver_Census_Tracts_Burglary` layer. The attribute table contains a number of fields that define potential variables that we believe may affect burglary incidents in Denver, CO. The fields of interest are described as follows:

   - `PCT_HISPAN`: This is the percentage of population of Hispanic origin.
   - `PCT_WHITE`: This is the percentage of population of non-Hispanic white origin.
   - `PCT_BLACK`: This is the percentage of population of non-Hispanic black origin.
   - `OCCUPIEDUN`: This is the percentage of occupied housing units.
   - `VACANTUNIT`: This is the number of vacant housing units.
   - `MED_AGE_MA`: This is the median age of male population.
   - `AVG_HH_SIZ`: This is the average household size.
   - `PCTRENTED`: This is the percent of housing units that are rented.
   - `COUNT_`: This is the total number of burglary incidents for one year in each census tract. This field will not be used as an explanatory variable nor is it the dependent variable.
   - `NORMBURG`: This is a normalized burglary count. This is the field that will be used as the dependent variable. The field was derived by dividing the value in the `Count_` field by the area of each census tract.
   - `HSDROP`: This is the number of high school dropouts.
   - `MEDHHINC`: This is median household income.
   - `PERCUNEMP`: This is the percentage of population unemployed.
   - `PERCPOV`: This is the percentage of population living below poverty.
   - `FEMALEHD`: This is the percentage of population with a female head of household.
   - `DIVORCED`: This is the percentage of population that is divorced.
   - `NEWARRIVE`: This is the percentage of population that has migrated to the area in the past year.
   - `POPULATION`: This is the total population of the census tract.
   - `DISTURBCOR`: This is the distance to the urban core.

Most of these fields will be used as potential explanatory variables. The NORMBURG field will be our dependent variable. This field contains a normalized value of burglaries for each census tract. The Count_ field contains the number of burglaries in each census tract. To remove the effect of geographic size on the count, these values have been divided by the area of each census tract to arrive at the contents of NORMBURG.

3. The Denver_Census_Tracts_Burglary layer contains a number of attributes that have already been prepared for you in the interest of saving time and will allow you to focus on running the OLS tool and interpreting the output. However, you should keep in mind that a typical project will normally require some pre-preparation of your dataset before running the OLS tool.

4. Disable background geoprocessing by navigating to **Geoprocessing | Geoprocessing Options.....** In the **Background Processing** section, make sure that **Enable** is *not* selected. If it is, unselect the checkbox.

5. In **ArcToolbox**, open the **Spatial Statistics Tools** toolbox and then open **Modeling Spatial Relationships**. Double-click on the **Ordinary Least Squares** tool to display the dialog. Enter the following parameters:

   - **Input Feature Class**: Denver_Census_Tracts_Burglary.
   - **Unique ID Field**: TractID.
   - **Output Feature Class**:
     C:\Users\<username>\Documents\ArcGIS\Default.gdb\Denver _Census_Tracts_Burglary_OLS.
   - **Dependent Variable**: NormBurg.
   - **Explanatory Variables**: Select all fields *except* the TractID, Count_, and NormBurg fields. The TractID field only contains unique identifiers for each record and the Count_ and NormBurg fields contain dependent variable information.
   - **Output Report File (optional)**:
     C:\GeospatialTraining\SpatialStats\OLS_Report.pd.
   - **Additional Options**: We won't specify anything in this section at this time.

6. Click on the **OK** button to execute the tool. In this first run of the OLS tool, we've included all the potential explanatory variables. That doesn't mean that all these variables (or any of them for that matter) will prove to be correlated to the incidence of burglary in Denver. You should think of this as an iterative process wherein you try different combinations of explanatory variables to get the best fit.

Examining the output generated by the tool

Let's examine the output generated by the OLS tool:

1. Time to examine the output of the OLS tool. There are six checks that you'll need to perform each time you run the OLS tool. The steps for these checks are listed briefly as follows, and we'll get into more detail in the next few steps:
   - Are the explanatory variables helping my model?
   - Is each explanatory variable statistically significant?
   - Each variable should tell a different part of the story
   - Are the residuals clustered in location or value?
   - Are the residuals normally distributed using the Jarque-Bera test?
   - Assess model performance

2. The progress dialog, along with the `OLS_Report.pdf` file will contain much of the information you need to examine. Under `Summary of OLS Results`, you'll see a listing of all the explanatory variables that have been included. The report also contains a scatterplot for each variable that gives a visual depiction of the relationships between the dependent variable and each explanatory variable.

3. Let's first examine the explanatory variable coefficients seen in the following screenshot. Each explanatory variable will be listed along with a coefficient:

Variable	Coefficient [a]	StdError	t-Statistic	Probability [b]	Robust_SE	Robust_t	Robust_Pr [b]	VIF [c]
Intercept	293.284349	120.389844	2.436122	0.016236*	46.761216	6.271957	0.000000*	--------
PCT_HISPAN	1.389755	2.371039	0.586138	0.558834	2.445638	0.568259	0.570874	36.691051
PCT_WHITE	1.197280	2.058731	0.581562	0.561903	1.916694	0.624659	0.533325	34.417892
PCT_BLACK	4.088821	2.260156	1.809088	0.072825	2.331051	1.754067	0.081856	7.208388
OCCUPIEDUN	0.171460	0.044949	3.814536	0.000219*	0.036901	4.646521	0.000010*	12.904671
VACANTUNIT	-0.054960	0.118608	-0.463375	0.643904	0.082773	-0.663983	0.507913	2.213684
MED_AGE_MA	-6.109064	2.574660	-2.372765	0.019159*	2.695107	-2.266724	0.025103*	3.289680
AVG_HH_SIZ	105.889631	47.542101	2.227281	0.027696*	42.871990	2.469902	0.014845*	12.015445
PCTRENTED	0.903956	0.938484	0.963208	0.337280	0.774467	1.167196	0.245334	4.243800
HSDROP	0.163679	0.095432	1.715140	0.088784	0.091161	1.795488	0.074977	4.103239
MEDHHINC	-0.001060	0.000795	-1.333561	0.184759	0.000643	-1.649305	0.101584	4.078811
PERCUNEMP	-5.018923	4.472815	-1.122095	0.263953	4.430655	-1.132772	0.259458	2.176544
PERCPOV	-0.779406	1.359191	-0.573434	0.567376	1.355302	-0.575079	0.566266	3.503081
FEMALEHD	-7.049433	2.233498	-3.156229	0.002006*	2.296160	-3.070097	0.002627*	3.786903
DIVORCED	-0.703364	2.280837	-0.308380	0.758309	2.314920	-0.303840	0.761758	1.267492
NEWARRIVE	1.326068	1.558455	0.850886	0.396438	1.451065	0.913858	0.362528	2.348636
POPULATION	-0.067532	0.020568	-3.283280	0.001336*	0.015989	-4.223574	0.000049*	11.960555
DISTURBCOR	-0.017744	0.002947	-6.021746	0.000000*	0.002825	-6.280481	0.000000*	2.276911

Summary of OLS Results

4. The coefficient provides a value that indicates the strength of the variable on the dependent variable along with a type, which can be either positive or negative. A positive example in the case of residential burglaries would be that a larger percentage of residential property renters (as a percentage of the population) would lead to a higher number of burglaries. A negative example would be fewer burglaries as the distance from an urban core increases. Negative relationships will always have a negative numeric value.

5. You need to ask yourself if these relationships are what you would expect using a common sense approach. Your preconceived expectations may or may not be correct, but more often than not, your relationship should be as expected. We're not ruling an explanatory variable out or in at this point. Instead, just examine each variable to see if the coefficient strength and type are what you would expect using common sense:

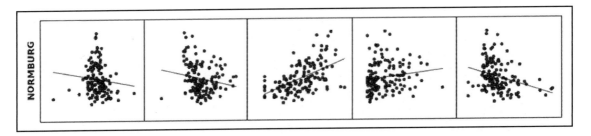

6. The next check for each explanatory variable is the `Probability` and `Robust Probability` fields. These statistics provides a measure of whether the variables are statistically significant. In other words, does each explanatory variable tell an important part of the story? This is easy to determine simply by looking for asterisks to the right side of each probability value for each explanatory variable. If you see an asterisk, it indicates that this variable has passed the check of statistical significance.

7. If you don't see an asterisk, you can generally conclude that this particular explanatory variable is not valid and probably needs to be removed. In other words, it doesn't play a role in the model. In this instance, `OCCUPIEDUN`, `MED_AGE_MA`, `AVG_HH_SIZ`, `FEMALEHD`, `POPULATION`, and `DISTURBCOR` were the only explanatory variables that have an asterisk. We'll include each of the variables in the next iteration of the OLS tool. That doesn't mean we'll leave out all the other variables though. As you'll see, there may be some reasons to include some of the other variables as well:

```
                              Summary of OLS Results
   Variable Coefficient [a]    StdError t-Statistic Probability [b] Robust_SE  Robust_t Robust_Pr [b]  VIF [c]
  Intercept    293.284349  120.389844    2.436122       0.016236* 46.761216   6.271957     0.000000*  --------
PCT_HISPAN       1.389755    2.371039    0.586138       0.558834  2.445638    0.568259     0.570874  36.691051
 PCT_WHITE       1.197280    2.058731    0.581562       0.561903  1.916694    0.624659     0.533325  34.417892
 PCT_BLACK       4.088821    2.260156    1.809088       0.072825  2.331051    1.754067     0.081856   7.208388
OCCUPIEDUN       0.171460    0.044949    3.814536       0.000219*  0.036901   4.646521     0.000010* 12.904671
VACANTUNIT      -0.054960    0.118608   -0.463375       0.643904  0.082773   -0.663983     0.507913   2.213684
MED_AGE_MA      -6.109064    2.574660   -2.372765       0.019159*  2.695107  -2.266724     0.025103*   3.289680
AVG_HH_SIZ     105.889631   47.542101    2.227281       0.027696* 42.871990   2.469902     0.014845* 12.015445
 PCTRENTED       0.903956    0.938484    0.963208       0.337280  0.774467    1.167196     0.245334   4.243800
    HSDROP       0.163679    0.095432    1.715140       0.088784  0.091161    1.795488     0.074977   4.103239
  MEDHHINC      -0.001060    0.000795   -1.333561       0.184759  0.000643   -1.649305     0.101584   4.078811
  PERCUNEMP     -5.018923    4.472815   -1.122095       0.263953  4.430655   -1.132772     0.259458   2.176544
   PERCPOV      -0.779406    1.359191   -0.573434       0.567376  1.355302   -0.575079     0.566266   3.503081
  FEMALEHD      -7.049433    2.233498   -3.156229       0.002006*  2.296160  -3.070097     0.002627*   3.786903
  DIVORCED      -0.703364    2.280837   -0.308380       0.758309  2.314920   -0.303840     0.761758   1.267492
 NEWARRIVE       1.326068    1.558455    0.850886       0.396438  1.451065    0.913858     0.362528   2.348636
POPULATION      -0.067532    0.020568   -3.283280       0.001336*  0.015989  -4.223574     0.000049* 11.960555
DISTURBCOR      -0.017744    0.002947   -6.021746       0.000000*  0.002825  -6.280481     0.000000*   2.276911
```

8. Each explanatory variable should tell a different part of the story. This is measured in the OLS tool through what is known as the **Variance Inflation Factor (VIF)**.

9. Sometimes, you will include multiple explanatory variables in your analysis that are essentially measuring the same thing. For example, in a study of residential home values, you might include the number of bedrooms as well as the square feet of the home. These are essentially measuring the same thing, which is the size of the house.

10. The VIF value for each explanatory value should be less than 7.5. If you have values beyond 7.5 you will always have more than one variable that is beyond 7.5. That's your indicator that these are the variables that are measuring the same thing. These are variables that are telling the same story. They are redundant. You'll want to remove them one at a time and re-run the OLS tool to see how removing one of the variables affects the model.

11. In this run of the OLS tool, several variables were identified as exceeding the 7.5 limits for VIF including PCT_HISPAN, PCT_WHITE, PCT_BLACK, OCCUPIEDUN, AVG_HH_SIZE, and POPULATION. The race percentages are all obviously measuring the same thing, which is of course race. We'll remove at least one of these in the next iteration of the OLS tool. It appears that OCCUPIEDUN, AVG_HH_SIZE, and POPULATION may also be measuring the number of people in an area. We'll need to make some decisions about which of these variables to include in the next iteration:

```
                           Summary of OLS Results
  Variable Coefficient [a]    StdError t-Statistic Probability [b] Robust_SE  Robust_t Robust_Pr [b]   VIF [c]
 Intercept     293.284349 120.389844    2.436122       0.016236* 46.761216  6.271957     0.000000*  --------
PCT_HISPAN       1.389755   2.371039    0.586138       0.558834  2.445638  0.568259     0.570874  36.691051
 PCT_WHITE       1.197280   2.058731    0.581562       0.561903  1.916694  0.624659     0.533325  34.417892
 PCT_BLACK       4.088821   2.260156    1.809088       0.072825  2.331051  1.754067     0.081856   7.208388
OCCUPIEDUN       0.171460   0.044949    3.814536       0.000219* 0.036901  4.646521     0.000010* 12.904671
 VACANTUNIT     -0.054960   0.118608   -0.463375       0.643904  0.082773 -0.663983     0.507913   2.213684
MED_AGE_MA      -6.109064   2.574660   -2.372765       0.019159* 2.695107 -2.266724     0.025103*  3.289680
AVG_HH_SIZ     105.889631  47.542101    2.227281       0.027696* 42.871990  2.469902     0.014845* 12.015445
 PCTRENTED       0.903956   0.938484    0.963208       0.337280  0.774467  1.167196     0.245334   4.243800
    HSDROP       0.163679   0.095432    1.715140       0.088784  0.091161  1.795488     0.074977   4.103239
  MEDHHINC      -0.001060   0.000795   -1.333561       0.184759  0.000643 -1.649305     0.101584   4.078811
  PERCUNEMP     -5.018923   4.472815   -1.122095       0.263953  4.430655 -1.132772     0.259458   2.176544
   PERCPOV      -0.779406   1.359191   -0.573434       0.567376  1.355302 -0.575079     0.566266   3.503081
  FEMALEHD      -7.049433   2.233498   -3.156229       0.002006* 2.296160 -3.070097     0.002627*  3.786903
   DIVORCED     -0.703364   2.280837   -0.308380       0.758309  2.314920 -0.303840     0.761758   1.267492
  NEWARRIVE      1.326068   1.558455    0.850886       0.396438  1.451065  0.913858     0.362528   2.348636
POPULATION      -0.067532   0.020568   -3.283280       0.001336* 0.015989 -4.223574     0.000049* 11.960555
DISTURBCOR      -0.017744   0.002947   -6.021746       0.000000* 0.002825 -6.280481     0.000000*  2.276911
```

12. The next thing to check is the residuals or random error. One of the outputs of the OLS tool is a new feature class, which is color-coded by residuals. The optional output report file will also contain a histogram and a normal bell curve.

13. Residuals should not be clustered in either location or value. If you see clustering on the map or if the histogram looks very different from the normal curve, you may have a biased model. Let's take a closer look at residuals. The output feature class that has been added in the **ArcMap** window in the **Table Of Contents** pane should appear as follows:

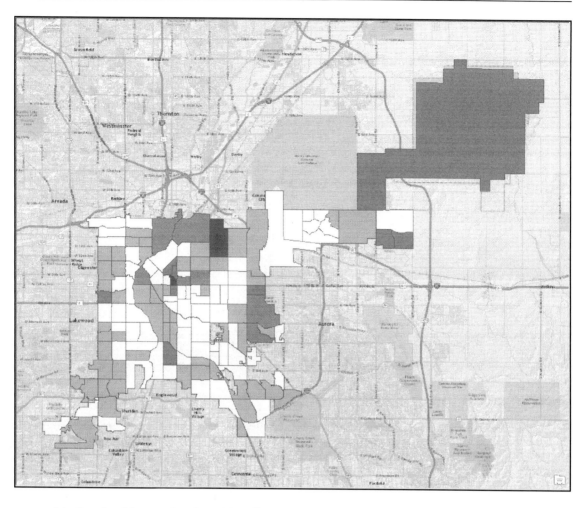

14. Just looking at the data visually, it is pretty apparent that we have some high value clustering near the center of the study area and some low value clustering in the tracts that bound the north side of the study area. However, we'll want to perform an additional test using the **Spatial Autocorrelation** tool to make sure that we do indeed have spatial clustering in our output residuals.

15. Remember, that we don't want clustering in the residuals. Instead, we want to see a random spatial pattern. We'll run the **Spatial Autocorrelation** tool in the next step. Before we do that though, you'll want to open the `C:\GeospatialTraining\SpatialStats\OLS_Report.pdf` file and find **Histogram of Standardized Residuals**. It should appear as follows:

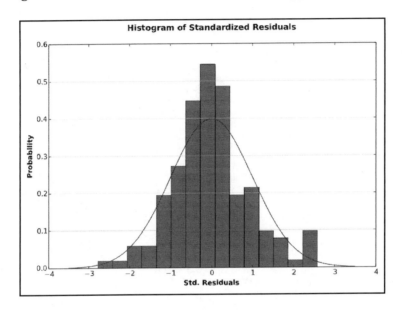

16. You'll notice that there are some values that are significantly different than the normal curve. This is yet another indicator that we have bias in our model, which is not surprising since this is the first iteration of the OLS tool when modeling this scenario.

17. In this step, we'll run the **Spatial Autocorrelation** tool against the residuals to determine if we have a random or clustered pattern. We want to see a random pattern, but based on what we can see, it's pretty clear that we do have clustering.

18. Find the **Spatial Autocorrelation** tool in the **Spatial Statistics Tools** toolbox and the **Analyzing Patterns** toolset. Open the tool and input the following parameters:

    - **Input Feature Class**: `Denver_Census_Tracts_Burglary_OLS1`
    - **Input Field**: `StdResid`
    - **Generate Report**: `Yes`
    - **Conceptualization of Spatial Relationships**: `CONTIGUITY_EDGES_CORNERS`

19. Don't change any of the other parameters. Click on the **OK** button to execute the tool.

20. The progress dialog will display the path and filename of the report. This will be an HTML file. Open the file to see the results shown in the following screenshot. Based on this report, we can see that we have a clustered pattern in our data. This is not what we want since we're looking for a random pattern. That isn't unexpected at this point though since this is our first iteration of the OLS tool. Right now, it's an indication that we have bias in our model:

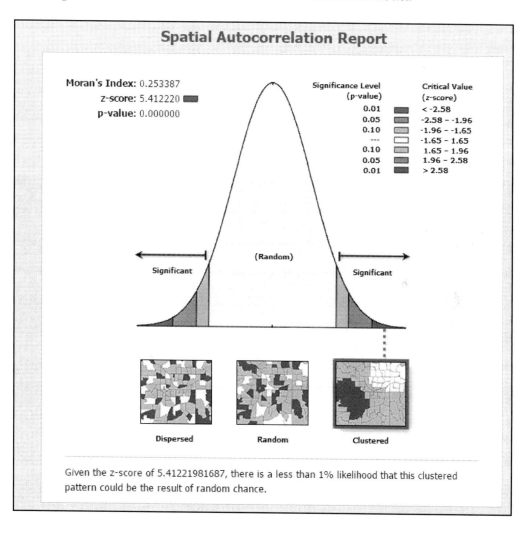

21. The next step in attempting to determine bias in your model is checking the `Jarque-Bera` statistic. This statistic should not have an asterisk. If it does, it is a strong indicator of bias in your model. It is not uncommon to have difficulty passing this test, or any of the others for that matter. OLS almost always requires multiple iterations with different combinations of variables before you ultimately arrive at a model without bias. For now, our model looks acceptable for the `Jarque-Bera` statistic:

	OLS Diagnostics		
Input Features:	Denver_Census_Tracts_Burglary	Dependent Variable:	NORMBURG
Number of Observations:	144	Akaike's Information Criterion (AICc) [d]:	1798.213325
Multiple R-Squared [d]:	0.613269	Adjusted R-Squared [d]:	0.561091
Joint F-Statistic [e]:	11.753388	Prob(>F), (17,126) degrees of freedom:	0.000000*
Joint Wald Statistic [e]:	300.930516	Prob(>chi-squared), (17) degrees of freedom:	0.000000*
Koenker (BP) Statistic [f]:	30.290102	Prob(>chi-squared), (17) degrees of freedom:	0.024327*
Jarque-Bera Statistic [g]:	5.519923	Prob(>chi-squared), (2) degrees of freedom:	0.063294

22. The final check you should perform is to find the `OLS Diagnostics` section and look for the `Multiple R-Squared [d]` and `Adjusted R-Squared [d]` values (`0.613269` and `0.561091` in this case). Values will range from 0.0 to 1.0. The closer to 1.0 you get, the better your model. Many people are tempted to check this value first, but the reality is that all your other checks must be acceptable before you can rely on the r-squared value as a strong indicator that your model is good.

23. In social sciences, values around 0.5 or 0.6 are generally considered to be very good as is the case in our example study of residential burglary. In social sciences, you deal with human behavior, meaning that there are many factors that must be considered. In the hard sciences, you are looking for values very close to 1.0. The r-squared is not the be-all end-all though. You must still go through the other five checks before you can feel comfortable with the results:

OLS Diagnostics			
Input Features:	Denver_Census_Tracts_Bu	Dependent Variable:	NORMBURG
Number of Observations:	144	Akaike's Information Criterion (AICc) [d]:	1798.213325
Multiple R-Squared [d]:	0.613269	Adjusted R-Squared [d]:	0.561091
Joint F-Statistic [e]:	11.753388	Prob(>F), (17,126) degrees of freedom:	0.000000*
Joint Wald Statistic [e]:	300.930516	Prob(>chi-squared), (17) degrees of freedom:	0.000000*
Koenker (BP) Statistic [f]:	30.290102	Prob(>chi-squared), (17) degrees of freedom:	0.024327*
Jarque-Bera Statistic [g]:	5.519923	Prob(>chi-squared), (2) degrees of freedom:	0.063294

24. The `Adjusted R-squared` value will always be somewhat lower but is the more accurate of the two. It is a reflection of model complexity (number of variables) as it relates to the data.

25. Clearly, we have some work to do in terms of selecting the appropriate explanatory variables and removing the bias that we found. For the second iteration of the OLS tool, we'll include the variables that were identified as statistically significant in the first run including `OCCUPIEDUN`, `MED_AGE_MA`, `AVG_HH_SIZ`, `FEMALEHD`, `POPULATION`, and `DISTURBCOR`. We're also going to include the race variable with the lowest VIF: `PCT_BLACK`. We'll also add in the `PCTRENTED` variable again because in past studies, a high percentage of residential renters have been shown to be strongly correlated with burglary incidents. Run the OLS tool again with the following parameters:

    - **Input Feature Class**: `Denver_Census_Tracts_Burglary`
    - **Unique ID Field**: `TractID`
    - **Output Feature Class**:
      `C:\Users\<username>\Documents\ArcGIS\Default.gdb\Denver_Census_Tracts_Burglary_OLS2`
    - **Dependent Variable**: `NormBurg`
    - **Explanatory Variables**: `OCCUPIEDUN`, `MED_AGE_MA`, `AVG_HH_SIZ`, `FEMALEHD`, `POPULATION`, `DISTURBCOR`, `PCT_BLACK`, and `PCTRENTED`
    - **Output Report File**:
      `C:\GeospatialTraining\SpatialStats\OLS_Report2.pdf`

26. Click on the **OK** button to execute the OLS tool. You'll want to go through the six steps again just like the first iteration of the tool. However, we will point out a number of things from the report. First, all of our explanatory variables are now statistically significant as noted with the asterisks for probability and robust probability. Next, we still have a couple of variables (OCCUPIEDUN and POPULATION) that have VIF values beyond 7.5. In the next iteration, we'll remove one of these. Finally, the Jarque-Bera statistic now has an asterisk indicating bias in the model:

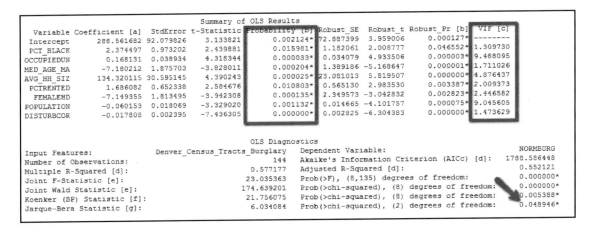

```
                                   Summary of OLS Results
  Variable  Coefficient [a]   StdError   t-Statistic   Probability [b]   Robust_SE   Robust_t   Robust_Pr [b]   VIF [c]
 Intercept   288.561682      92.079826    3.133821       0.002124*       72.887399    3.959006     0.000127*    --------
  PCT_BLACK    2.374497       0.973202    2.439881       0.015981*        1.182061    2.008777     0.046552*    1.309730
OCCUPIEDUN     0.168131       0.038934    4.318344       0.000033*        0.034079    4.933506     0.000003*    9.488095
 MED_AGE_MA   -7.180212       1.875703   -3.828011       0.000204*        1.389186   -5.168647     0.000001*    1.711026
  AVG_HH_SIZ 134.320115      30.595145    4.390243       0.000025*       23.081013    5.819507     0.000000*    4.876437
  PCTRENTED    1.686082       0.652338    2.584676       0.010803*        0.565130    2.983530     0.003387*    2.009373
   FEMALEHD   -7.149355       1.813495   -3.942308       0.000135*        2.349573   -3.042832     0.002823*    2.446582
 POPULATION   -0.060153       0.018069   -3.329020       0.001132*        0.014665   -4.101757     0.000075*    9.045605
 DISTURBCOR   -0.017808       0.002395   -7.436305       0.000000*        0.002825   -6.304383     0.000000*    1.473629


                                       OLS Diagnostics
Input Features:                 Denver_Census_Tracts_Burglary   Dependent Variable:                                NORMBURG
Number of Observations:                            144          Akaike's Information Criterion (AICc) [d]:      1788.586448
Multiple R-Squared [d]:                       0.577177          Adjusted R-Squared [d]:                           0.552121
Joint F-Statistic [e]:                       23.035363          Prob(>F), (8,135) degrees of freedom:             0.000000*
Joint Wald Statistic [e]:                   174.639201          Prob(>chi-squared), (8) degrees of freedom:       0.000000*
Koenker (BP) Statistic [f]:                  21.756075          Prob(>chi-squared), (8) degrees of freedom:       0.005388*
Jarque-Bera Statistic [g]:                    6.034084          Prob(>chi-squared), (2) degrees of freedom:       0.048946*
```

27. You'll also want to run the **Spatial Autocorrelation** tool a second time against the new output feature class. You should continue to see a clustered pattern. So we obviously still have work to do, but we're getting closer.

28. For the next iteration of the OLS tool, we'll remove the OCCUPIEDUN variable (in favor of POPULATION). While this may seem like a lot of work, it is not uncommon to run the OLS tool dozens of times using various combinations of variables. In the third iteration of the OLS tool, input the following input parameters:

   - **Input Feature Class**: Denver_Census_Tracts_Burglary
   - **Unique ID Field**: TractID
   - **Output Feature Class**:
     C:\Users\<username>\Documents\ArcGIS\Default.gdb\Denver_Census_Tracts_Burglary_OLS3

- **Dependent Variable**: NormBurg
- **Explanatory Variables**: MED_AGE_MA, AVG_HH_SIZ, FEMALEHD, POPULATION, DISTURBCOR, PCT_BLACK, and PCTRENTED
- **Output Report File**: C:\GeospatialTraining\SpatialStats\OLS_Report3.pdf

29. For the third iteration, all our VIF values are now less than 7.5 and our Jarque-Bera statistic is now acceptable. However, some of our explanatory variables are now showing up as not statistically significant. By now, you're probably getting a good feel for how this process works and an understanding of how difficult it can be to create a set of explanatory variables that are correlated to the dependent variable:

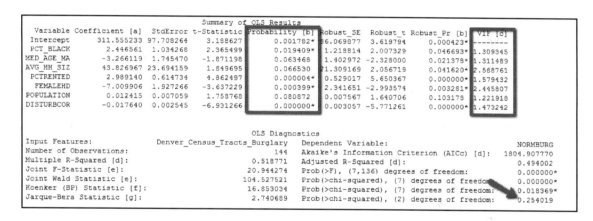

Variable	Coefficient [a]	StdError	t-Statistic	Probability [b]	Robust_SE	Robust_t	Robust_Pr [b]	VIF [c]
Intercept	311.555233	97.708264	3.188627	0.001782*	96.069877	3.619794	0.000423*	--------
PCT_BLACK	2.446561	1.034268	2.365499	0.019409*	1.218814	2.007329	0.046693*	1.309345
MED_AGE_MA	-3.266119	1.745470	-1.871198	0.063468	1.402972	-2.328000	0.021378*	1.311489
AVG_HH_SIZ	43.826967	23.694159	1.849695	0.066530	21.309169	2.056719	0.041620*	2.588761
PCTRENTED	2.989140	0.614734	4.862497	0.000004*	0.529017	5.650367	0.000000*	1.579432
FEMALEHD	-7.009906	1.927266	-3.637229	0.000399*	2.341651	-2.993574	0.003281*	2.445807
POPULATION	0.012415	0.007059	1.758768	0.080872	0.007567	1.640706	0.103178	1.221918
DISTURBCOR	-0.017640	0.002545	-6.931266	0.000000*	0.003057	-5.771261	0.000000*	1.473242

OLS Diagnostics

Input Features:	Denver_Census_Tracts_Burglary	Dependent Variable:	NORMBURG
Number of Observations:	144	Akaike's Information Criterion (AICc) [d]:	1804.907770
Multiple R-Squared [d]:	0.518771	Adjusted R-Squared [d]:	0.494002
Joint F-Statistic [e]:	20.944274	Prob(>F), (7,136) degrees of freedom:	0.000000*
Joint Wald Statistic [e]:	104.527521	Prob(>chi-squared), (7) degrees of freedom:	0.000000*
Koenker (BP) Statistic [f]:	16.853034	Prob(>chi-squared), (7) degrees of freedom:	0.018369*
Jarque-Bera Statistic [g]:	2.740689	Prob(>chi-squared), (2) degrees of freedom:	0.254019

30. In the output report, take a look at the relationships between the dependent variable and each of the independent variables, as shown in the following screenshot. See that the PCT_BLACK and POPULATION fields exhibit fairly week correlations, so let's remove those two variables in our next iteration to see the effect:

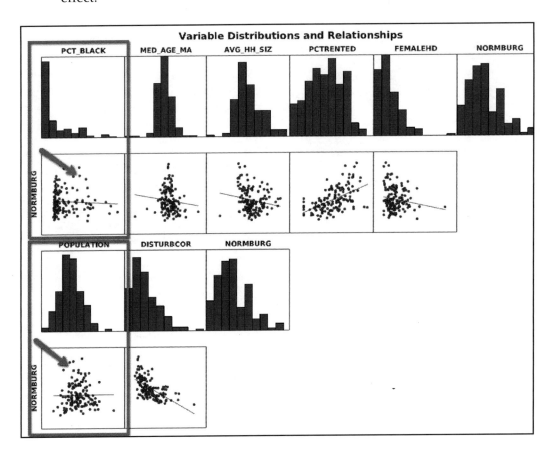

31. In the fourth iteration of the OLS tool, input the following input parameters:

  - **Input Feature Class**: `Denver_Census_Tracts_Burglary`
  - **Unique ID Field**: `TractID`
  - **Output Feature Class**:
    `C:\Users\<username>\Documents\ArcGIS\Default.gdb\Denver_Census_Tracts_Burglary_OLS4`
  - **Dependent Variable**: `NormBurg`
  - **Explanatory Variables**: `MED_AGE_MA`, `AVG_HH_SIZ`, `FEMALEHD`, `DISTURBCOR`, and `PCTRENTED`
  - Output Report File:
    `C:\GeospatialTraining\SpatialStats\OLS_Report4.pdf`

32. Most of the output looks good at this point with no variables beyond 7.5 for VIF and an acceptable `Jarque-Bera` statistic. We do still have the `MED_AGE_MA` variable as not statistically significant, and if you run the **Spatial Autocorrelation** tool on the output feature class, you'll still find clustering:

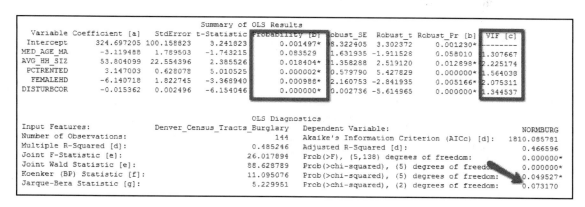

Summary of OLS Results

Variable	Coefficient [a]	StdError	t-Statistic	Probability [b]	Robust_SE	Robust_t	Robust_Pr [b]	VIF [c]
Intercept	324.697205	100.158823	3.241823	0.001497*	98.322405	3.302372	0.001230*	--------
MED_AGE_MA	-3.119488	1.789503	-1.743215	0.083529	1.631935	-1.911528	0.058010	1.307667
AVG_HH_SIZ	53.804099	22.554396	2.385526	0.018404*	21.358288	2.519120	0.012898*	2.225174
PCTRENTED	3.147003	0.628078	5.010525	0.000002*	0.579790	5.427829	0.000000*	1.564038
FEMALEHD	-6.140718	1.822745	-3.368940	0.000988*	2.160753	-2.841935	0.005166*	2.075311
DISTURBCOR	-0.015362	0.002496	-6.154046	0.000000*	0.002736	-5.614965	0.000000*	1.344537

OLS Diagnostics

Input Features:	Denver_Census_Tracts_Burglary	Dependent Variable:	NORMBURG
Number of Observations:	144	Akaike's Information Criterion (AICc) [d]:	1810.085781
Multiple R-Squared [d]:	0.485246	Adjusted R-Squared [d]:	0.466596
Joint F-Statistic [e]:	26.017894	Prob(>F), (5,138) degrees of freedom:	0.000000*
Joint Wald Statistic [e]:	88.628789	Prob(>chi-squared), (5) degrees of freedom:	0.000000*
Koenker (BP) Statistic [f]:	11.095076	Prob(>chi-squared), (5) degrees of freedom:	0.049527*
Jarque-Bera Statistic [g]:	5.229951	Prob(>chi-squared), (2) degrees of freedom:	0.073170

33. Let's mix things up a little bit in the next iteration by leaving most of the current explanatory variables but adding several variables back into the tool and removing others. In the fifth iteration of the OLS tool, input the following parameters:

    - **Input Feature Class**: `Denver_Census_Tracts_Burglary`
    - **Unique ID Field**: `TractID`
    - **Output Feature Class**:
      `C:\Users\<username>\Documents\ArcGIS\Default.gdb\Denver_Census_Tracts_Burglary_OLS5`
    - **Dependent Variable**: `NormBurg`
    - **Explanatory Variables**: `PCT_BLACK`, `PCT_RENTED`, `MEDHHINC`, `FEMALEHD`, `POPULATION`, and `DISTURBCOR`.
    - **Output Report File**:
      `C:\GeospatialTraining\SpatialStats\OLS_Report5.pdf`

34. This iteration looks pretty good for the most part, but not perfect. Take a look at the following screenshot for the output values. In general, these values are acceptable. The probabilities for each of the explanatory variables are all within the acceptable range, all VIF values are less than 7.5, the `Jarque-Bera` statistic is good, and the r-squared value is at a decent level. Another way of viewing the r-squared value is to say that roughly 50% of burglary incidents are explained by the explanatory variables we have provided. It was mentioned earlier that in the social sciences a value of 50-60% is considered good. However, there are obviously other factors that help explain burglary, we just haven't found what they are yet. Also, if you run the **Spatial Autocorrelation** tool against the residual, you will still get clustering, so it's not perfect:

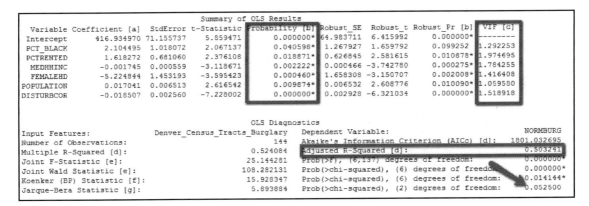

Summary of OLS Results

Variable	Coefficient [a]	StdError	t-Statistic	Probability [b]	Robust_SE	Robust_t	Robust_Pr [b]	VIF [c]
Intercept	416.934970	71.155737	5.859471	0.000000*	64.983711	6.415992	0.000000*	--------
PCT_BLACK	2.104495	1.018072	2.067137	0.040598*	1.267927	1.659792	0.099252	1.292253
PCTRENTED	1.618272	0.681060	2.376108	0.018871*	0.626845	2.581615	0.010878*	1.974695
MEDHHINC	-0.001745	0.000559	-3.118671	0.002222*	0.000466	-3.742780	0.000275*	1.784255
FEMALEHD	-5.224844	1.453193	-3.595423	0.000460*	1.658308	-3.150707	0.002008*	1.416408
POPULATION	0.017041	0.006513	2.616542	0.009874*	0.006532	2.608776	0.010090*	1.059580
DISTURBCOR	-0.018507	0.002560	-7.228002	0.000000*	0.002928	-6.321034	0.000000*	1.518918

OLS Diagnostics

Input Features:	Denver_Census_Tracts_Burglary	Dependent Variable:		NORMBURG
Number of Observations:	144	Akaike's Information Criterion (AICc) [d]:		1801.032695
Multiple R-Squared [d]:	0.524084	Adjusted R-Squared [d]:		0.503241
Joint F-Statistic [e]:	25.144281	Prob(>F), (6,137) degrees of freedom:		0.000000*
Joint Wald Statistic [e]:	108.282131	Prob(>chi-squared), (6) degrees of freedom:		0.000000*
Koenker (BP) Statistic [f]:	15.928347	Prob(>chi-squared), (6) degrees of freedom:		0.014144*
Jarque-Bera Statistic [g]:	5.893884	Prob(>chi-squared), (2) degrees of freedom:		0.052500

35. The point of this exercise is to get you familiar with the OLS tool and to understand the iterative process required for ultimately coming up with a model that explains (at least in part) the variables that affect the dependent variable. If you'd like to continue analyzing different sets of variables that are already attached to the `Denver_Census_Tracts_Burglary` layer, you can continue to do so at this time. There is an **American Community Survey** (**ACS**) layer in the map document file that contains many additional variables that you could join to the census tracts layer. The associated ACS metadata table gives detailed descriptions of the attribute fields in this layer. Feel free to attach these variables and add them to your analysis as well.

In the next section of this chapter, you'll learn how to use the **Exploratory Regression** tool to analyze variables for good model fit and explore relationships in your data.

Using the Exploratory Regression tool

The Exploratory Regression tool can be used to evaluate combinations of exploratory variables for OLS models that best explain the dependent variable. This data-mining tool does a lot of work for you in finding variables that are well suited. This tool can save you a lot of time. The results of this tool are written to the progress dialog, the **Result** window, and an optional report file. In this section, you will use the **Exploratory Regression** tool to analyze the variables attached to the `Denver_Census_Tracts` layer used in the OLS section of the course to identify combinations of variables that may be appropriate for a model of burglary incidents.

Running the Exploratory Regression tool

Let's learn how to run the **Exploratory Regression** tool by performing the following steps:

1. If necessary, open **ArcMap** with the
   `C:\GeospatialTraining\SpatialStats\DenverCrimeModel.mxd` file. You
   should see a feature class called `Denver_Census_Tracts_Burglary`, as shown
   in the following screenshot, along with an American Community Survey layer
   and metadata table that we'll use later in the exercise:

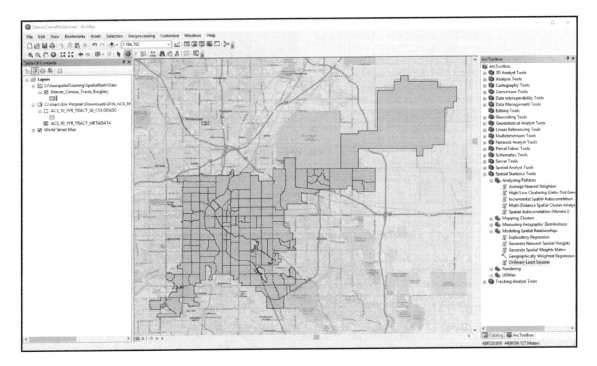

2. Find the **Exploratory Regression** tool found in the **Spatial Statistics Tools**
   toolbox under the **Modeling Spatial Relationships** toolset. Double-click on
   Exploratory Regression and define the following parameters:
   - **Input Features**: `Denver_Census_Tracts_Burglary`
   - **Dependent Variable**: `NormBurg`
   - **Candidate Explanatory Variables**: Select all variables *except* `Count_`,
     `NormBurg`, and `TractID`
   - **Output Report File (option)**:
     `C:\GeospatialTraining\SpatialStats\ExploratoryRegressio`
     `n.txt`

- **Search Criteria**: Leave all the default parameters, as shown in the following screenshot:

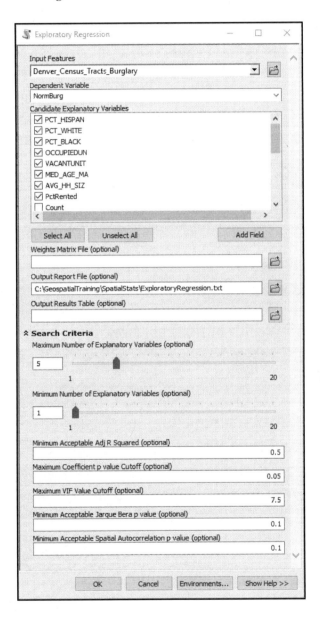

3. Click on the **OK** button to execute the tool.

Examining the output generated by the tool

Let's examine the output generated by the Exploratory Regression tool:

- The progress dialog will display the results as the tool is executing, as shown in the following screenshot. The information will also be written to the output report file. There are several sections of the output report file that need to be examined:

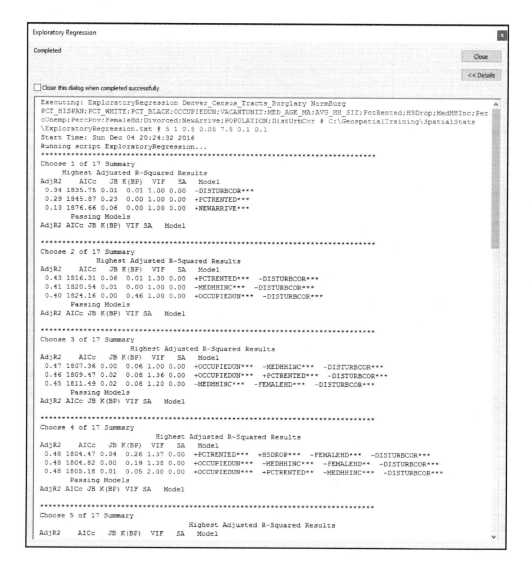

- The OLS tool is run against each of the possible combinations and assesses the output against the values in your **Search Criteria** section. The combinations of exploratory variable are grouped by the number of variables examined. For example, initially, the tool will test each of the explanatory variables individually and output any that match your input search criteria. Next, it looks at all the combinations of two variables. It will continue examining combinations of variables until it reaches the maximum number of exploratory variables that has been defined under the **Search Criteria** section. For instance, if you examine the following screenshot, a section is outlined that outputs the results for combinations of three exploratory variables. You'll see that three combinations of variables have met our search criteria. The first includes the exploratory variables OCCUPIEDUN, MEDHHINC, and DISTURBCOR. This section lists only combinations of three variables. The next section contains combinations of four variables:

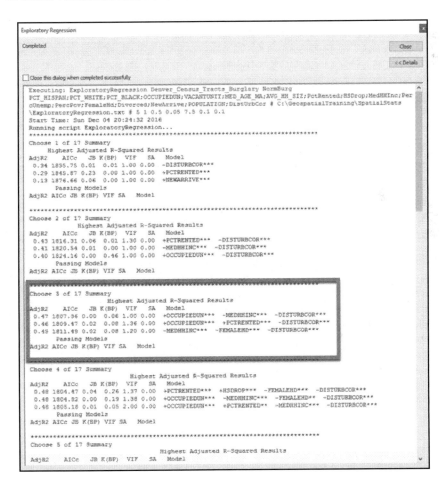

- Any models that are listed under the `Passing Models` section in the output report have met all your specified search criteria. To get a properly specified OLS model, a group of explanatory variables must meet the default values supplied for the tool. So, if you change one of the search criteria, just keep in mind that even though you may get a passing model, it won't meet the requirements for a properly specified OLS model.

  - The next section in the output report file that is important is `Summary of Variable Significance` seen in the following screenshot. This provides a listing of all the explanatory variables along with the percentage of the time that each was statistically significant and what percentage of the time it was either positively or negatively significant. This is important information because it gives a good indicator of the variables that should be used in the development of your OLS model. In this case, the `DISTURBCOR`, `PCTRENTED`, `FEMALEHD`, `VACANTUNIT`, `MEDHHINC`, and `NEWARRIVE` fields are all significant in over 75% of the OLS runs. What this means is that you should probably be using these variables in the development of your OLS model:

Variable	% Significant	% Negative	% Positive
DISTURBCOR	100.00	100.00	0.00
PCTRENTED	99.28	0.00	100.00
FEMALEHD	77.71	99.32	0.68
VACANTUNIT	77.20	0.08	99.92
MEDHHINC	77.08	96.34	3.66
NEWARRIVE	75.33	5.88	94.12
OCCUPIEDUN	73.50	0.00	100.00
HSDROP	59.59	0.44	99.56
PCT_HISPAN	39.21	22.45	77.55
AVG_HH_SIZ	37.86	79.02	20.98
POPULATION	28.01	49.86	50.14
PERCPOV	27.14	25.86	74.14
PCT_WHITE	25.71	49.98	50.02
MED_AGE_MA	14.86	90.27	9.73
DIVORCED	13.79	0.87	99.13
PERCUNEMP	10.25	39.01	60.99
PCT_BLACK	3.89	56.10	43.90

Summary of Variable Significance

- The **Exploratory Regression** tool is an excellent tool for analyzing various combinations of exploratory variables and can speed up the development of your OLS model.
- You should also take a look at the summary of the `Multicollinearity` section. This gives a summary of each variable, the average VIF, and how often it violated the VIF criteria. Note that `PCT_WHITE`, `PCT_HISPAN`, and `PCT_BLACK` are at the top of the list. That's because all three of these variables are all essentially measuring the same thing, which is race.

Using the Geographically Weighted Regression tool

Geographically Weighted Regression (GWR) is a local form of linear regression for modeling spatially varying relationships. GWR constructs a separate equation for each feature. What this means is that the relationships we're trying to model can and often change across the study area. For example, in our study, we might find that a high percentage of renters are an important predictor of burglary in one area of the county but a weak predictor in others.

GWR works by creating a local model of the variables or process that you are attempting to understand. It fits a regression equation to every feature in the study area. The variables of features that fall within the *bandwidth* of each target feature are incorporated into the equation. The shape and size of the *bandwidth* are dependent upon user input for criteria such as the kernel type, bandwidth method, distance, and number of neighbors.

GWR creates an output feature class and table. The output table contains a summary of the tool execution. When running GWR, you should use the same explanatory variables that you specified in your OLS model.

 The **Geographically Weighted Regression** tool requires an advanced ArcGIS license. You will not be able to complete this exercise without this license level.

Running the Geographically Weighted Regression tool

Let's see how to run the **Geographically Weighted Regression** tool by performing the following steps:

1. If necessary, open **ArcMap** with the
   `C:\GeospatialTraining\SpatialStats\DenverCrimeModel.mxd` file. You
   should see a feature class called `Denver_Census_Tracts_Burglary`, as shown
   in the following screenshot, along with an American Community Survey layer
   and metadata table:

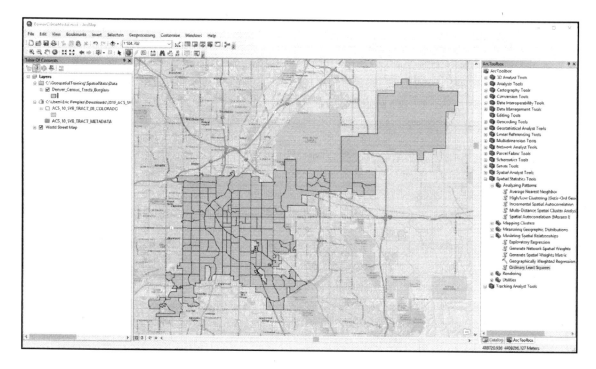

2. Find the **Geographically Weighted Regression** tool in the **Spatial Statistics
   Tools** toolbox and **Measuring Spatial Relationships**. Double-click on the
   Geographically Weighted Regression tool and define the following parameters:
   - **Input Feature Class**: `Denver_Census_Tracts_Burglary`
   - **Dependent Variable**: `NormBurg`
   - **Candidate Explanatory Variables**: Select the `PCT_BLACK`, `PctRented`,
     `MedHHInc`, `FemaleHD`, and `DistUrbCor` variables.

- **Output Feature Class**:
  `C:\Users\<username>\Documents\ArcGIS\Default.gdb\Geogra`
  `phicallyWeightedRegression`
- **Kernel type**: `FIXED`
- **Bandwidth method**: `AICc`
- Don't change any of the remaining parameters.

3. Click on the **OK** button to execute the tool.

Examining the output generated by the tool

Let's examine the output generated by the **Geographically Weighted Regression** tool:

1. There are a lot fewer diagnostics in the GWR report than what we saw with the OLS and Exploratory Regression tools. However, you'll notice that the adjusted r-squared value has gone up to almost 58%, meaning that we are telling more of the residential burglary story by allowing the relationships to vary across space.

2. The output feature class will be added to the **ArcMap** window in the **Table Of Contents** pane and symbolized using the `StdResid` field that shows where our model is over predicting and where it is under predicting burglary. The orange and red colors on the map indicate areas where the model is over predicting burglary and the blue colors indicate under prediction:

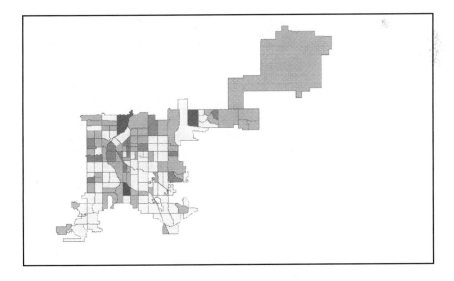

3. The attribute table for this layer also contains a number of other fields including coefficients for each explanatory variable, local r-squared, condition number, and residuals. Take a few minutes to examine this table. We'll go into detail about the contents of the table as we move through this exercise.

4. The GWR tool also creates a new table containing the results of the tool and also prints this information out to the progress dialog. For now, the most important record in the table is the `R2Adusted` variable that indicates a value of `0.577` or almost `58%`.

5. You can also map the coefficients for each variable. In the **ArcMap** window in the **Table Of Contents** pane, right-click on the new `GeographicallyWeightedRegression` layer and select **Copy**.

6. Right-click on the **Layers** data frame and select **Paste Layer(s)**. This will add a copy of the layer to the data frame.

7. Double-click on the new version of the `GeographicallyWeightedRegression` layer to display the **Layer Properties** dialog box. Select the **Symbology** tab and change the **Value** drop-down list to `Coefficient #2 PctRented`. Also, change the **Color Ramp** drop-down list to a red color ramp that gradually changes the color from the lightest to darkest. Finally, select the **General** tab and rename the layer as `Coefficient #2 PctRented` and click on the **OK** button.

8. You should see something similar to the following screenshot. Every feature will have a different coefficient value for each explanatory variable. The darker areas are areas where the relationship between the percentage of population renting a residential property (instead of owning) and burglary is the strongest. These are the areas where a local campaign to increase burglary awareness or perhaps create neighborhood watch groups might be effective in reducing burglary:

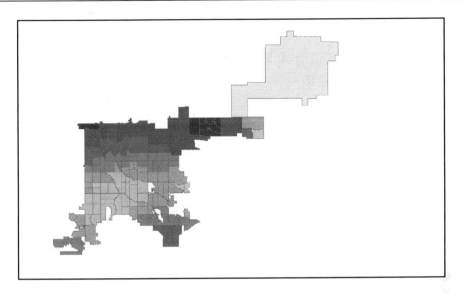

9. Repeat steps 5 and step 7 for each of the explanatory variables in the study to create the maps shown in the following screenshots. In all cases, the darker red areas indicate the strongest relationship between the explanatory variable and the incidence of burglary. The following screenshot displays the PCT_BLACK explanatory variable:

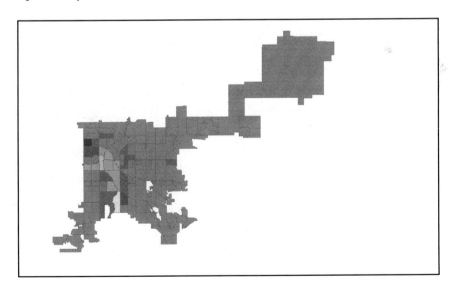

10. The following screenshot displays the `MED_HHInc` explanatory variable:

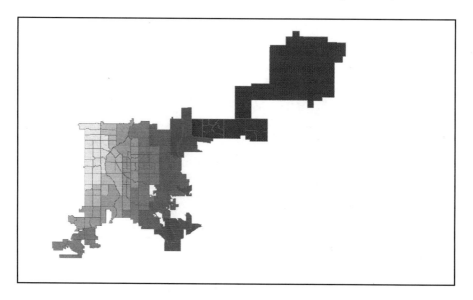

11. The following screenshot displays the `FemaleHD` explanatory variable:

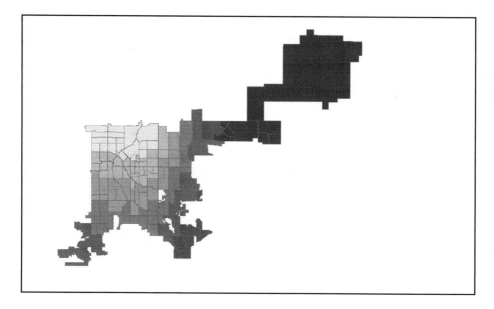

12. The following screenshot displays the `DistUrbCo` explanatory variable:

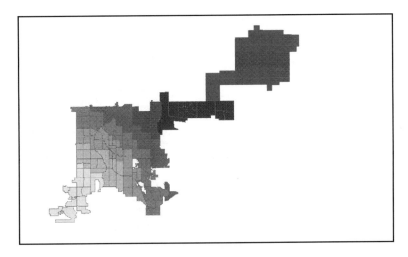

13. The GWR tool can also be used for prediction. This helps us model and understand the potential impact of changes. For example, what would be the predicted impact on residential burglary if the median household income increased by 20%.

- **Dependent Variable**: `NormBurg`
- **Candidate Explanatory Variables**: Select the `PCT_BLACK`, `PctRented`, `MedHHInc`, `FemaleHD`, and `DistUrbCor` variables
- **Output Feature Class**: `C:\Users\<username>\Documents\ArcGIS\Default.gdb\GeographicallyWeightedRegression1`
- **Kernel type**: `FIXED`
- **Bandwidth method**: `AICc`
- **Additional Parameters**: Under this section, include the following (these are the prediction parameters):
    - **Prediction locations**: `Denver_Census_Tracts_Burglary`.
    - **Prediction Explanatory Variables**: `PCT_BLACK`, `PctRented`, `HHIncInc`, `FemaleHd`, and `DisturbCor`. The `HHIncInc` field contains the information modeling a 20% increase in household income from the `MedHHInc` field. This field is the prediction field and is the only explanatory variable that is different.

- **Output Prediction Feature Class**:
  `C:\Users\<username>\Documents\ArcGIS\Default`
  `.gdb\PredictionHHIncome`.

14. To model this predictive scenario, the `HHIncInc` field in the `Denver_Census_Tracts_Burglary` layer has been populated to include the values in the `MedHHInc` field multiplied by 20%.

15. Run the **Geographically Weighted Regression** tool again and include the following parameters:**Input Feature Class**: `Denver_Census_Tracts_Burglary`

16. Click on the **OK** button to execute the tool. This will execute the GWR tool functionality just as it did before to calibrate the model, so the progress dialog will display the same diagnostics it did before, including the `R2Adjusted` variable. It then predicts the impact based on any new variables we have provided, which in this case is the `HHIncInc` field.

17. The output feature class, `PredictionHHIncome`, contains a new field called `Predicted`. To compare this new prediction of the incidence of burglary based on an increase in household income, we need to symbolize the `Denver_Census_Tracts_Burglary` layer based on the `NormBurg` field. In the **ArcMap** window in the **Table Of Contents** pane, double-click on the `Denver_Census_Tracts_Burglary` layer to display the **Layer Properties** dialog.

18. Select the **Symbology** tab and then navigate to **Quantities | Graduated Colors**.

19. Select `NormBurg` in the **Value** dropdown under **Fields**. Accept the default color ramp and classification. Click on the **OK** button to apply the symbology.

20. Double-click on the `PredictionHHIncome` layer to display the properties dialog.

21. Click on the **Symbology** tab and then the **Import...** button.

22. On the **Import Symbology** dialog that is displayed, make sure that **Import symbology definition from another layer in the map or from a layer file** is selected and then select the `Denver_Census_Tracts_Burglary` layer and click on the **OK** button.

23. The **Import Symbology Matching Dialog** dialog box will be displayed. It will prompt you to select a field from the current layer to match to the field used in the imported symbology definition. Select **Predicted** from the list of available values and click on the **OK** button.

24. Click on the **OK** button to dismiss the **Layer Properties** dialog.

25. Compare the layers to see the predicted change in the incidence of burglary. Your output should appear as shown in the following series of the screenshots:

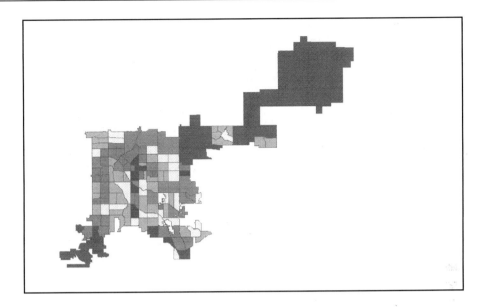

Take a look at the following screenshot which depicts a change in the incidence of burglary:

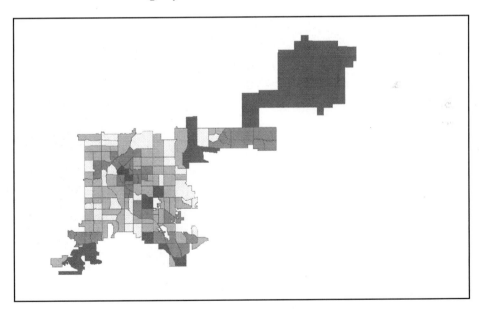

The predicted incidence of burglary based on a predicted median household increased by 20% with all other variables remaining consistent.

As you can see from the output, many of the census tracts that currently have the highest incidence of burglary are predicted to have a decrease based on a rise in the median household income.

Summary

In this chapter, two linear regression tools were used to model the relationships between various demographic, socio-economic, and geographic factors and the incidence of burglary in Denver County, CO. Using the OLS tool, a combination of variables were identified as the best model for understanding burglary in this context. The model was then improved using the **Geographically Weighted Regression** tool, which introduced spatial variability into the model. Finally, the **Exploratory Regression** tool was used to quickly identify combinations of variables that best fit a model. In the next chapter, we'll examine a variety of data conversion tools found in the **Utilities** toolset. These tools are often used in conjunction with other tools found in the **Spatial Statistics Tools** toolbox.

6
Working with the Utilities Toolset

The tools found in the **Utilities** toolset are primarily used for data conversion tasks in support of other tools found in the **Spatial Statistics Tools** toolbox. Tools in this toolset include **Calculate Distance Band from Neighbor Count**, **Collect Events**, and **Export Feature Attributes to ASCII**.

The **Calculate Distance Band from Neighbor Count** tool returns the minimum, maximum, and average distance to the specified nth nearest neighbor. Before doing so, it generates a list of all features in the dataset plus the distances to those features' nearest n neighbors. This tool is used as a support tool when using the **Hot Spot Analysis**, **Cluster and Outlier Analysis**, and **Spatial Autocorrelation** tools. The maximum distance reported by the **Calculate Distance Band from Neighbor Count** tool can be used as input to the **Distance Band or Threshold** parameter for these tools.

The **Collect Events** tool converts event data points to weighted point data. This tool creates an output feature class containing all unique locations. By unique locations, we mean that the point locations must have the exact same x,y location. The output feature class will contain a field that is the sum of all incidents at each unique location. Tools such as **Hot Spot Analysis**, **Cluster and Outlier Analysis**, and **Spatial Autocorrelation** require weighted points for use in their analysis rather than individual incidents, so the Collect Events tool can be used to create the weighted points.

The **Convert Spatial Weights Matrix to Table** tool converts spatial weights matrix files to a tabular structure. A .swm file is a binary file containing a representation of the spatial structure of your data. The contents are a quantification of the spatial relationships that exist among features in your dataset.

The **Export Feature Attribute to ASCII** tool exports the geometry and attributes of a feature class to an ASCII text file that can be delimited by comma, space, or semicolon.

In this chapter, you will learn how to use many of these utility tools to support your **Spatial Statistics Analysis** tools. The following tools will be covered in this chapter:

- The **Calculate Distance Band from Neighbor Count** tool
- The **Collect Events** tool
- The **Export Feature Attribute to ASCII** tool

The Calculate Distance Band from Neighbor Count tool

The **Calculate Distance Band from Neighbor Count** tool returns the minimum, maximum, and average distance to the specified *n*th nearest neighbor. This tool requires several inputs including an input feature class, the number of neighbors to analyze, and the distance method. If the input feature class is a polygon or polyline, it will use the centroid of the feature as the input feature. This tool is used as a support tool when using the **Hot Spot Analysis**, **Cluster and Outlier Analysis**, and **Spatial Autocorrelation** tools. The maximum distance reported by the **Calculate Distance Band from Neighbor Count** tool can be used as an input to the **Distance Band or Threshold** parameter for these tools. In this exercise, you'll learn how to use the tool to generate the distance band for the **Hot Spot Analysis** tool.

Running the Calculate Distance Band from Neighbor Count tool

Let's see how to use the **Calculate Distance Band from Neighbor Count** tool by performing the following steps:

1. If necessary, open **ArcMap** with the
   `C:\GeospatialTraining\SpatialStats\DenverCrimeModel.mxd` file. You should see a feature class called `Denver_Census_Tracts_Burglary`, as shown in the following screenshot, along with an American community survey layer and metadata table:

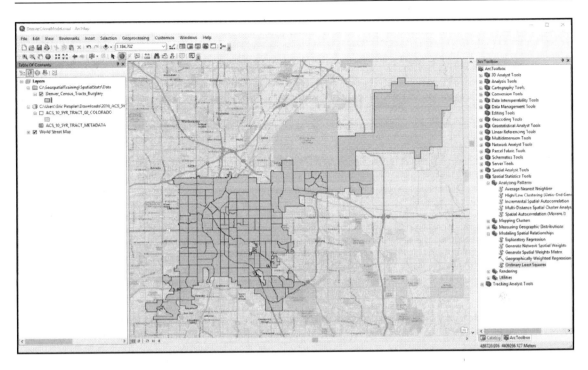

2. If necessary, disable background geoprocessing by navigating to **Geoprocessing | Geoprocessing Options....** In the **Background Processing** section, make sure that **Enable** is *not* selected. If it is, unselect the checkbox.

3. In the **ArcToolbox** toolset, find the **Spatial Statistics Tools** toolbox and the **Utilities** toolset. Open the **Utilities** toolset and double-click on the **Calculate Distance Band from Neighbor Count** tool. Enter the following parameters for the tool:

   - **Input Features**: `Denver_Census_Tracts_Burglary`
   - **Neighbors**: `8`
   - **Distance Method**: `EUCLIDEAN_DISTANCE`

Let's take a look at the following screenshot which depicts the preceding mentioned parameters:

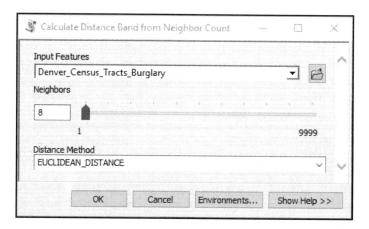

4. Click on the **OK** button to execute the tool. The results should appear as shown in the following screenshot. Make a note of the maximum neighbor distance of 14024.893460 meters. You'll use this value in the next step when running the **Hot Spot Analysis** tool:

```
        Calculate Distance Band Summary
Minimum 8 neighbor distance:   1201.903560
Average 8 neighbor distance:   2754.409500
Maximum 8 neighbor distance:  15009.157840
```

Using the maximum distance as the distance band in the Hot Spot Analysis tool

Let's take a look at the following steps to learn how to use the maximum distance as the distance band in the **Hot Spot Analysis** tool:

1. Find the **Hot Spot Analysis** tool in the **Mapping Clusters** toolset and double-click on the tool to display the dialog. Enter the following parameters:
   - **Input Feature Class**: Denver_Census_Tracts_Burglary.
   - **Input Field**: NormBurg.

- **Output Feature Class**:
  `C:\Users\<username>\Documents\ArcGIS\Default.gdb\Denver`
  `_Census_Tracts_Burglary_HS`.
- **Conceptualization of Spatial Relationships**: `FIXED_DISTANCE_BAND`.
- **Distance Method**: `EUCLIDEAN_DISTANCE`.
- **Distance Band or Threshold Distance**: `14024.89346`. This value will ensure that at least six neighbors will be considered in the generation of the neighborhood for each feature when the hot spot analysis is executed.

2. Click on the **OK** button to execute the tool. The output should appear as shown in the following screenshot. In this exercise, the **Calculate Distance Band from Neighbor Count** tool was used to define the distance band used with the `FIXED_DISTANCE_BAND` spatial relationship for the **Hot Spot Analysis** tool:

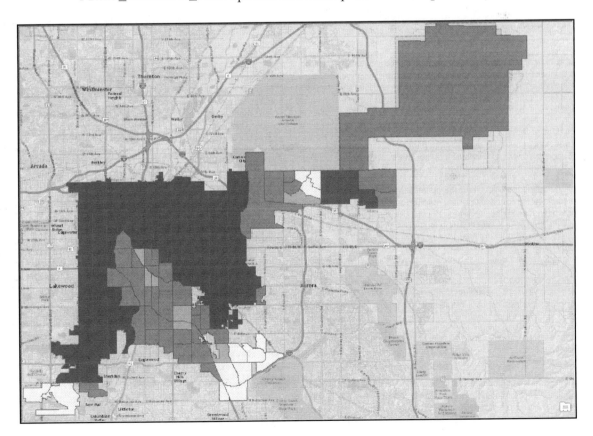

The Collect Events tool

The **Collect Events** tool converts event data points to weighted point data. This tool creates an output feature class containing all unique locations. By unique locations, we mean that the point locations must have the exact same *x,y* location. If your data has many points that are close together but not identical, you could consider using the **Integrate** tool to snap nearby features together before using the **Collect Events** tool.

The output feature class will contain an ICOUNT field that contains the sum of all incidents at each unique location. Tools such as Hot Spot Analysis, Cluster and Outlier Analysis, and Spatial Autocorrelation require weighted points for use in their analysis rather than individual incidents, so the Collect Events tool can be used to create the weighted points. In this exercise, you'll use the **Collect Events** tool to group residential real estate sales.

Data preparation

Let's get prepared for using the **Collect Events** tool by performing the following steps:

1. If necessary, open **ArcMap** with the
   `C:\GeospatialTraining\SpatialStats\SanAntonioRealEstate.mxd` file.
   This file contains a `ResidentialSales` layer and a
   `BexarCountyCensusBlockGroups` layer. The `ResidentialSales` layer
   contains approximately 27,000 points, with each representing a residential real
   estate sale. Most of the real estate sales in this dataset have a unique *x,y* location
   since the data was pulled from a single year of sales information. Obviously,
   most homes don't sell more than once per year.
2. The **Collect Events** tool creates a graduated symbol map for unique locations, so
   there won't be much differentiation in the output symbology unless we group the
   features beforehand. Since many sales occur within close proximity of other sales,
   we can use the **Integrate** geoprocessing tool to snap nearby features together
   before running the **Collect Events** tool.
3. The **Integrate** tool alters the existing dataset, so it's best to create a copy of the
   dataset beforehand. Right-click on the `ResidentialSales` layer in the
   ArcMap window in the **Table Of Contents** pane and navigate to **Data | Export
   Data....** Save the shapefile at
   `C:\GeospatialTraining\SpatialStats\Data\ResidentialSalesCopy.sh`
   `p`.

4. Add the copy of the shapefile to **ArcMap**.

5. Find the **Integrate** tool found in the **Data Management Tools** toolbox. Double-click on the tool and enter the following parameters:

   - **Input Features**: `ResidentialSalesCopy`.
   - **XY Tolerance (optional)**: `0.25` **Miles**. This will snap together all residential sales that are within a quarter mile of each other:

   Take a look at the following screenshot which depicts the preceding mentioned parameters:

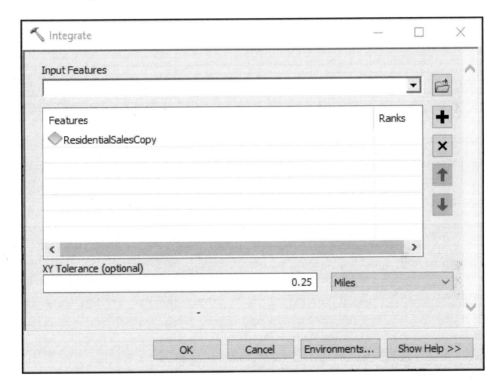

6. Click on **OK** to execute the tool. Remember that this will alter the dataset you provide as the input features. It does not create a new output dataset. The `ResidentialSalesCopy` layer should now appear as shown in the following screenshot:

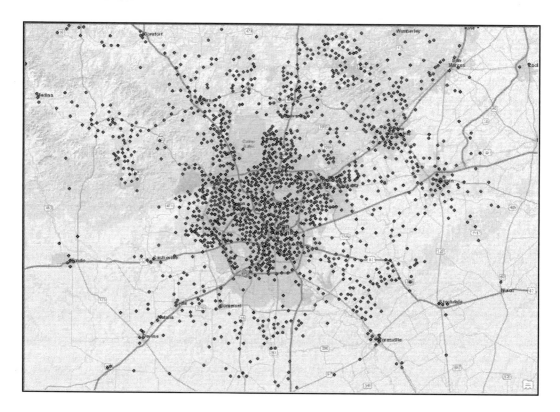

Executing the Collect Events tool

Let's see how to execute the Collect Events tool by performing the following steps:

1. Find the **Collect Events** tool in the **Utilities** toolset found in the **Spatial Statistics Tools** toolbox. Double-click on the tool to display the dialog and enter the following parameters:
   - **Input Incident Features**: `ResidentialSalesCopy`
   - **Output Weighted Point Feature Class**:
     `C:\Users\<username>\Documents\ArcGIS\Default.gdb\Reside ntialSales_CollectEvents`

Let's take a look at the following screenshot which depicts the preceding mentioned parameters:

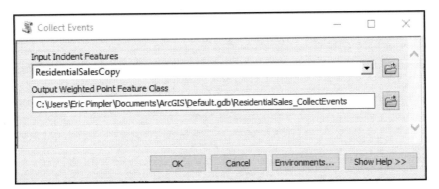

2. Click on **OK** to run the tool.
3. You may want to zoom in on an area to see the distinction between the graduated symbols, but in general, you should see something similar to the following screenshot. The **Collect Events** tool will automatically apply the graduated symbology:

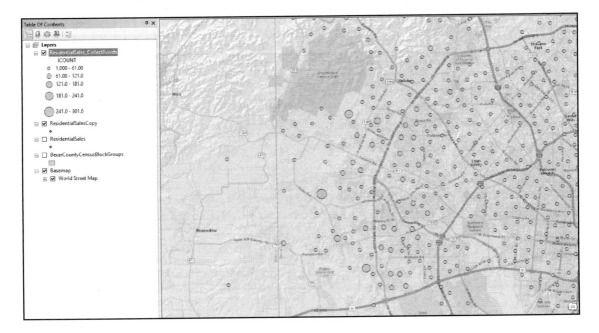

4. For this particular analysis, we only want to create a hot spot analysis for Bexar County, TX, so any points outside the county boundary need to be discarded. Zoom to the extent of the `BexarCountyCensusBlockGroups` layer.

5. Right-click on the `BexarCountyCensusBlockGroups` layer and navigate to **Selection | Select All**.

6. From the main ArcMap menu, navigate to **Selection | Select by Location...** and fill in the parameters as shown in the following screenshot:

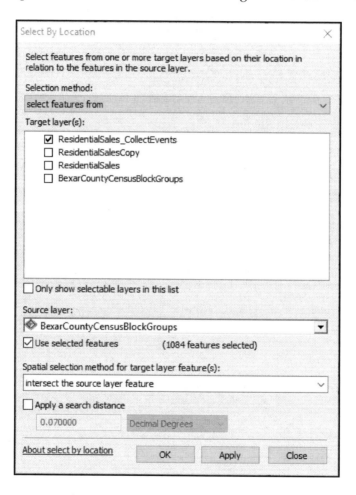

7. Right-click on `ResidentialSales_CollectEvents` and navigate to **Data** | **Export Data....** Define the output feature class as `C:\GeospatialTraining\SpatialStats\Data\Bexar_RS_CE.shp`. Leave the other default parameters in place for the remaining properties on the **Export Data** dialog.

8. Click on **OK** to export the layer and add it to the **ArcMap** window in the **Table Of Contents** pane when prompted.

9. Navigate to **Selection** | **Clear Selected Features** from the main **ArcMap** menu.

10. To reduce clutter, you may want to turn off the `ResidentialSales_CollectEvents` layer.

Using the Collect Events results in the Hot Spot Analysis tool

Tools such as **Hot Spot Analysis**, **Optimized Hot Spot**, **Cluster and Outlier Analysis**, and **Spatial Autocorrelation** can use weighted points for use in their analysis rather than individual incidents, so in this step, the weighted points layer created by the **Collect Events** tool will be used as input to the **Hot Spot Analysis** tool:

1. Find the **Hot Spot Analysis** tool and double-click on it to display the dialog for the tool. Enter the following parameters:
   - **Input Feature Class**: `Bexar_RS_CE`
   - **Analysis Field**: `ICOUNT`
   - **Output Feature Class**: `C:\Users\<username>\Documents\ArcGIS\Default.gdb\ResidentialSales_CE_HS`
   - **Conceptualization of Spatial Relationships**: `INVERSE_DISTANCE`
   - **Distance Method**: `EUCLIDEAN_DISTANCE`

2. Click on **OK** to execute the tool.

3. The output should appear as shown in the following screenshot:

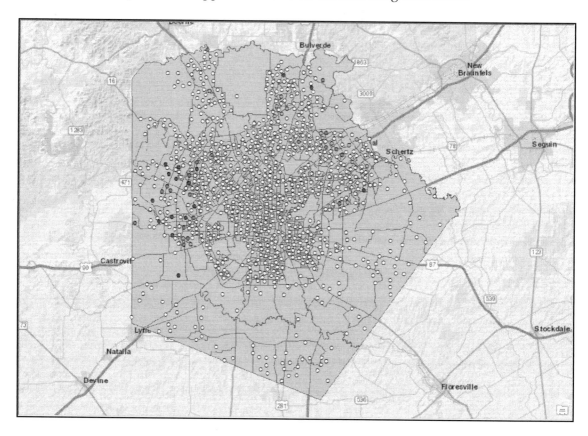

The Export Feature Attribute to ASCII tool

The **Export Feature Attribute to ASCII** tool exports the geometry and attributes of a feature class to an ASCII text file that can be delimited by comma, space, or semicolon. In this exercise, you'll use the **Export Feature Attribute to ASCII** tool to export a feature class to a comma delimited text file.

Exporting a feature class

Let's take a look at the following steps to learn about exporting a feature class:

1. If necessary, open ArcMap with the
   `C:\GeospatialTraining\SpatialStats\DenverCrimeModel.mxd` file. For
   this exercise, the `Denver_Census_Tracts_Burglary` layer will be exported to a
   comma-delimited text file.

2. Find the **Export Feature Attribute to ASCII** tool found in the **Utilities** toolset in
   the **Spatial Statistics Tools** toolbox and double-click on it to display the dialog
   box.

3. Define the following input parameters for the **Export Feature Attribute to ASCII**
   tool:
   - **Input Feature Class**: `Denver_Census_Tracts_Burglary`.
   - **Value Field**: Select several fields from the list. It doesn't matter which
     field you select.
   - **Delimiter**: **Comma**.
   - **Output ASCII File**:
     `C:\GeospatialTraining\SpatialStats\Data\DenverCensusTra`
     `ctsBurglary.txt`
   - **Add Field Names to Output**: Checked.

4. Click on **OK** to execute the tool. Open the output file in a text editor and you
   should see something similar to the following screenshot:

```
XCoord,YCoord,PCT_HISPAN,PCT_WHITE,OCCUPIEDUN,VACANTUNIT
499960.75825164,4400394.70541678,6.670000,81.360000,3070.000000,548.000000
500585.96561776,4399468.95584665,9.730000,75.220000,2363.000000,894.000000
500356.33638923,4397897.84842974,34.000000,56.400000,1727.000000,124.000000
499260.66213226,4398144.16131310,48.660000,24.330000,1014.000000,38.000000
499291.71677939,4399546.43517753,8.790000,78.720000,60.000000,9.000000
500754.24280500,4398387.29901059,9.580000,78.000000,1140.000000,205.000000
499705.46993513,4394803.58355332,73.610000,22.590000,1252.000000,88.000000
499154.76635081,4393711.50742763,71.430000,18.370000,1971.000000,146.000000
498897.66251360,4392898.64124337,66.090000,24.470000,1353.000000,70.000000
500591.48267150,4392397.32862797,30.570000,60.280000,1044.000000,245.000000
501132.60962088,4403406.55379822,67.830000,25.770000,1040.000000,117.000000
501261.53119564,4401341.36651556,22.000000,62.090000,3771.000000,400.000000
497242.69443532,4400291.34415769,35.970000,54.570000,2598.000000,180.000000
498352.76924922,4400248.35214425,55.600000,38.830000,1182.000000,176.000000
496045.47716294,4398838.41405300,52.930000,39.700000,1737.000000,168.000000
497242.73886506,4398962.55249824,68.530000,21.910000,1966.000000,178.000000
```

Summary

The tools provided in the **Utilities** toolset support various tools found in the **Spatial Statistics Tools** toolbox. While these tools are not analysis tools, they do provide an important supporting role in the analysis process. In the next chapter, you'll learn the basics of the R programming language for spatial statistics.

7
Introduction to the R Programming Language

The R Project for Statistical Computing, or simply named R, is a free software environment for statistical computing and graphics. It is also a programming language that is widely used among statisticians and data miners for developing statistical software and data analysis.

Although there are other programming languages for handling statistics, R has become one of the most popular languages for statistical routines, offering a package repository with over 6,400 packages. The R language also offers versatile and powerful plotting tools.

In this chapter, you will learn the fundamentals of the R programming language and how it can be applied to GIS analysis. However, this chapter is not a comprehensive guide to the R language. Instead, it will focus on introducing you to some of the most important constructs of the language and the various data types you can expect to encounter. In future chapters, you'll integrate R programming scripts with ArcGIS to create custom script tools via ArcBridge.

Installing R and the R interface

R is cross-platform and can be run on Windows, Mac, or Linux. For our purposes, the Windows version will need to be installed so that the scripts can eventually be executed inside ArcGIS. The R installer will install both the 32-bit and the 64-bit versions. ArcGIS Desktop uses the 32-bit version, while ArcGIS Pro uses the 64-bit version. ArcGIS Desktop can use the 64-bit version if background geoprocessing is installed and the script has been configured for background geoprocessing.

Perform the following steps to install R for Windows:

1. Open a browser and go to `http://cran.cnr.berkeley.edu`.
2. Click on the **Download R for Windows** (`http://cran.cnr.berkeley.edu/`) link.
3. Click on the **base** link (`http://cran.cnr.berkeley.edu/`).
4. Click on **Download R 3.3.3 for Windows**. This will download an executable file (`R-3.3.2-win.exe`, for example).

 The current version as of this writing is 3.3.2, but you may see a different version.

5. Double-click on the downloaded executable file and follow the prompts to install the R software.
6. R includes a very simple interface with a console window for testing small chunks of code and the option to create script windows for full-length scripts.

   Take a look at the following screenshot of the application interface:

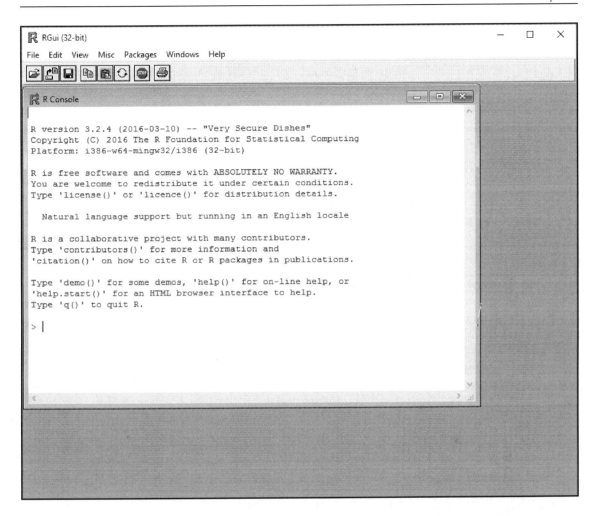

There are only a few buttons and menu items, so it's styled more like a command-line interface. With all command-line interfaces, there is a learning curve involved, but in general, it's reasonably easy to learn how to use the interface.

7. Scripts are windows you use to write and execute a series of commands. They are useful for automating your data analysis and give you the ability to save your work for future use. You should get into the habit of creating scripts for all your work. To create a new script window, navigate to **File** | **New Script**. You should see a window similar to what you see in the following screenshot:

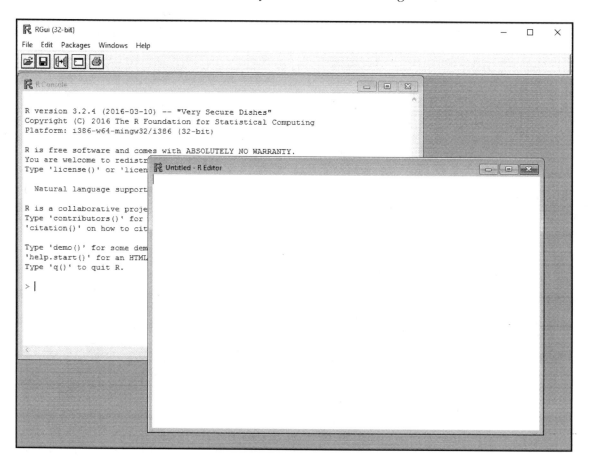

Variables and assignment

In the R programming language, like other languages, variables are given a name and assigned data. Each variable has a name that represents its area in memory. In R, variables are case sensitive, so use care in naming your variables and referring to them later in your code. There are two ways in which this can be done, and both are illustrated in the following screenshot:

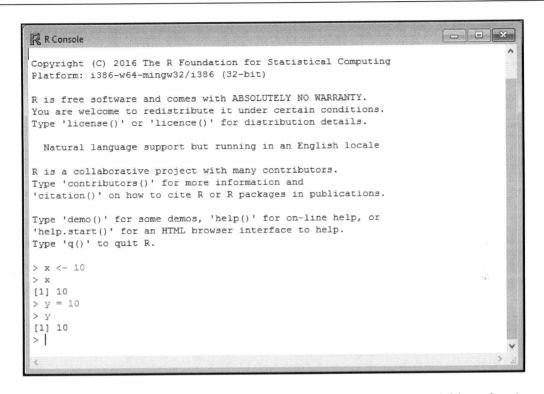

Let's take a look at the following ways in which we can use to name a variable and assign data to it:

1. In the first code example, a variable named x is created. The use of a less-than sign immediately followed by a dash then follows the variable name. This is the operator used to assign data to a variable in R. On the right-hand side of this operator is the value being assigned to the variable. In this case, the value 10 has been assigned to the variable x. To print the value of a variable in R, you can simple type the variable name and then press the *Enter* key on your keyboard.

2. The other way of creating and assigning data to a variable is to use the equals sign. In the second code example, we create a variable called y and assigned the value 10 to the variable. This second method of creating and assigning data to a variable is probably more familiar to you if you've used other languages like Python or JavaScript.

3. Variables are created inside a workspace. This directory can be changed by navigating to **File | Change dir...** in the **R Console** window. You can get a listing of all the variables currently in the workspace by calling the `ls()` function. This is illustrated in the code sample shown in the following screenshot:

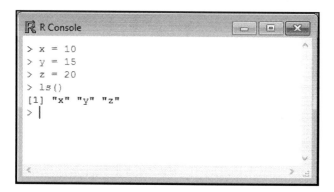

```
> x = 10
> y = 15
> z = 20
> ls()
[1] "x" "y" "z"
>
```

4. You can also remove a variable from a workspace using the `rm()` function, as shown in the following screenshot of the code example:

```
> x = 10
> y = 15
> z = 20
> ls()
[1] "x" "y" "z"
> rm(x)
> ls()
[1] "y" "z"
>
```

5. R code can be commented through the use of the # sign prior to the line you want to comment. Commented lines of code are used only for your documentation purposes and are ignored by the R interpreter:

```
R Console

> x = 10
> y = 15
> z = 20
> ls()
[1] "x" "y" "z"
> # this is a comment line of code...it will be ignored by R
```

We've already seen a few R functions in action, including c(), ls(), and rm(), but we haven't really discussed functions yet. Functions are a sequence of commands executed as a group. R includes many functions that you can use, or you can write your own if needed. Most of these functions return some sort of value or result. For example, when you call the ls() function, it returns a list of all the variables in the current workspace.

Many functions also require input parameters, sometimes called arguments. These are values that you pass into the function so that it can do its task. These become variables inside the function. We've already seen several functions up to this point, including the c(), ls(), and rm() functions. However, this is just the start. We'll see many functions as we work our way through the course.

In the first exercise of this chapter, you will learn how to create variables in R and assign data to them by performing the following steps:

1. Start the R application (use the 32-bit version since that is what we'll use with ArcGIS Desktop) and find the **R Console** window.
2. In the **R Console** window, create a variable called x and assign a value of 10.
3. Create a second variable called y and assign it a value of 20.
4. Create a third variable called z and assign it a value that is the sum of the variables x and y.
5. Print out the value of the z variable using the print() function.

6. Get a list of the current variables in your workspace with the `ls()` function.

7. On a new line, create a comment using the # sign with the following text: `The variable below contains my name.`

8. Create a new variable called `name` and assign your name to the variable. Your actual name should be enclosed by double quotes, as in `"John Doe"`.

9. Type the following value into the **R Console** window and click on the *Enter* key on your keyboard:

   ```
   Name
   ```

   > You probably got an error when you did this. Remember that R is a case sensitive language, so there is no variable called `Name`. However, there is a variable called `name`.

10. Now type `name` into the **R Console** window and click on the *Enter* key. Now you should see the value that has been assigned to the `name` variable.

11. If you need to check your work, you can open the `Ch7_1.R` solution file found in the `C:\GeospatialTraining\SpatialStats\Code\solutions` folder.

12. To open the file, navigate to **File | Open script...** in R.

13. To execute the `.R` file, select **Edit | Run all**.

R data types

There are many types of data that can be assigned to variables in R. The most basic types are characters, numbers, and logicals. Characters, also known as strings, are a sequence of characters surrounded by quotes. Numbers are exactly what you'd expect. Numeric data types can be any type of number. Logical data types are `Boolean` values of either `true` or `false`. The `true` and `false` values can include any of the iterations from the following code example:

```
c('T', 'True', 'TRUE', 'true')
c('F','False','FALSE','false')
```

There are also a number of data classes, which are structures used to hold multiple values. These include vectors, matrices, data frames, factors, and lists. We'll examine each of these data types.

Vectors

In R, a vector is a sequence of data elements that have the same data type. To create a vector in R, you call the `c()` method and pass in a list of values of the same type. Several examples have been provided in the following code:

```
c(5,6,7,8)
c('TRUE','TRUE','FALSE','FALSE','FALSE','TRUE')
c('A','B','C','D')
```

After a vector has been created, you can get the number of items in the vector by calling the `length()` function, as shown in the following example. Remember that the data values assigned to the vector must be of the same type:

```
length(c('A','B','C','D'))
[4]
```

Vectors can be assigned to variables, as shown in the following code example, where the variable x has been assigned a vector of string values. It is easy to pluck a value out of the vector simply by referring to the variable name followed by the index number of the item you want to retrieve inside square brackets:

```
x = c('A','B','C','D')
x[2]
[1] "B"
```

Values can also be removed from a vector using a negative integer value, as shown in the following code example:

```
x = c('A','B','C','D')
x[-2]
[1] "A" "C" "D"
```

Vector slicing refers to the ability to pull out a sequence of values from a vector. This is accomplished by passing in two offset values inside square braces. In the following code example, the values 2 and 4 are passed in as an offset inside the square braces and are separated by a colon. This will pull out the second, third, and fourth values from the vector. B, C, and D in this case:

```
x = c('A','B','C','D')
x[2:4]
[1] "B" "C" "D"
```

Vectors can also be combined with other vectors. Note in the next code example that R automatically converts the numbers to strings since vectors must always be of the same type:

```
x = c('A','B','C','D')
y = c(1,2,3)
z = c(x,y)
z
[1] "A" "B" "C" "D" "1" "2" "3"
```

When performing vector arithmetic, if two vectors are of unequal length, R will perform vector recycling. Vector recycling repeats the values from the vector with few items:

```
x = c(5,10,15,20)
y = c(10,20,30,40,50,60,70,80)
x + y
[1] 15 30 45 60 55 70 85 100
```

In the next exercise, you will learn how to create and use vectors by performing the following steps:

1. Start the R application (use the 32-bit version since that is what we'll use with ArcGIS Desktop) and find the **R Console** window.
2. In the **R Console** window, create a variable called `layers` and use the `c()` function to create a vector containing the following values:
   - Parcels
   - Streets
   - Railroads
   - Streams
   - Buildings
3. Get the length of the vector using the `length()` function.
4. Retrieve the `Railroads` value from the vector.
5. Retrieve the `Railroads`, `Streams`, and `Buildings` values.
6. Remove `Streams` from the vector.
7. Create a second vector variable called `layerIDS` containing the values 1, 2, 3, and 4.
8. Create a new variable called `combinedVector` and combine the `layers` and `layerIDS` variables. Remember that the contents of a vector must be of the same datatype. R will automatically convert your numbers to strings in this case.
9. You can check your work by opening the `Ch7_2.R` solution file found in the `C:\GeospatialTraining\SpatialStats\Code\solutions` folder.

10. To open the file, navigate to **File | Open script...** in R.

11. To execute an .R file, navigate to **Edit | Run all**.

12. Clear the **R Console** window by right-clicking on the **R Console** window and selecting the **Clear** window.

13. Create two new variables: x and y. Assign the 10,20,30,40,50 values to the x variable and assign the 100,200,300,400,500 values to the y variable.

14. Add the values of the vectors.

15. You can check your work by opening the Ch7_3.R solution file found in the C:\GeospatialTraining\SpatialStats\Code\solutions folder.

16. To open the file, navigate to **File | Open script...** in R.

17. To execute an .R file, navigate to **Edit | Run all**.

Matrices

A matrix in R is a structure very similar to a table, in that it has columns and rows. Keep in mind that this is an in-memory structure though. This type of structure is commonly used in spatial statistical operations. A matrix is created using the matrix() function. The number of columns and rows can be passed in as arguments to the function to define the attributes and data values of the matrix. A matrix might be created from the values found in the attribute table of a feature class. Rows and columns in a matrix can be named. The colnames() function is used to name columns, and this is the most common of the two operations. Rows can also be named using the rownames() function.

Matrices have some basic statistical functions that can be called, including rowSums(), colSums(), colMeans(), and sum().

In the following exercise, you'll learn the basics of working with matrices in R:

1. Start the R application (use the 32-bit version since that is what we'll use with ArcGIS Desktop) and find the **R Console** window.

2. In the **R Console** window, create a variable called A and use the matrix() function to create a matrix containing the following values: 2, 4, 3, 1, 5, 7. The matrix should have two rows and three columns. The following code shows how to create this matrix:

```
A = matrix(c(2,4,3,1,5,7), nrow=2, ncol=3,
byrow=TRUE)
```

3. Use the `print()` function to print out the value of A, so you can see the structure. You should see an output that appears as follows:

```
     [,1] [,2] [,3]
[1,]   2    4    3
[2,]   1    5    7
```

4. You can name the columns in a matrix using the following code:

```
colnames(A) = c("POP2000", "POP2005", "POP2010")
```

5. Now when you print out the structure of the matrix, you should see columns as seen in the following code output:

```
     POP2000 POP2005 POP2010
[1,]    2       4       3
[2,]    1       5       7
```

6. Retrieve a value from the matrix with the following code. The format is `matrix(row, column)`:

```
A[2,3]
POP2010
      7
```

7. You can also extract an entire row using the following code. Here, we just provide a row value but no column indicator:

```
A[2,]
POP2000   POP2005   POP2010
      1         5         7
```

   You can also extract an entire column using the following format:
```
A[ ,3]
[1] 3   7
```

8. You can also extract multiple columns at a time as follows:

```
A[, c(1,3)]
POP2000   POP2010
[1,]     2         3
[2,]     1         7
```

9. You can also access columns or rows by name, if you have named them, as follows:

```
A[ , "POP2005"]
[1] 4 5
```

10. You can use the `colSums()`, `colMeans()`, or `rowSums()` functions against the data as well:

```
colSums(A)
POP2000   POP2005   POP2010
      3         9        10


colMeans(A)
POP2000   POP2005   POP2010
    1.5       4.5       5.0
```

11. You can check your work by opening the `Ch7_4.R` solution file found in the `C:\GeospatialTraining\SpatialStats\Code\solutions` folder.

12. To open the file, navigate to **File** | **Open script...** in R.

13. To execute an `.R` file, select **Edit** | **Run all**.

Data frames

Data frames in R are very similar to tables, in that they have columns and rows. This makes them very similar to matrix objects as well. However, with data frames, all columns must be the same length.

In statistics, a dataset will often contain multiple variables. For example, if you are analyzing real estate sales for an area, there will be many factors including income, job growth, immigration, and others. These individual variables are stored as columns in a data frame. Data frames can be created through your code or you can manually enter the values. When manually entering the data, the R console will display a spreadsheet-style interface that you can use to define the column names as well as the row values.

R includes many built-in datasets that you can use for learning purposes and these are stored as data frames. In the **R Console** window, you can type the data() function to see a list of the built-in datasets that you can use. To load one of the sample datasets, simply call the data() function and pass in the name of the dataset you want to load. You'll get a chance to do this in the exercise for this section. To view the data in the dataset, you then type the name of the dataset. You can see an example of this in the following screenshot:

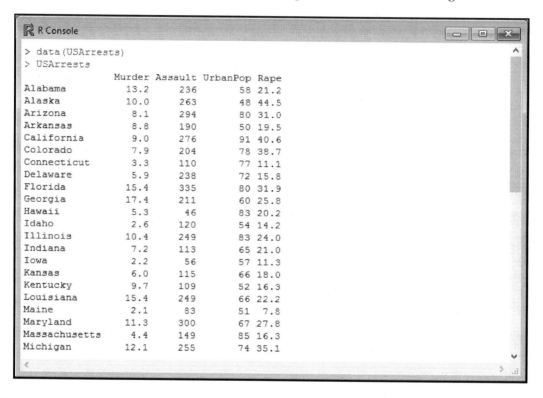

Often, you'll need to access specific portions of data from a data frame. To access the data from a specific column, you issue the name of the data frame followed by a dollar sign followed by the name of the column. This is illustrated in the code example provided in the following screenshot:

```
R Console
> USArrests$Murder
 [1] 13.2 10.0  8.1  8.8  9.0  7.9  3.3  5.9 15.4 17.4  5.3  2.6 10.4  7.2  2.2
[16]  6.0  9.7 15.4  2.1 11.3  4.4 12.1  2.7 16.1  9.0  6.0  4.3 12.2  2.1  7.4
[31] 11.4 11.1 13.0  0.8  7.3  6.6  4.9  6.3  3.4 14.4  3.8 13.2 12.7  3.2  2.2
[46]  8.5  4.0  5.7  2.6  6.8
>
```

You can also access specific rows and columns. The next code example uses two offsets, 50 and 1 to retrieve the fiftieth row and the first column from that row. This value is 6.8. The final line of code passes in a single offset, which is a value of 50. The second offset is left off in this case. This will retrieve all the columns for the 50th row:

```
R Console
> USArrests[50,1]
[1] 6.8
> USArrests[50,]
        Murder Assault UrbanPop Rape
Wyoming    6.8     161       60 15.6
>
```

You may be wondering what the difference is between a data frame and a matrix. They both have a table-like appearance, so here are some guidelines you can use to determine which of the two to use.

If you expect that the columns in your data will be of different data types, then you'll need to use a data frame. For example, if one column is numeric and another is character and a third is logical then a data frame is the way to go. Data stored in a matrix must be of the same type. Frequently, this will be numeric data, but you can't mix different data types.

Often, the function you're calling will dictate which data class to use. If a parameter requires that you pass a data frame rather than a matrix, then this is what you'll need to use.

Matrices do tend to be more memory efficient, if you have a large number of columns, and they are more efficient from a coding perspective as well. Data frames tend to be more convenient if you frequently refer to columns by name since you can use the $ operator to do so. Finally, data frames tend to be better for reporting or printing tabular information.

Factors

A factor in R is a more advanced type of vector in that it has categories. This type of structure is used for categorical data. The levels parameter is used to define the categories for a factor. In this exercise, you'll learn how to create and use a factor by performing the following steps:

1. In the **R Console** window, create a variable called land.type and use the factor() function to create the factor as seen in the following code:

```
>land.type = factor(c('Residential', 'Commercial',
'Agricultural', 'Commercial', 'Commercial',
'Residential'),
levels=c('Residential','Commercial'))

>table(land.type)
land.type
Residential   Commercial
          2        3
```

2. There may be times when you want to order the output of the factor. For example, you may want to order the results by month. Enter the code shown in the following screenshot:

```
R Console                                                                    ▭ ▢ ✕

> mons = c("March", "April", "January", "November", "January", "September", "October",
+ "September", "November", "August", "January", "November", "November", "February",
+ "May", "August", "July", "December", "August", "August", "September", "November",
+ "February", "April")
> mons = factor(mons)
> table(mons)
mons
    April     August  December  February   January     July     March     May  November
        2         4        1        2         3        1        1       1        5
  October September
        1         3
> |
```

3. The output is less than desirable in this case. It would be preferable to have the months listed in the order in which they occur during the year. Creating an ordered factor resolves this issue. Add the following code to see how this works:

```
> mons = factor(mons,levels=c("January", "February", "March", "April", "May", "June",
+ "July","August", "September", "October", "November", "December"), ordered=TRUE)
> table(mons)
mons
  January  February     March     April       May      June      July   August September
        3         2         1         2         1         0         1        4         3
  October  November  December
        1         5         1
```

Lists

A list is an ordered collection of elements. If you've used the Python programming language in the past with ArcGIS, this type of data should be very familiar to you as they are essentially the same. With lists you can include any combination of data types. This differs from other data structures like vectors, matrices, and factors, which must contain the same data type. So lists are highly versatile and useful data types. The following code example shows the creation of a list that contains strings, numbers, and Booleans:

```
my.list = list("John Doe", 2000, "Jane Doe", 5000,
TRUE, FALSE)
```

To extract a value from a list, you simply refer to the variable name followed by the index number that corresponds to the value you want to extract, as shown in the following code:

```
my.list[5]
[[1]]
[1] TRUE
```

Lists can be manipulated after creation. Two lists can be joined together using the `append()` function. You can also add items to an existing list, remove items from a list, or update items in a list. Take a look at the following examples:

```
#Add item to a list
my.list[6] = "January"

#remove the last element
my.list[6] = NULL

#update the 3rd item
my.list[3] = "Mary Doe"
```

Reading, writing, loading, and saving data

There are three basic formats that we'll examine for reading data into and out of R. The first is text files, and this is typically going to be comma or tab-delimited text files. The next format is R data files, and the final format is spatial data files with shapefiles being the most common.

Data stored in text files can be read into R or you can write data to a text file. Typically, your text files will be either comma or tab-delimited. To open a text file for analysis in R, you can use the `read.table()` function to load the dataset into a data frame. The header line, if included in the text file, will load a dataset into a data frame object. Default values will be used for the column headers if these are not provided. The `file.choose()` function is a handy function that you can use to interactively select the file you want imported rather than having to hardcode the path to the dataset. You can also use the `read.csv()` function to load a CSV file into R or the `write.csv()` function to write data to a file.

Variables stored in the current workspace of your R console can be saved to a designated file with an extension of `.RData`. This can be done in one of two ways: navigating to **File | Save Workspace...** from the **R Console** window or the `save()` function in your code. The `save()` function is more versatile because you can decide which variables you want to save rather than saving all of them, which is the case when navigating to **File | Save Workspace...**. The `.Rdata` file is a binary file that is very efficient at data storage. Existing `.Rdata` files can be loaded into your R scripts or the console using the `load()` function.

R also has the ability to load many different spatial data formats including shapefiles and geodatabases. The `GISTools` package can be used to accomplish this task. You'll first need to install the `GISTools` package, and because it has dependencies, you'll need to install them as well. You can use the `install.packages()` function as shown in the following screenshot to complete the installation. Then, you'll want to reference the library:

```
install.packages("GISTools", depend=T)
library(GISTools)
```

In your next exercise, you'll have a chance to install this package and put it to use:

1. The first time you use any package in R, it needs to be downloaded and then installed. The `GISTools` package adds a number of utilities for handling and visualizing geographic data including choropleth mapping with legends. In the **R Console** window, execute the `install.packages()` function to install the package, as shown in the following screenshot. The messages you see reported may differ from mine:

```
> install.packages("GISTools", depend=T)
Installing package into 'C:/Users/Eric Pimpler/Documents/R/win-library/3.2'
(as 'lib' is unspecified)
--- Please select a CRAN mirror for use in this session ---
trying URL 'https://cran.revolutionanalytics.com/bin/windows/contrib/3.2/GISTools_0.7-4.zip'
Content type 'application/zip' length 3460214 bytes (3.3 MB)
downloaded 3.3 MB

package 'GISTools' successfully unpacked and MD5 sums checked

The downloaded binary packages are in
        C:\Users\Eric Pimpler\AppData\Local\Temp\Rtmp2dX8cw\downloaded_packages
```

2. Now you can reference the `GISTools` library with the `library()` function. You will see some messages when you load the package, letting you know that the packages that `GISTools` makes use of have been loaded as well:

```
> library(GISTools)
Loading required package: maptools
Loading required package: sp
Checking rgeos availability: TRUE
Loading required package: RColorBrewer
Loading required package: MASS
Loading required package: rgeos
rgeos version: 0.3-19, (SVN revision 524)
 GEOS runtime version: 3.5.0-CAPI-1.9.0 r4084
 Linking to sp version: 1.2-3
 Polygon checking: TRUE

Warning messages:
1: package 'GISTools' was built under R version 3.2.5
2: package 'maptools' was built under R version 3.2.5
3: package 'sp' was built under R version 3.2.5
4: package 'rgeos' was built under R version 3.2.5
```

3. The `GISTools` package has a `readShapePoly()` function that can be used to read shapefile data into a `SpatialPolygonsDataFrame` object. We'll use this in conjunction with the `file.choose()` function to select a shapefile to read. In the **R Console** window, add the following code to read the `Denver_Census_Tracts` shapefile into a variable:

```
denverCensusTracts = readShapePoly(file.choose())
```

4. This will display the following file chooser dialog. Navigate to `C:\GeospatialTraining\SpatialStats\Data` to find the `Denver_Census_Tracts.shp` file, select the file, and click on **Open**. This will load the shapefile data into a `SpatialPolygonsDataFrame` object from the `GISTools` library:

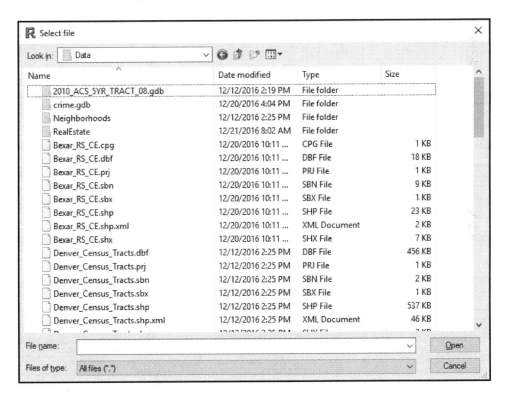

5. Next, we'll create a choropleth map based on the `PCT_WHITE` attribute column in the shapefile. Issue the following code in the **R Console** window:

```
choropleth(denverCensusTracts,
denverCensusTracts$PCT_WHITE)
```

This will display a plot window with the census tract data, which is color coded as shown in the following screenshot:

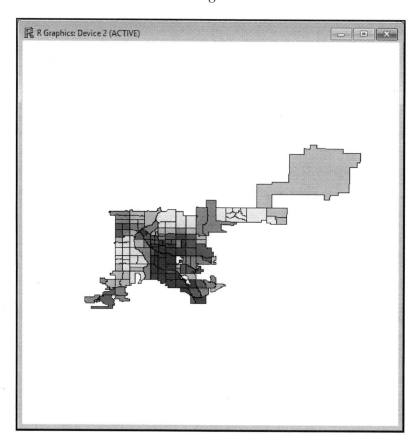

6. Let's make things a little more interesting by changing up the color scheme, adding a legend, title, and north arrow, and defining the number of categories. Add the following code block to accomplish this and then we'll discuss the code:

```
denverCensusTracts = readShapePoly(file.choose())
pctWhite = denverCensusTracts$PCT_WHITE
shades = auto.shading(pctWhite, n = 6, cutter =
rangeCuts, cols = brewer.pal(6, "Greens"))
```

```
choropleth(denverCensusTracts, pctWhite, shades)
choro.legend(-104.85, 39.75, shades, fmt =
"%4.1f", title = "Percent White Population")
title("Percent White Population in Denver")
north.arrow(-104.98, 39.62, 0.010)
```

7. Let's see what the following code lines used in the preceding code example depict:

- denverCensusTracts = readShapePoly(file.choose()): This code simply uses the file chooser to allow you to select the shapefile and assign it to the denverCensusTracts variable.

- pctWhite = denverCensusTracts$PCT_WHITE: This code creates a new variable called pctWhite that will hold the attribute information for the PCT_WHITE attribute column in the shapefile.

- shades = auto.shading(pctWhite, n = 6, cutter = rangeCuts, cols = brewer.pal(6, "Greens")): This code defines the color ramp for the data to reference the PCT_WHITE field, 6 color buckets, how to divide the data, and the color ramp, which is Green in this case.

- choropleth(denverCensusTracts, pctWhite, shades): Using this code, we create a new choropleth map by passing in the denverCensusTracts, pctWhite, and shades variables. These define the shapefile to display, the field to use for the choropleth map, and the color scheme.

- choro.legend(-104.85, 39.75, shades, fmt = "%4.1f", title = "Percent White Population"): This code creates the legend.

- title("Percent White Population in Denver"): This code creates the title.

- north.arrow(-104.98, 39.62, 0.010): This code creates the north arrow.

The final output should appear as shown in the following screenshot:

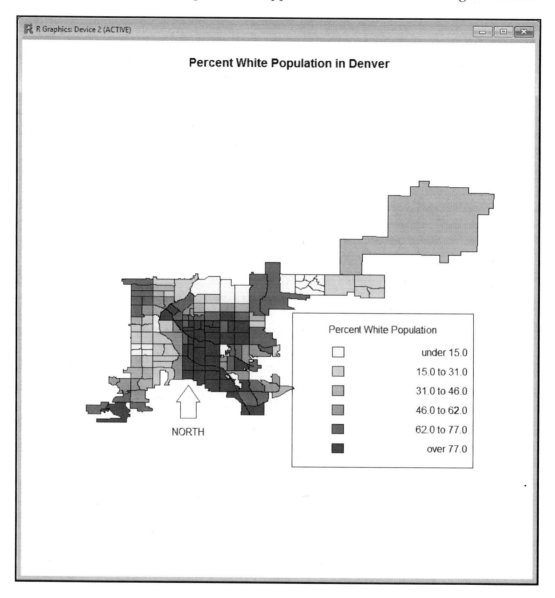

8. Next we'll create a histogram by issuing the following statement in the **R Console** window:

```
hist(denverCensusTracts$PCT_WHITE, col="red")
```

The plot window should now display a histogram as shown in the following screenshot:

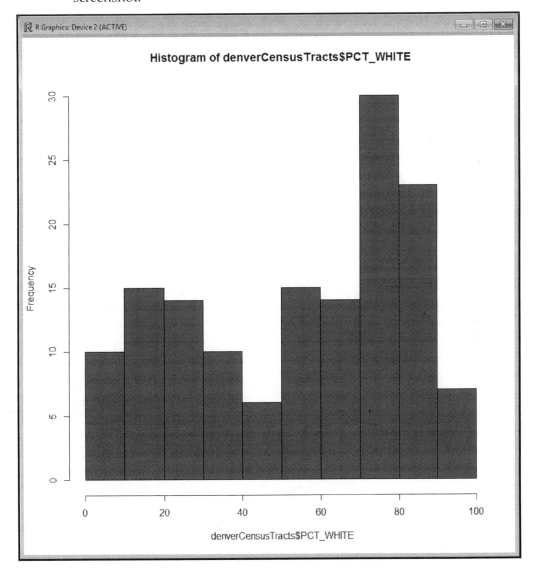

9. You can check your work by opening the `Ch7_5.R` solution file found in the `C:\GeospatialTraining\SpatialStats\Code\solutions` folder.
10. To open the file, navigate to **File | Open script...** in R.
11. To execute an `.R` file, navigate to **Edit | Run all**.

Additional R study options

The intent of this chapter was to provide you with an overview of the R programming language, but it is by no means a comprehensive study of the topic. The entire scope of the R programming language is far beyond what we can be provided in a single chapter. For more information on the topic, refer to the following resources:

- The Owen Guide (`https://cran.r-project.org/doc/contrib/Owen-TheRGuide.pdf`)
- R Bloggers (`https://www.r-bloggers.com/`)
- Stackoverflow for R (`https://stackoverflow.com/questions/tagged/r`)
- The R Project (`https://www.r-project.org/`)

Summary

R is a set of tools for data manipulation, statistical calculation, simulation, and visualization. In this chapter, the basic constructs of the R programming language have been introduced. In later chapters, you'll use the R programming skills you have acquired in this chapter to build a custom ArcGIS script tool with an R script.

8
Creating Custom ArcGIS Tools with ArcGIS Bridge and R

R-ArcGIS Bridge is a free, open source R package that connects ArcGIS and R. It was released together with an R-ArcGIS community website on GitHub, encouraging a collaboration between the two communities. The package serves the following three purposes:

- ArcGIS developers can now create custom tools and toolboxes that integrate ArcGIS and R
- ArcGIS users can access R code through geoprocessing scripts
- R users can access the GIS data managed in traditional GIS ways

The creation of custom script tools in ArcGIS has been possible for a long time using the Python programming language. Now, using the R-ArcGIS Bridge package you can also use the R programming language to build custom script tools that allow you to integrate GIS data with R scripts. The new `arcgisbinding` package facilitates the movement of data between these two platforms. You can also access traditional GIS data formats through your standalone R scripts.

In this chapter, you will learn how to install the R-ArcGIS Bridge package and then use the `arcgisbinding` package along with ArcGIS Desktop to build a custom script tool.

Installing the R-ArcGIS Bridge package

There are some pre-requisites for installing the R-ArcGIS Bridge package. The first thing you'll want to do is install R 3.1 or later. If you completed the exercises in `Chapter 7`, *Introduction to the R Programming Language*, you will have already completed this step. If not, visit `https://cran.r-project.org/` the **Comprehensive R Archive Network (CRAN)**, download the binary distribution for Windows, and install R.

The Windows installer for R will install both the 32-bit and the 64-bit versions by default. ArcGIS Desktop uses the 32-bit version, while ArcGIS Pro uses the 64-bit version. ArcGIS Desktop can use the 64-bit version if background geoprocessing is installed and the script has been configured for background geoprocessing.

After installing R, you can download the R-ArcGIS Bridge package by going to the GitHub page for the project (`https://github.com/R-ArcGIS/r-bridge-install`). You'll want to select the Python link from the GitHub page. Detailed installation instructions are provided at the download page (`https://github.com/R-ArcGIS/r-bridge-install`). There is also a video that details the installation process. It's important to know where you can run the package. You need to have at least version 3.1 of the R software installed, along with either ArcGIS Desktop 10.3.1 or ArcGIS Pro 1.1 (or later versions of both).

After installing the package, it is possible to connect both environments. Starting from within R, you can connect to ArcGIS by loading the R-ArcGIS Bridge library and initializing a connection to ArcGIS. Similar to working with data cursors in Python, there are two stages for opening GIS data if you want to work in R. First, you need to select a GIS data source (such as a feature class, layer, or table). Second, you need to filter the data to the set you want to work with. The reason for this is that R runs and processes data in-memory, so an in-memory data frame is created rather than storing an entire file in-memory. This data frame retains references back to the geometry data.

In order to analyze data in R with spatial data, it needs to be represented as the `sp` object. This conversion is done with `arc.data2sp`. After finishing your work in R, the results need to go back to ArcGIS, either by writing to an existing data source or a new one. The results can be written to a new feature class using the `arc.write` statement in R.

By building R script tools for ArcGIS, you can run R scripts inside ArcGIS and make use of the R functionality, for example, by using data input from a GIS, processing it with R, and having it sent back to ArcGIS without having to change from one environment to another - the script tool takes care of that. You can also put different geospatial and statistical workflows together with **ModelBuilder** in ArcGIS, for example by making an R script part of a large geospatial analysis workflow, thus making it an even more powerful methodology.

In this exercise, you will download and install the R-ArcGIS Bridge library by performing the following steps:

1. Open a browser and go to `https://r-arcgis.github.io/`.

   You should see something similar to the following screenshot:

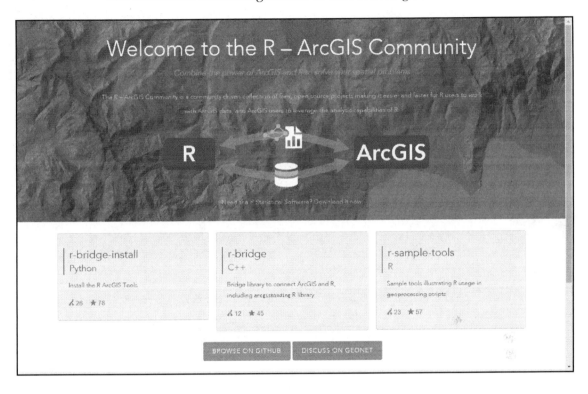

2. Click on the **Python** link from the page to display the page seen in the following screenshot:

3. Click on the **Clone or download** button and select **Download ZIP** as shown in the following screenshot. This will download a file called `r-bridge-install-master.zip`:

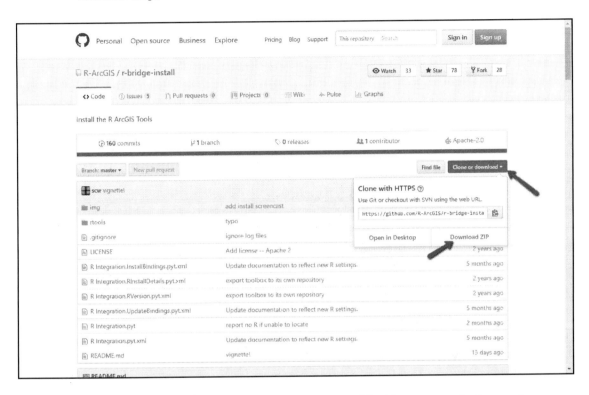

4. Unzip the `r-bridge-install-master.zip` file. You can unzip it anywhere you'd like but the **Downloads** folder is fine. This will create an `r-bridge-install-master` folder. Inside `r-bridge-install-master` is a Python toolbox called `R Integration.pyt`.

5. Open the **ArcMap** window and display the **Catalog** view.

6. If necessary, add a folder connection to the **Downloads** folder (or wherever you extracted the ZIP file).

7. Inside the new folder connection, navigate to the `r-bridge-install-master` folder and open it. You should see the `R Integration.pyt` toolbox. Open the toolbox.

8. You should see several script tools, as shown in the following screenshot:

9. Double-click on the **Install R bindings** script tool and click on **OK** to execute the tool. If all your pre-requisites have been installed, you should see some messages in the progress dialog box that indicate a successful installation.

10. There are several other tools in the R Integration toolbox, which are as follows:

   - **Print R Version**: This tool simply displays the current version of R being used

   - **R Installation Details**: This tool provides summary information about the package

   - **Update R bindings**: This tool can be used to update the bindings with new versions as they become available

Building custom ArcGIS tools with R

Scripts written in R can be called from ArcGIS via custom script tools in much the same way that Python can be used. There are three components of R scripts tools, including the R script, a custom toolbox, and parameters for the script. The `arcgisbinding` package provides the mechanism for communication between R and ArcGIS.

Introduction to the arcgisbinding package

The `arcgisbinding` package allows you to access ArcGIS format data from an R script. Using this package, you can access geodatabases and shapefiles for read and write purposes. You can also select subsets of GIS datasets using a `select()` function that acts much the same as cursor objects in Python. Basically, they are in-memory copies of datasets. You can also convert ArcGIS data to `sp` objects, perform analysis, and write data back to ArcGIS format datasets. Other capabilities include the ability to convert between WKT and `proj.4` and interact with geometries and attributes.

The arcgisbinding package functionality - checking for licenses

The `arc.check_product()` function is used to initialize a connection to ArcGIS from scripts run directly from R. This is for scripts not called directly from an ArcGIS geoprocessing script. This function returns the product, which will be either ArcGIS Desktop or ArcGIS Pro, the license level, build number, and DLL.

The arcgisbinding package functionality - accessing ArcGIS format data

ArcGIS format data including geodatabases, shapefiles, and standalone tables can be accessed through several functions. The `arc.open()` function is used to open an existing ArcGIS format dataset, such as a shapefile and returns an `arc.dataset` object. The following code example shows the use of the `arc.open()` function. This code sample opens a shapefile and returns an `arc.dataset` object:

```
ozone.file = system.file("extdata",
"ca_ozone_pts.shp", package="arcgisbinding")
d = arc.open(ozone.file)
cat('all fields: ', names(d@fields, fill = TRUE)
#print all fields
```

The `arc.select()` function is used in conjunction with the `arc.dataset` object returned by `arc.open()`. Using this object, you can apply a filter on the returned attribute fields, along with a `where` clause that restricts the number of records. The returned records are held in memory where they can be used as input to various analyses. There is also a selected attribute that can be used to define whether only the selected records should be returned. This function loads the dataset to a standard R data frame object. Finally, the `arc.write()` function can be used to write out data to a feature dataset or table. The following code example shows the use of the `arc.open()`, `arc.select()`, and `arc.write()` functions to open, select, and write data:

```
##write as a shapefile
fc = arc.open(system.file("extdata",
"ca_ozone_pts.shp", package="arcgisbinding"))
d = arc.select(fc, 'ozone')
d[1,] = 0.6
arc.write(tempfile("ca_new", fileext=".shp"), d)
##write as a table
arc.write(tempfile("tlb", fileext=".dbf"),
list('f1'=c(23,45), 'f2'=c('hello', 'bob')))
```

```
##from scratch as feature class
arc.write(tempfile("fc_pts", fileext=".shp"),
list('data'=rnorm(100)),
list(x=runif(100, min=0, max=10), y=runif(100, min=0,
max = 10)),
list(type='Point'))
```

The arcgisbinding package functionality - shape classes

There are various shape objects that can be used to access geometry information associated with ArcGIS format data or R format spatial data. The `arc.shape()` function returns an `arc.shape` class from an `arc.dataframe` object. Essentially, this is the shape field information found on feature classes. There are two functions that can be used to convert data to and from ArcGIS and R spatial formats. The `arc.shape2sp()` function converts the contents of an `arc.shape` class to the `sp` spatial geometry classes including `SpatialPoints`, `SpatialLines`, and `SpatialPolygons`. To convert R spatial format data to ArcGIS format, you can use `arc.sp2data()`. Finally, `arc.shapeinfo()` returns details on the geometry type of the dataset as well as the spatial reference. The following code example shows the use of the `arc.shape` class:

```
d = arc.open(system.file("extdata",
"ca_ozone_pts.shp", package="arcgisbinding"))
df = arc.select(d, 'ozone')
shp = arc.shape(df)
length(shp$x)
```

The arcgisbinding package functionality - progress bar

There are a couple functions that you can use when working with the progress bar and label. This is the dialog box that appears when a geoprocessing tool is executed. The label is a text string and can be set with the `arc.progress_label()` function. It's good for presenting the current status of a tool that is executing and also good for debugging. You can also set the value of the progress bar to a value between 0 and 100 using `arc.progress_pos()`.

Introduction to custom script tools in ArcGIS

Scripts written in R can be called from ArcGIS via custom script tools in much the same way that Python can be used. There are three components to R scripts tools: the R script, a custom toolbox, and parameters for the script.

The tool_exec() function

R script tools follow the same general format with three primary components including the `tool_exec()` function along with the `in_params` and the `out_params` lists. The `tool_exec()` function is the primary function and is executed when called from the ArcGIS custom tool. This is the entry point to the R script when the user clicks on the **OK** button on the tool dialog box.

Input parameters are defined as a list and passed as the first parameter to the `tool_exec()` function. Any output parameters will be passed in as a list. This is the second parameter passed to the `tool_exec()` function, and it is only required if data is being output from the tool. The following code example shows a typical `tool_exec()` function with the input and output parameters highlighted:

```r
tool_exec = function(in_params, out_params)
{
  if (!requireNamespace("sp", quietly= TRUE))
    install.packages("sp")
  if (!requireNamespace("mclust", quietly=TRUE))
    install.packages("mclust")
    require(mclust)
    require(sp)

  source_dataset = in_params[[1]]   nclust =
  in_params[[2]]   out_table = out_params[[1]]
  out_ellipses = out_params[[2]]   out_dens =
  out_params[[3]]   out_sim = out_params[[4]]

arc.progress_label("Loading Dataset")
d = arc.open(source_dataset)
data = arc.select(d, names(d@fields[d@fields ==
"OID"]))
data_shp = arc.shape(data)
data.xy = cbind(data_shp$x, data_shp$y)

  arc.progress_label("Bayesian information Criterion
  for model")
  patternBIC = mclustBIC(data.xy)
```

```
    }
```

The `arc.progress_label()` and `arc.progress_pos()` functions can be used to update
the progress information while the tool is executing, as shown in the highlighted lines of the
preceding code:

```
tool_exec = function(in_params, out_params)
{
  if (!requireNamespace("sp", quietly= TRUE))
  install.packages("sp")
  if (!requireNamespace("mclust", quietly=TRUE))
  install.packages("mclust")
  require(mclust)
  require(sp)
  source_dataset = in_params[[1]]
  nclust = in_params[[2]]
  out_table = out_params[[1]]
  out_ellipses = out_params[[2]]
  out_dens = out_params[[3]]
  out_sim = out_params[[4]]
arc.progress_label("Loading Dataset")
  d = arc.open(source_dataset)
  data = arc.select(d, names(d@fields[d@fields ==
  "OID"]))
  data_shp = arc.shape(data)
  data.xy = cbind(data_shp$x, data_shp$y)
arc.progress_label("Bayesian information Criterion
  for model")
  patternBIC = mclustBIC(data.xy)
}
```

Any plots created by the R script will be displayed in a window inside ArcGIS, as shown in the following screenshot:

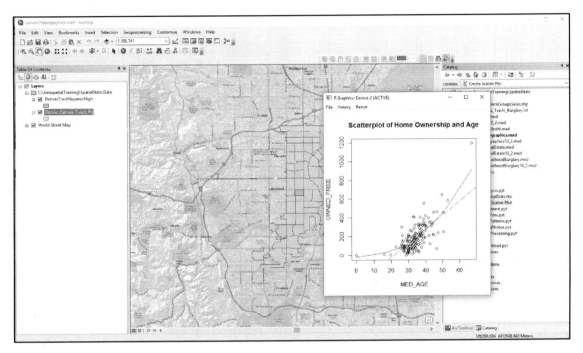

Creating the custom toolbox and tool

Now, let's walk through the process of creating an R script tool in ArcGIS:

1. You first have to add a new script inside a custom toolbox. The custom script has to go inside a custom toolbox, not a system toolbox. System toolboxes are read-only structures. You'll get a chance to go through the specific steps for creating a custom toolbox and tool in the next exercise.

2. The second step in the **Add Script** wizard is to define the location of the .R script. You must make sure that you run the script in process as well.

3. The final step in creating the custom R script tool is to define the parameters for the tool. Make sure that the parameters are defined in the same order found in the R script. Each parameter has a display name (what the user sees), a data type, and parameter properties including the type, direction, multivalue, default, environment, and others.

Exercise - creating a custom ArcGIS script tool with R

In this exercise, you'll build a custom ArcGIS script tool and attach it to an R script. The script will create a simple scatterplot from two variables selected from the `Denver_Census_Tracts_Prj` layer:

1. Open **ArcMap** with the `DenverDemographics` map document file.
2. Open the **Catalog** view and navigate to **Toolboxes | My Toolboxes**. Right -click on **My Toolboxes** and select **New Toolbox**. Call the toolbox `DenverSpatialStats`. We'll return to this new toolbox after we create the R script.
3. Open the **R Console** window and navigate to **File | New script**.
4. In the new script window, create a new function called `tool_exec` as shown in the following code:

```
tool_exec = function(in_params, out_params)
  {


  }
```

5. This tool will require several input parameters including an input feature class, fields for the x and y axes, and a title for the scatterplot. Add the following highlighted code to capture these parameters as they come into the script:

```
tool_exec = function(in_params, out_params)
  {
      source_dataset = in_params[[1]]    xField =
      in_params[[2]]    yField = in_params[[3]]
      title = in_params[[4]]
  }
```

6. Load the input dataset using `arc.open()`, as follows:

```
tool_exec = function(in_params, out_params)
  {
      source_dataset = in_params[[1]]
      xField = in_params[[2]]
      yField = in_params[[3]]
      title = in_params[[4]]

      # read data
      arc.progress_label("Loading Dataset")
      d = arc.open(source_dataset)

  }
```

7. Retrieve an R data frame object from the dataset using the `arc.select()` function:

```
tool_exec = function(in_params, out_params)
{
    source_dataset = in_params[[1]]
    xField = in_params[[2]]
    yField = in_params[[3]]
    title = in_params[[4]]

    # read data
    arc.progress_label("Loading Dataset")
    d = arc.open(source_dataset)

    # get a data frame object with fields needed
    data = arc.select(d, c(xField, yField))


}
```

8. Retrieve the field names as strings, so we can use them to label the x and y axes:

```
tool_exec = function(in_params, out_params)
{
    source_dataset = in_params[[1]]
    xField = in_params[[2]]
    yField = in_params[[3]]
    title = in_params[[4]]

    # read data
    arc.progress_label("Loading Dataset")
    d = arc.open(source_dataset)

    # get a data frame object with fields needed
    data = arc.select(d, c(xField, yField))
    xAxisTitle = colnames(data)[[1]]
    yAxisTitle = colnames(data)[[2]]


}
```

9. Use the R `plot()` function to create the scatterplot by passing in the input parameters:

```
tool_exec = function(in_params, out_params)
  {
        source_dataset = in_params[[1]]
        xField = in_params[[2]]
        yField = in_params[[3]]
        title = in_params[[4]]

        # read data
        arc.progress_label("Loading Dataset")
        d = arc.open(source_dataset)

        # get a data frame object with fields needed
        data = arc.select(d, c(xField, yField))
        xAxisTitle = colnames(data)[[1]]
        yAxisTitle = colnames(data)[[2]]

        plot(data[[1]], data[[2]], main=title,
        xlab=xAxisTitle, ylab=yAxisTitle)


  }
```

10. Finally, add a couple of fit lines to the scatter plot so that we can better understand the relationship between the two variables:

```
tool_exec = function(in_params, out_params)
  {
        source_dataset = in_params[[1]]
        xField = in_params[[2]]
        yField = in_params[[3]]
        title = in_params[[4]]

        # read data
        arc.progress_label("Loading Dataset")
        d = arc.open(source_dataset)

        # get a data frame object with fields needed
        data = arc.select(d, c(xField, yField))
        xAxisTitle = colnames(data)[[1]]
        yAxisTitle = colnames(data)[[2]]

        plot(data[[1]], data[[2]], main=title,
        xlab=xAxisTitle, ylab=yAxisTitle)
        abline(lm(data[[2]]~data[[1]]), col="red")
        lines(lowess(data[[1]],data[[2]]),
```

```
    col="blue")

}
```

11. Save your script with a name of
    `C:\GeospatialTraining\SpatialStats\ScatterPlot.R`.
12. Return to **ArcMap** and right-click on the `DenverSpatialStats` toolbox you
    created earlier. Navigate to **Add | Script** to display the **Add Script** wizard dialog.
13. Give your script tool a name, label, and description as shown in the following
    screenshot:

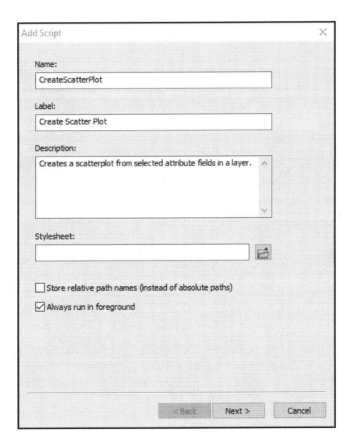

14. Click on **Next** and then browse to `C:\GeospatialTraining\SpatialStats` and select the `ScatterPlot.R` file, as shown in the following screenshot:

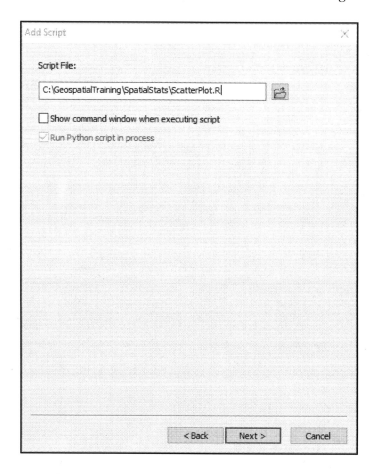

15. Click on **Next** to display the final dialog in the **Add Script** wizard. Add the following parameters:

- **First parameter**:
    - **Display Name**: Input Feature Class
    - **Data Type**: Feature Layer
    - **Type: Required**
    - **Direction: Input**
    - Leave all other parameter properties to their default settings

- **Second parameter**:
    - **Display Name**: X Field
    - **Data Type**: Field
    - **Type: Required**
    - **Direction: Input**
    - **Filter: Field**
        - Short, Long, Float, and Double
    - **Obtained From**: Input Feature Class

- **Third parameter**:
    - **Display Name**: Y Field
    - **Data Type**: Field
    - **Type: Required**
    - **Direction: Input**
    - **Filter: Field**
        - Short, Long, Float, and Double
    - **Obtained From: Input Feature Class**

- **Fourth Parameter**:
    - **Display Name**: Title
    - **Data Type**: String
    - **Type: Required**
    - **Direction: Input**
    - **Default: Scatterplot of Demographic Data**

Take a look at the following screenshot, which depicts the parameters that need to be inserted:

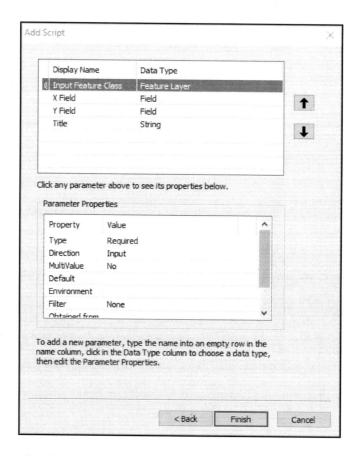

16. Click on **Finish**.

17. Insert the `DenverSpatialStats` toolbox. You should now see a new custom script tool called `Create Scatter Plot`:

18. Double-click on the tool to display the input dialog and add the input parameters shown in the following screenshot:

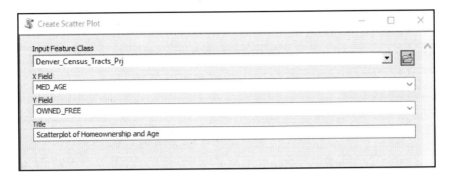

19. Click on **OK** to execute the tool. If everything has been coded correctly and your custom script tool parameters have been defined correctly, the output scatterplot should appear in a separate window inside of ArcGIS, as shown in the following screenshot:

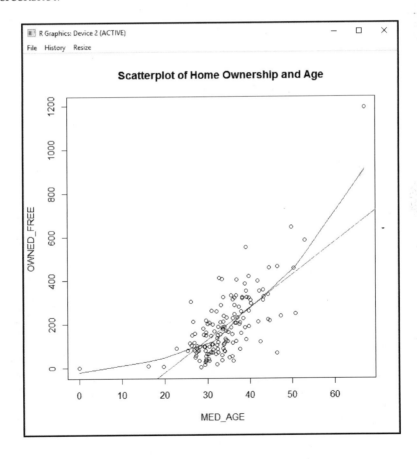

Sometimes, the **R Console** window will appear behind the **ArcMap** window.

Summary

The R-ArcGIS Bridge package enables communication between R and ArcGIS. Using the bridge, R users can now easily access GIS format data from their stand alone R scripts and ArcGIS users can use R to create custom script tools that take advantage of R functionality. This is made possible through the `arcgisbinding` package that is installed by the R-ArcGIS Bridge package. In the next chapter, we'll look at a case study that will allow you to apply the skills you've learned in this book to the analysis of crime in a major city.

9
Application of Spatial Statistics to Crime Analysis

Vehicle theft in Seattle, WA, increased in 2016 compared to previous years. According to the West Seattle blog (http://westseattleblog.com/), car thefts in King County (Seattle area) increased by 18.9% during the first four months of 2016 compared to the first four months of 2015 - from about 2,500 to about 2,900. By the end of the year, Seattle had experienced over 7,000 vehicle thefts in 2016. Understanding more about where these thefts occurred can be of assistance to local police and city officials. However, knowing where vehicle theft occurs doesn't necessarily help us understand why it is occurring. Using spatial statistics tools provided by ArcGIS allows analysts and officials to understand where vehicle theft occurs, but also where they cluster, and which variables explain why they occur.

This chapter will differ somewhat from the previous chapters in a number of ways. First, rather than providing a specific set of steps that you follow in sequence, it will assume that over the first eight chapters of the book, you have developed a new set of skills that you can use in addition to your existing ArcGIS Desktop knowledge. Instructions will be provided in a more generic fashion, and you'll use your skills and knowledge of basic ArcGIS functionality, along with your new spatial statistics tools, to get a better understanding of vehicle theft in Seattle and eventually develop a general model that, at least to some degree, explains this type of crime. Finally, the previous chapters discussed the tools provided by the Spatial Statistics Tools toolbox in isolation, whereas this chapter takes a more integrated approach to using these tools and others provided by ArcGIS Desktop to gain a higher level of understanding of a particular topic.

In this chapter, you will tackle the topic of vehicle theft in Seattle, WA, including the following topics:

- Downloading and preparing several datasets for the city of Seattle, including crime data, census data, and others
- Using the **Central Feature** and **Directional Distribution** tools to obtain basic descriptive information about the vehicle theft dataset
- Determine if the vehicle theft is clustered, distributed, or randomly spaced using the **Average Nearest Neighbor** tool
- Find hot spots, cold spots, and outliers using the **Hot Spot Analysis** and **Cluster and Outlier Analysis** tools
- Use the **Exploratory Regression** and **Ordinary Least Squares** regression tools to model the variables correlated with vehicle theft

Obtaining the crime dataset

For this case study, we'll use data obtained from the city of Seattle, WA, open source database. Seattle is one of the many cities committed to providing easy access to their data through an online portal:

1. Open a web browser and go to `http://data.seattle.gov`. You should see a page similar to the following screenshot, but keep in mind that websites change frequently so your version may look different:

2. For this case study, we are interested in obtaining crime data, which can be found in a file named `Seattle Policy Department Policy Report Incident`. You can navigate directly to this file at `https://data.seattle.gov/Public-Safety/Seattle-Police-Department-Polic e-Report-Incident/7ais-f98f`.

3. You can also use the search textbox and type in the term `Seattle Police Department Police Report Incident`. The report should be the first item returned in the search results.

4. From the incident report page, click on **View Data** and you'll be presented with a page that looks similar to the following screenshot:

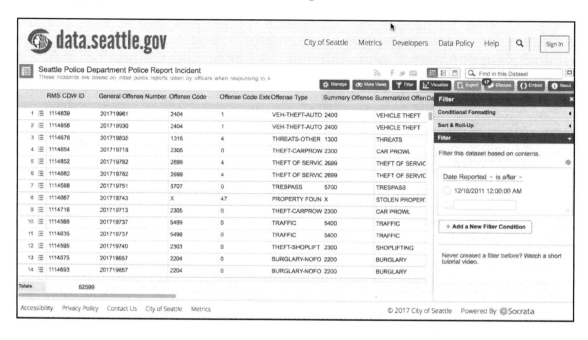

5. In this step, we'll filter the data using a date range. In the **Filter** pane, set the **Year** parameter to **2016,** as seen in the following screenshot:

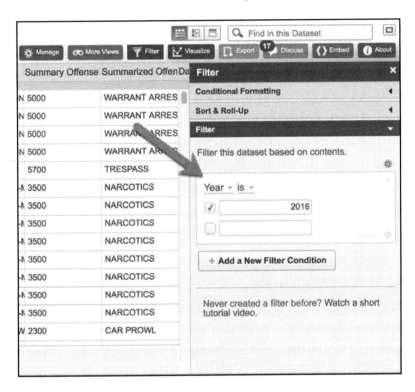

6. This should return 71,765 records, but keep in mind that your results may differ slightly.

7. Click on the **Export** button and then select **CSV** to download the file as shown in the following screenshot:

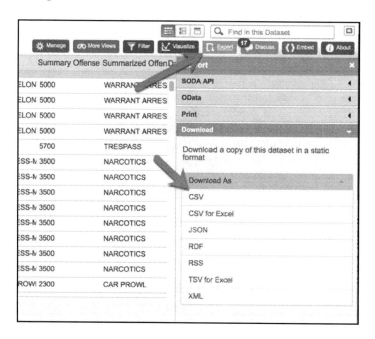

8. In your `C:\GeospatialTraining\SpatialStats\Data` folder, create a new folder and name it `SeattleCrime`. Copy the downloaded `Seattle_Police_Department_Police_Report_Incident.csv` file to this folder.

9. Open **ArcMap** with the `SeattleNeighborhoodBurglary.mxd` file. This file contains a feature class called `Seattle Neighborhood Burglary` that we used in a previous exercise in this book. Open the attribute table for this feature class and remove the `Count_` field by right-clicking on the field and selecting **Delete Field**. This field was used in a previous exercise. In this exercise, we'll recreate the field with new data.

10. In this step you'll add the CSV file that you exported from the Seattle open source database. In the **ArcMap** window, navigate to **File | Add XY Data** and go to `C:\GeospatialTraining\SpatialStats\Data\SeattleCrimeSeattle_Police_Department_Police_Report_Incident.csv` and click **Add**.

11. Specify **Longitude** for **X Field** and **Latitude** for **Y Field** as shown in the following screenshot:

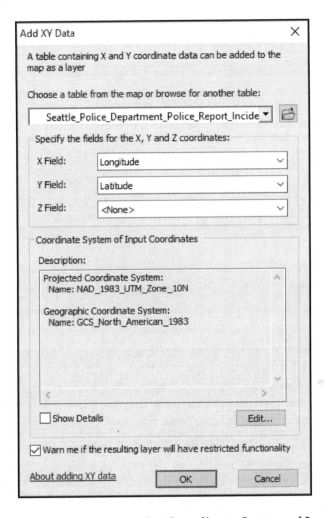

12. Click on the **Edit...** button to set the **Coordinate System of Input Coordinates** option.
13. Scroll to the top of the **XY Coordinate System** tab and navigate to **Geographic Coordinate Systems | World | WGS 1984** and click **OK**.

14. Click on **OK** to add the file. You may be prompted with a message regarding the **Object-ID** field. Click **OK** on this dialog. This will add the points to the map as shown in the following screenshot:

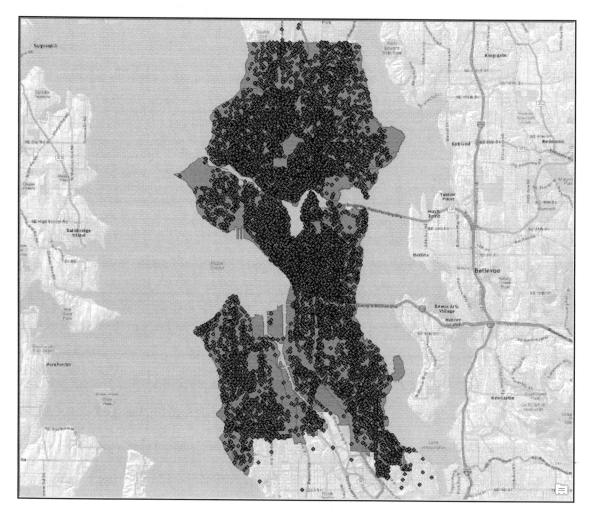

15. In the **ArcMap** window in the **Table Of Contents** pane, right-click on the Seattle_Police_Department_Police_Report_Incident.csv event layer and navigate to **Data | Export Data....** Save the file as Police_Incident_Report.shp in the C:\GeospatialTraining\SpatialStats\Data\SeattleCrime folder.

16. Add the layer to the map when prompted and remove the events layer.

Data preparation

In this section of the case study, you will do some data preparation in advance of the spatial statistical analysis. This analysis will concentrate on vehicle theft:

1. In the **ArcMap** window navigate to **Selection** | **Select by Attributes....**

2. In the **Select by Attributes** dialog box, select `Police_Incident_Report` in the **Layer** option and fill in the additional attributes as shown in the following screenshot. Click on **OK**. This will select all vehicle theft crimes:

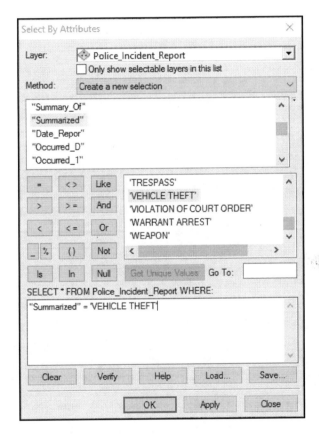

3. This should select 7473 records. Right-click on `Police_Incident_Report` and navigate to **Data** | **Export Data....** Specify the output shapefile as `Vehicle_Theft.shp` and place it in the `SeattleCrime` folder you created earlier. Add the layer to **ArcMap** when prompted.

4. Remove the `Police_Incident_Report` layer from the ArcMap **Table Of Contents** pane.

5. Tools in the **Spatial Statistics Tools** toolbox should be used with data that has been projected into a coordinate system. In **ArcMap** navigate to **Geoprocessing | Search for Tools** and find the **Project** tool. It should be in the **Data Management** toolbox.

6. Project the `VehicleTheft` layer to a new feature class called `VehicleTheft_Prj` and save it in the `SeattleCrime` folder. For the output coordinate system, select `NAD_1983_UTM_ZONE_10N`. The other layers in the **Table Of Contents** pane have already been projected to this coordinate system, so you should be able to simply select it from one of the existing layers, as shown in the following screenshot:

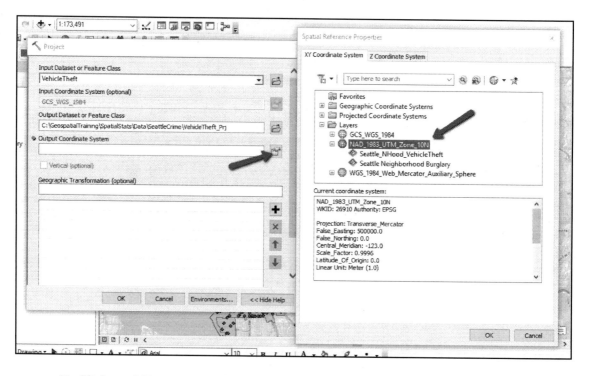

7. Click on **OK** to execute the tool and then add the new feature class to ArcMap.

8. Remove the `VehicleTheft` layer from the ArcMap **Table Of Contents** pane.

9. In this step, you'll spatially join the `VehicleTheft_Prj` layer to the `Seattle Neighborhood Burglary` layer. Right-click on `Seattle Neighborhood Burglary` and navigate to **Joins and Relates | Join**.

10. In the **Join Data** dialog, select **Join data from another layer based on spatial location** and fill in the additional parameters as shown in the following screenshot. This will create a `Count_` field in `Seattle Neighborhood Burglary` that contains a summary of the number of vehicle thefts in each neighborhood. Click on **OK** to execute the spatial join:

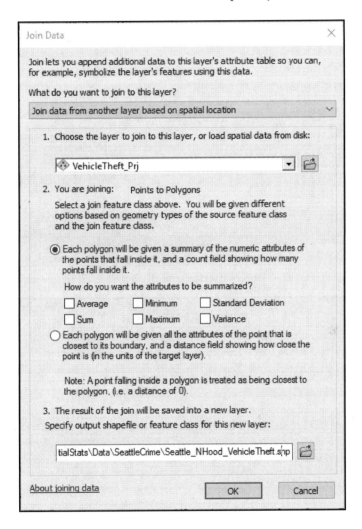

11. The new `Seattle_NHood_VehicleTheft` layer will contain a `Count_` field containing a count of the number of vehicle thefts in each neighborhood during 2016.

12. While most of the neighborhoods are relatively equal in size, there is enough of a size difference to normalize the counts. Open the attribute table for the `Seattle_NHood_VehicleTheft` layer and add a new field called `NormVT`. Make it a `Float` data type field.

13. Right-click on the `NormVT` field and select **Field Calculator**. Click on **Yes** if prompted with a warning. In the **Field Calculator** dialog, set `NormVT` equal to the `Count_` field divided by the `AREA` field as shown in the following screenshot:

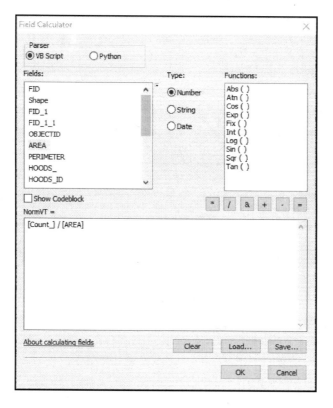

14. Click on **OK** to execute the calculator. This will normalize the number of thefts by the area of each neighborhood, to remove the size as the dominant factor in the number of incidents.

15. Before applying the spatial statistical tools to the datasets, we can create a graduated color map to get a general feel for the data. Open the **Properties** dialog box for the `Seattle_NHood_VehicleTheft` layer and select the **Symbology** tab.

16. In the **Symbology** tab, navigate to **Quantities | Graduated colors**.

17. Under **Fields**, select NormVT as the **Value** field and click on the **Apply** button. The central part of the study area appears to be a hot spot for vehicle theft in the Seattle area as shown in the following screenshot. Let's not jump to conclusions though, until we apply some statistical analysis to the data:

Getting descriptive spatial statistics about the crime dataset

Before moving on to more advanced spatial statistical analysis, we'll run some descriptive statistical tools to get a general feel for vehicle theft data in Seattle from 2016:

1. Find the **Spatial Statistics Tools** toolbox in **ArcToolbox** and open the **Measuring Geographic Distributions** toolset.

2. Run the **Central Feature** tool against the `VehicleTheft_Prj` layer. You can name the output feature class to whatever name you'd like. If you need to review how to execute or interpret the output of this tool, refer to `Chapter 2`, *Measuring Geographic Distributions with ArcGIS Tools*. The output should be as follows:

3. Run the **Direction Distribution** tool against the `VehicleTheft_Prj` layer. You can name the output feature class to whatever name you'd like. If you need to review how to execute or interpret the output of this tool, refer to `Chapter 2`, *Measuring Geographic Distributions with ArcGIS Tools*. The output should be as follows:

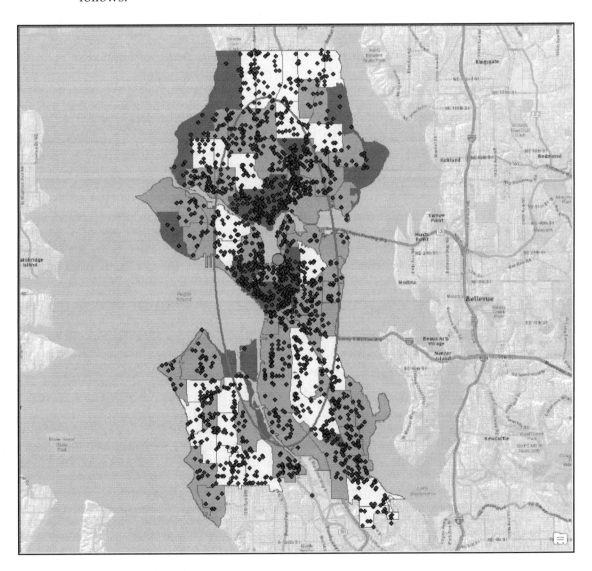

What basic information can you derive by analyzing the output of these descriptive spatial statistics tools?

Using the Analyzing Patterns tool in the crime dataset

In this section, you'll use the **Analyzing Patterns** toolset to determine if the vehicle theft data exhibits a clustered, dispersed, or random spatial pattern. Remember that with the tools in the **Analyzing Patterns** toolset, the null hypothesis is **Complete spatial randomness (CSR)** in the dataset being analyzed. Our analysis should tell us if the null hypothesis can be rejected. If necessary, go back to Chapter 3, *Analyzing Patterns with ArcGIS Tools*, for an overview of how to use these tools.

Let's take a look at the following steps, to learn how to use the Analyzing Patterns toolset in the crime dataset to determine the type of spatial pattern the vehicle theft data might exhibit:

1. Rejecting the null hypothesis requires a subjective judgment. You must determine what degree of risk you are willing to accept for being wrong. Before the pattern analysis tool is run, you will want to select a confidence value and not reject the null hypothesis unless the output matches or exceeds the confidence value. Typical confidence values include 90%, 95%, and 99%, with 99% being the most conservative. In other words, if you selected a 99% confidence level, you would not reject the null hypothesis unless the probability that the pattern was created by random chance is less than **1%**. Take some time now to select a confidence level for this analysis. The level should be 90%, 95%, or 99%.

2. Use the **Average Nearest Neighbor** tool with the VehicleTheft_Prj layer as the input feature class to determine if the dataset exhibits a **Clustered**, **Dispersed**, or **Random** spatial pattern. The output should be as follows:

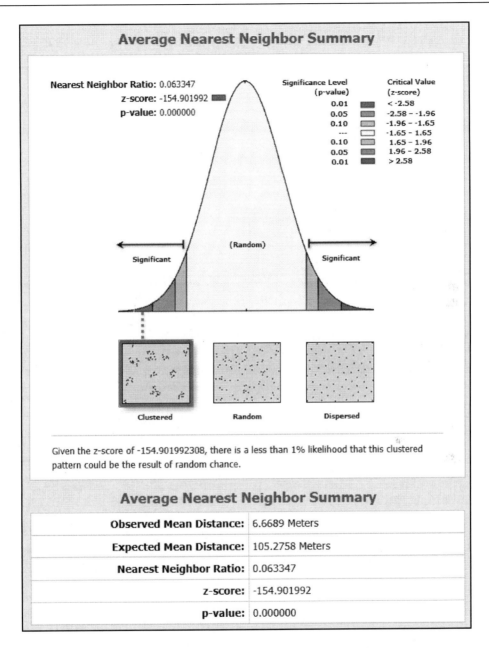

Average Nearest Neighbor Summary

Nearest Neighbor Ratio: 0.063347
z-score: -154.901992
p-value: 0.000000

Given the z-score of -154.901992308, there is a less than 1% likelihood that this clustered pattern could be the result of random chance.

Average Nearest Neighbor Summary

Observed Mean Distance:	6.6689 Meters
Expected Mean Distance:	105.2758 Meters
Nearest Neighbor Ratio:	0.063347
z-score:	-154.901992
p-value:	0.000000

What does the result of your analysis reveal? Does the data exhibit a clustered, dispersed, or random spatial pattern?

Using the Mapping Clusters tool in vehicle theft data

In the last section, our analysis revealed that vehicle theft in Seattle is clustered. Now, we'll expand our analysis to include the use of several tools found in the **Mapping Clusters** toolset, including **Hot Spot Analysis**, **Grouping Analysis**, and **Cluster and Outlier Analysis**:

1. Let's start the clustering analysis by running the **Hot Spot Analysis** tool. Define `Seattle_NHood_VehicleTheft` as the input feature class and `NormVT` as the analysis field. You can define the name and location of the output feature class. For the **Conceptualization of Spatial Relationships** parameter, use your knowledge of the neighborhood boundaries and the dataset to select an appropriate value. The following screenshot shows the output using `CONTIGUITY_EDGES_CORNERS`. You may also want to run this tool multiple times with different values for the spatial relationship parameter to see the effect on the output:

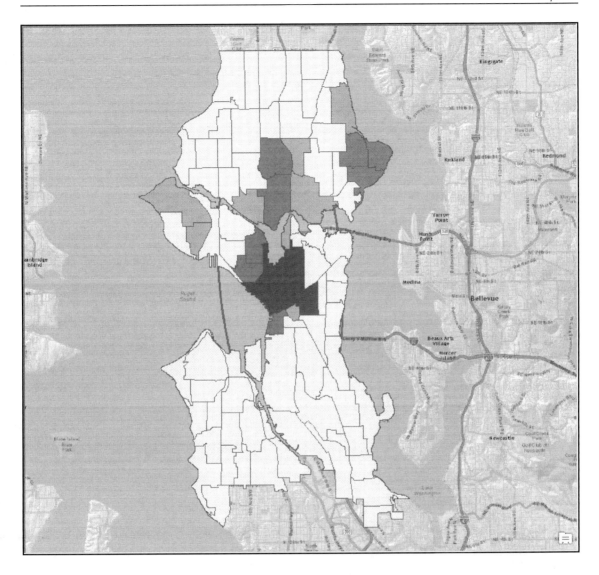

2. Now run the **Cluster and Outlier Analysis** tool with the same input parameters. The following screenshot displays the output using the `CONTIGUITY_EDGES_CORNERS` spatial relationship:

Modelling vehicle theft with Regression Analysis

Up until this point in the chapter, we have examined tools that help us answer *where* questions. For example, where do vehicle thefts cluster in Seattle? However, you may have noticed that they didn't address the logical progression of the problem such as *why* is vehicle theft occurring in the first place? What are the factors that determine why vehicle theft is prevalent in a particular area? Answering these types of questions helps us model the relationships in our data. The **Measuring Spatial Relationships** toolset contains a number of regression analysis tools that help you examine and/or quantify the relationships among features. They help measure how features in a dataset relate to each other in space. In this section, your goal is to create a model that describes the most important determinants of vehicle theft in Seattle.

Data preparation

Let's get prepared to learn about modeling vehicle theft with Regression Analysis by performing the following steps:

1. The first step in this section is to find, download, and prepare a census blocks dataset for the Seattle, WA area, containing a range of demographic and socio-economic variables. It's beyond the scope of this chapter to go through every detail of how to accomplish this task. Instead, I'll provide a broad overview of this process, and then you'll use your ArcGIS Desktop skills to accomplish the task.

2. The **American Community Survey (ACS)** is a monthly survey conducted by the U.S. Census Bureau. It is sent to 3.5 million addresses per year to produce detailed population and housing estimates. This data is released twice each year. Data collected includes a variety of social, demographic, economic, and housing variables. Data is collected for a variety of geographies, including census tracts and census block groups.

3. In this step, you will download ACS data at a census block group level for the State of Washington. Open a browser and navigate to `http://census.gov`. Downloading the data can be a little challenging, but you can download a guide that describes the process. Instructions for downloading the data from the census bureau begin on *page 11* of the guide. Download census block group data for the State of Washington.

4. If you'd prefer to skip this part of the process, we have already downloaded the data for you and placed it on the course website (`https://www.dropbox.com/s/b j4gjemrpqwrgm5/ACS_2014_5YR_BG_53.gdb.zip?dl=0`). In either case, whether you download the data directly from the U.S. Census Bureau or from our course website, the downloaded data incudes a single feature class called `ACS_2014_5YR_BG_53_WASHINGTON` along with a large group of tables that can be joined to the feature class. After downloading the file, unzip it to your `C:\GeospatialTraining\SpatialStats\Data\SeattleCrime` folder. The following screenshot depicts the contents of this file:

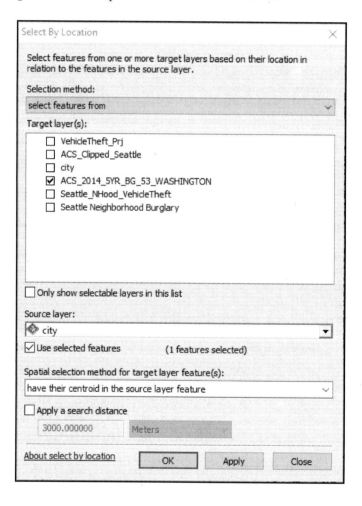

5. Each ACS table, prefixed with X<nn> contains a series of columns that can only be interpreted by viewing the metadata provided in the BG_METADATA_2014 table. The following screenshot depicts the metadata table. Open the BG_METADATA_2014 table in the **ArcMap** window and view the contents:

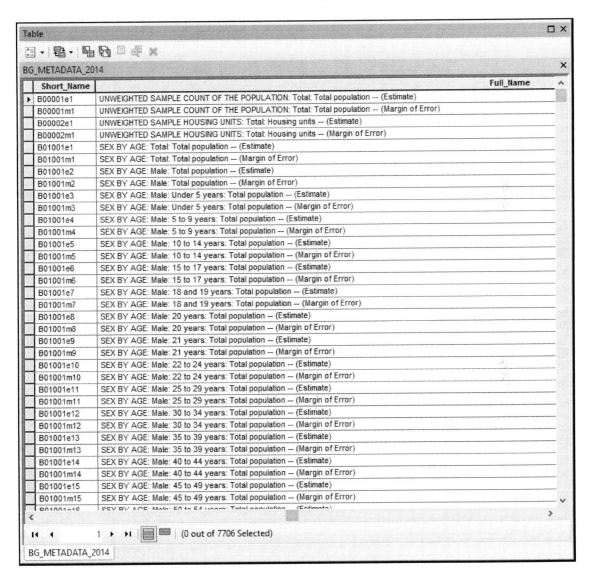

- Review the metadata for variables that you think might be highly correlated with vehicle theft and make a note of them somewhere. At this point, you want to select a broad array of potential variables, so if you think there is even a possibility that a variable may play a role in vehicle theft, leave it in the analysis for now.

6. For example, after a quick review of the metadata table, I found a handful of variables that would be interesting to include in the analysis. The following are listed variables, but keep in mind that this is just a sampling and at this stage of the process, you want to include many possible variables, so find additional variables if you can:

- **Means of Transportation to Work**: Car, truck, or van:
  - **Workers 16 and over**: B08301e2
- **Means of Transportation to Work**: Public transportation:
  - **Workers 16 and over**: B08301e10
- **Means of Transportation to Work**: Worked at home:
  - **Workers 16 and over**: B08301e21
- **Means of Transportation to Work**: 90 or more minutes:
  - **Workers 16 and over**: B08303e13
- **Educational Attainment for the Population 25 years and over**: B15003e22
- **Household Language by Household Limited English Speaking Status**: B16002e1
- **Poverty Status int he Past 12 months**: B17010e1
- **Aggregate Income Deficit**: B17011e1
- **Household Income in the Past 12 Months**: B19001e1
- **Public Assistance Income in the Past 12 Months**: B19057e1
- **Median Family Income in the Past 12 Months**: B19113e1
- **Receipt of Food Stamps/Snap in the past 12 months**: B22010e2
- **Tenure by Vehicle Available: No Vehicle Available**: B25044e3

When selecting a variable from the metadata table, you want to make sure that you select variables that end with the term **Estimate** and not **Margin of Error**. For example, if you were interested in the median age by sex, by total population, you'd select **MEDIAN AGE BY SEX: Total: Total Population - (Estimate)** which is defined in the B01002e1 column (Short_Name) and not the **MEDIAN AGE BY SEX: Total: Total Population - (Margin of Error)** record, which is represented by B01002m1. The Margin of Error is simply a figure indicating potential error in the output data, while the Estimate table contains the actual demographic and socioeconomic data for a particular variable.

7. Find the tables associated with the variables you want to test and make a note of them somewhere.

8. While these variables will provide a good starting point in terms of socio-economic and demographic data, you should also consider adding other variables like distance to city center, proximity to nearest bus stop, proximity to police stations, and perhaps other crime variables such as burglary, rape, homicide, and others. The point being that you should include as many potential variables as you can possibly find.

9. The ACS_2014_5YR_BG_53_WASHINGTON feature class includes a GEOID_Data field. Use the join functionality in **ArcMap** to join the feature class to the tables you identified earlier that contain the variables you are interested in testing. I would suggest joining them one at a time and then turning off the visibility of the columns you don't intend to use. This is described in more detail in the next step.

10. There will be a lot of columns attached to the feature class at this point, so you'll want to turn off any columns that you don't need. Right-click on the ACS_2014_5YR_BG_53_WASHINGTON layer and select **Properties** and go to the **Fields** tab. Turn off any fields you don't want visible.

11. The columns have seemingly arbitrary names, so you may also want to add an alias for each of the columns that are still visible simply to make it easier to understand the data in the column without having to constantly refer back to the metadata. This can be done in the Fields tab as well.

12. This completes the initial data preparation for this section, but there are a couple more data preparation things we need to do before running our regression analysis. In this step, spatially join the `VehicleTheft_Prj` layer to the `ACS_2014_5YR_BG_53_WASHINGTON` layer. This will create a `Count_` column containing the number of vehicle thefts for each block group in the `ACS_2014_5YR_BG_53_WASHINGTON` layer. Use the ArcGIS Desktop help system if you don't know how to spatially join a point feature class to a polygon feature class.

13. Normalize the count by creating a new `Float` data type field in the `ACS_2014_5YR_BG_53_WASHINGTON` layer (name is `NormVT`) and populating it by dividing the `Count_` field by the `AREA` of each block group.

14. Next, open a browser window and navigate to `http://www5.kingcounty.gov/gisdataportal`. Under **Option 2** on this page, scroll down to **Incorporated Areas of King County** and download this layer in shapefile format. It will actually download a ZIP archive file called `city_SHP.zip`.

15. Unzip the `city_SHP.zip` file somewhere on your computer. You can leave it in the `Downloads` folder if you'd like, because this file will only be used temporarily to define the extent of the study area.

16. In **ArcMap**, add the city shapefile that you just downloaded and select the polygon that defines the city of Seattle.

17. Use the **Select by Location...** tool in **ArcMap** to select features from the `ACS_2014_5YR_BG_53_WASHINGTON` layer that intersect with the selected city of Seattle polygon from the city layer. This can be accomplished by selecting the parameters as shown in the following screenshot. You'll want to make sure that the **Spatial selection method for target layer feature (s)** option is set to **have their centroid in the source layer feature**:

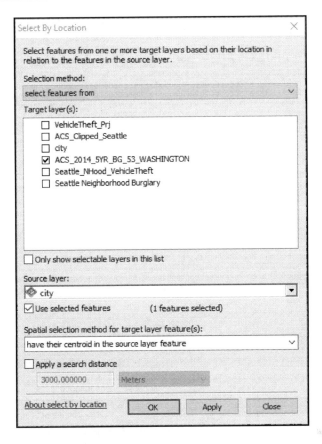

18. Export the selected features from ACS_2014_5YR_BG_53_WASHINGTON to a new layer. You can call the layer ACS_Seattle. You can save it wherever you'd like.

19. Project the new ACS_Seattle layer to NAD_1983_UTM_Zone_10N using the **Project** tool and name the output shapefile ACS_Seattle_Prj. Save it to your C:\GeospatialTraining\SpatialStats\Data\SeattleCrime folder.

20. Add the projected ACS_Seattle_Prj file to **ArcMap** and remove the ACS_Seattle, city, and ACS_2014_5YR_BG_53_WASHINGTON layers. These will no longer be needed.

Spatial Statistical Analysis

As you can see from the preceding detailed steps, data preparation is often the most time consuming aspect of analyzing a problem. With that out of the way, we can turn our attention to the actual analysis. In the following steps, you will use the Exploratory Regression tool to find combinations of exploratory variables for OLS:

1. The **Exploratory Regression** tool found in the **Modeling Spatial Relationships** toolset is an excellent way to quickly determine groups of variables that are important in Ordinary Least Squares regression. Without this tool, you'd need to manually select many different combinations of variables and run the OLS tool on each to determine their suitability for a model. If necessary, go back to Chapter 5, *Modeling Spatial Relationships with ArcGIS Tools*, for a full explanation of the Exploratory Regression tool before continuing.

2. Find the **Exploratory Regression** tool in the **Modeling Spatial Relationships** toolset and run the tool with the ACS_Seattle_Prj layer as the input features, and the normalized column of vehicle theft count (NormVT) you created in step 10 in the preceding section as the dependent variable. Select the potential fields to be used, review and adjust the search criteria according to what you learned in Chapter 5, *Modeling Spatial Relationships with ArcGIS Tools*, and run the tool.

3. Explore the output of the tool to check whether there are groups of explanatory variables suitable for an OLS model. Make a note of these groups (if any).

4. Now open the **Ordinary Least Squares** tool found in the **Modeling Spatial Relationships** toolset. Use ACS_Seattle_Prj as the input feature class, define the unique ID field, select NormVT as the dependent variable, and select a grouping of the explanatory variables you found from running the **Exploratory Regression** tool in step 1. Make sure that you include an output report file. Refer to Chapter 5, *Modeling Spatial Relationships with ArcGIS Tools*, if you need more information about how to run the OLS tool or interpret the output.

5. You will probably need to run the OLS tool multiple times using different sets of variables to find a good model, and you may even need to introduce some additional variables that you didn't include in your initial analysis.

6. Analyze your final OLS model. What did you learn about the variables that affect vehicle theft? Report your findings to the author at eric@geospatialtraining.com, so that your results can be compared with other readers and shared through the book website.

Summary

In this chapter, we used many of the tools found in the **Spatial Statistics Tools** toolbox to analyze vehicle theft in Seattle, WA. After downloading the data and doing some initial data preparation, which is often the most time consuming aspect of any GIS project, we used a variety of tools to get a better understanding of the data. Initially, we used some basic descriptive statistical tools to get a general understanding of the data. The **Central Feature** tool gave us an idea of where vehicle theft is centered in the area, and the **Directional Distribution** tool was used as a basic tool for understanding both the distribution and the directionality of the data. Later, we used the **Average Nearest Neighbor** tool to determine if the data formed a clustered, dispersed, or randomly spaced pattern. In our case, the data exhibited a strongly clustered pattern. Next, the **Hot Spot Analysis** tool was run, and it produced an output that indicated hot spots of vehicle theft in the central and north central areas of the city with cold spots in the northeast and northwest areas. Finally, after some additional data downloads and preparation, the **Exploratory Regression** and **Ordinary Least Squares** tools were used to define a general model that explains vehicle theft.

10
Application of Spatial Statistics to Real Estate Analysis

Lone Stone Realty, a fictional real estate brokerage located in the Stone Oak area of San Antonio, Texas, has contracted you to provide an analysis of residential sales for the metropolitan area. Using sales information for the past year, they would like to use your services to get a better understanding of the underlying geographic patterns that influence their business, guide their potential expansion efforts, and assist with marketing efforts.

Lone Star Realty currently has a single office location in the Stone Oak area and a large percentage of their business is conducted in this area. The brokerage focuses on assisting buyers and sellers within a price range of $250,000 to $400,000, and for the most part, within a roughly 5 square miles radius of the neighborhood. They would like to have you analyze a dataset of all residential sales from the past year to determine what areas have experienced a high volume of sales and which areas have been slow. They are also interested in finding any hidden neighborhoods where sales have been strong despite generally weak sales activity in the surrounding area. This information will then be used to drive marketing efforts for the next year.

The client is also interested in the possibility of expansion through the opening of a new office somewhere on the north side of the metropolitan area. Because they have been successful assisting buyers and sellers in this price range, they want to find a location that is similar to the existing Stone Oak location in terms of real estate characteristics.

They would like to have you assist with identifying potential locations for a second office somewhere on the north side of San Antonio. This second office location should have the same real estate characteristics as their existing office in Stone Oak.

You will provide the following output products for Lone Stone Realty:

- Hot spot/cold spot maps for all sales in the San Antonio metropolitan area grouped by the Zillow neighborhood.
- Hot spot/cold spot maps for sales in a range of $250,000 to $400,000 grouped by the Zillow neighborhood.
- Outlier maps for all sales in the range of $250,000 to $400,000 grouped by the Zillow neighborhood. Outlier maps will depict neighborhoods that are either experiencing high or low sales volume when the neighborhoods surrounding them would predict the opposite.
- Identification of potential neighborhoods for a new office location that are similar to the existing Stone Oak office.
- Identification of neighborhood groups that are similar in real estate characteristics that would be good for potential marketing efforts.

Our analysis will start by identifying neighborhoods that are similar to the existing office location in Stone Oak. We will also group the Zillow neighborhoods using the **Grouping Analysis** tool to identify similar groups of neighborhoods for marketing efforts.

Obtaining the Zillow real estate datasets

For this case study, we'll use two datasets including a point dataset containing all residential real estate sales in the San Antonio, TX area, and a Zillow neighborhood boundaries dataset for the same area:

1. Open a web browser and go to
   http://www.zillow.com/howto/api/neighborhood-boundaries.htm.
2. You should see a link for **Texas Neighborhood Boundaries**. Click on this link to download a file called ZillowNeighborhoods-TX.zip.
3. Extract this file to the C:\GeospatialTraining\SpatialStats\RealEstate folder.
4. This will create a new Zillowneighborhoods-TX folder, inside which is a single shapefile containing the Zillow neighborhood boundaries for Texas.

Data preparation

As with almost all GIS projects, there is a considerable amount of data preparation work that must be done before the analysis can begin:

1. Open **ArcMap** with the SanAntonioRealEstate.mxd file found in your C:\GeospatialTraining\SpatialStats folder.

2. Remove or turn off the visibility of the BexarCountyCensusBlockGroups layer.

3. Add the ZillowNeighborhoods-TX shapefile. You should now have layers for ResidentialSales, ZillowNeighborhoods-TX, and a basemap layer.

 The Zillow neighborhoods data doesn't include full coverage of every area within the San Antonio metropolitan area.

4. Obtain a count of the number of sales along with the average and sum of each numeric attribute for each neighborhood using the spatial join functionality in ArcMap. To accomplish this, right-click on the ZillowNeighborhoods-TX layer and navigate to **Joins and Relates | Join**.

5. In the **Join Data** dialog, define the input parameters as shown in the following screenshot. The output feature class can be called `ZillowNeighborhoods_Joined.shp` and placed in the `ZillowNeighborhoods-TX` folder:

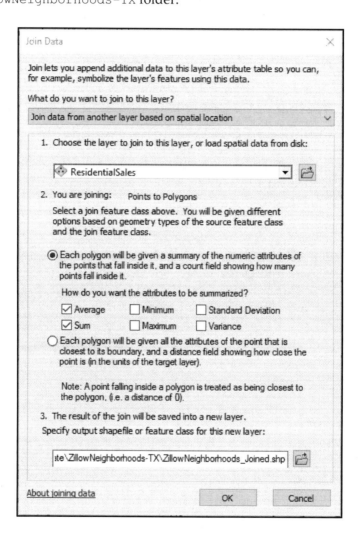

6. You may want to turn off some of the fields that are created in the `ZillowNeighborhoods_Joined.shp` file so that only the fields that we need for the analysis are visible. These include `NAME`, `Count_`, `Avg_DOM`, and `Avg_SqFt`, and `Avg_Sold_P`, `Avg_BR`, `Avg_FB`, and `Avg_HB`. To do this, open the **Properties** dialog box for the layer. Go to the **Fields** tab, and turn off all layers except those specified earlier. When you perform an **Identify** operation on any of the features in this layer, you should now see something similar to the following screenshot:

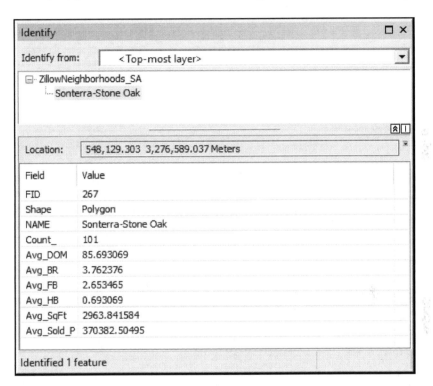

7. Next, we'll normalize the number of sales by the size of each neighborhood to take out size as the primary determinant of the number of sales. This shapefile doesn't contain an `AREA` field or any other field that we can use for the normalization. However, we can create and calculate the contents of an `AREA` field. Add a new field to the attribute table of the `ZillowNeighborhoods_Joined` shapefile and call it `AREA`. It should be defined as a `DOUBLE` data type.

8. Right-click on the new field and select **Calculate Geometry**. Select the parameters as shown in the following screenshot and click on **OK** to populate the records:

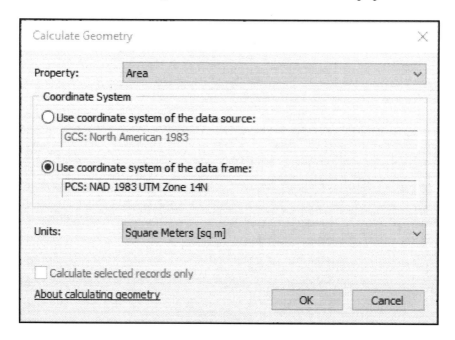

9. Create a new field called NormCnt (define it as a DOUBLE data type) and populate this field by dividing the Count_ field by the AREA field.

10. Since we're only interested in neighborhoods in the San Antonio metro area. Let's isolate these by manually selecting all the neighborhoods as shown in the following screenshot and exporting them to a new shapefile called ZillowNeighborhoods_SA.shp. You can save it in the C:\GeospatialTraining\SpatialStats\Data\RealEstate\ZillowNeighborhoods-TX folder. Add the new layer to ArcMap when prompted:

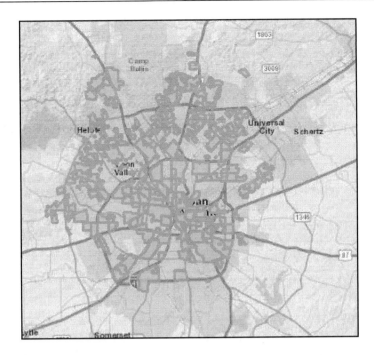

11. Remove the `ZillowNeighborhoods_Joined` and `ZillowNeighborhoods-TX` layers from **ArcMap**. These layers will no longer be needed. Now we're ready to start the analysis.

Finding similar neighborhoods

In this section of the project, you will identify neighborhoods that are similar to the Stone Oak neighborhood where Lone Star Realty has it's current office location with respect to some basic real estate characteristics of the area. The results of this analysis will be used later in the chapter when we combine some additional analysis with the similarity search.

You will also generate a dataset that groups neighborhoods based on various real estate sales characteristics. Lone Star Realty will then use these groups to focus marketing efforts on those areas most common to its existing market area. Later in the chapter, we'll also identify neighborhoods where sales in the target market for Lone Star Realty have been strong over the past year and match those with the grouped neighborhoods defined by the grouping analysis.

The Similarity Search tool

The **Similarity Search** tool is used to identify candidate features that are most similar or most dissimilar to one or more input features based on the attributes of a feature. Part of the analysis for this project involves finding neighborhoods that are similar to others so that we can make some recommendations for potential new office locations. This type of analysis is also useful for agents who are showing properties to potential buyers. When filtering lists of potential properties to show buyers, the output from this analysis can help agents narrow the potential neighborhoods based on their search criteria:

1. Find the Stone Oak neighborhood in the `ZillowNeighborhoods_SA` layer and select this feature. The easiest way to do this is to use the **Select by Attributes...** tool and define an attribute search where `NAME` is set to `Stone Oak`. There are several attributes that contain the term Stone Oak such as Stone Oak Communities and others. However, to keep the analysis simple, simply use the term `Stone Oak`. This neighborhood is found in the far northern end of the San Antonio metropolitan area, as shown in the following screenshot:

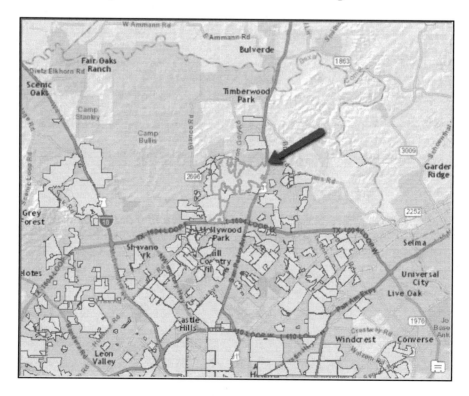

2. Right-click on the `ZillowNeighborhoods_SA` layer and navigate to **Selection |
Create Layer from Selected Features**. This will create a new layer called
`ZillowNeighborhoods_SA selection` and add it to the ArcMap **Table Of
Contents** pane.

3. Switch the selection set on the `ZillowNeighborhoods_SA` layer. To accomplish
this, right-click on the `ZillowNeighborhoods_SA` layer and then navigate to
Selection | Switch Selection. This step creates a selection set containing all
features except the Stone Oak neighborhood. You don't want to match the same
feature that is being used as the input feature.

4. Open the **Similarity Search** tool from the **Spatial Statistics Tools** toolbox and fill
in the parameters as defined here and shown in the following screenshot. The
tool will use the `Stone Oak` feature found in the new selection layer as the input
feature and then match other features from the `ZillowNeighborhoods_SA`
layer that are similar to Stone Oak:

   - **Input Features to Match**: `ZillowNeighborhoods_SA selection`
   - **Candidate Features**: `ZillowNeighborhoods_SA`
   - **Output Features**: In the default database, create a feature class called
     `ZillowNeighborhoods_Similar`
   - **Most Or Least Similar**: `MOST _SIMILAR`
   - **Match Method**: `ATTRIBUTE_VALUE`
   - **Number Of Results**: 5
   - **Attributes Of Interest**: `Avg_DOM, Avg_BR, Avg_FB, Avg_HB,
     Avg_SqFt, Avg_Sold_P, NormCnt.`
   - **Additional Options: Fields to Append**: `Name, Avg_DOM, Avg_BR,
     Avg_FB, Avg_HB, Avg_SqFt, Avg_Sold_P,` and `NormCnt`

You'll see something like this:

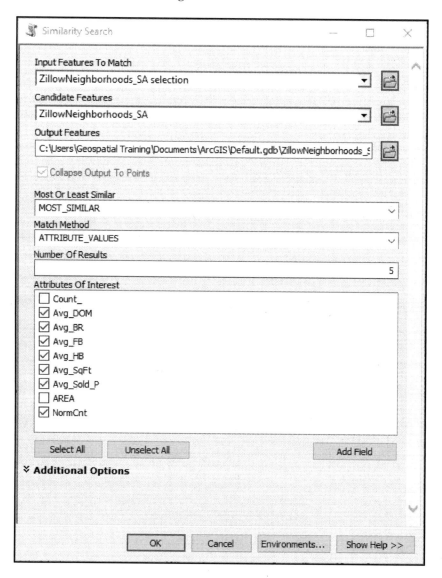

5. Click on **OK** to execute the tool.
6. The output from this tool will include statistics that are written to the progress dialog along with a new layer that is added to the map. In the following screenshot, you will see the output written to the progress dialog. This includes a summary of attributes of interest as well as a ranking of the most similar locations. You may not see exactly the same results as are displayed in the following screenshot:

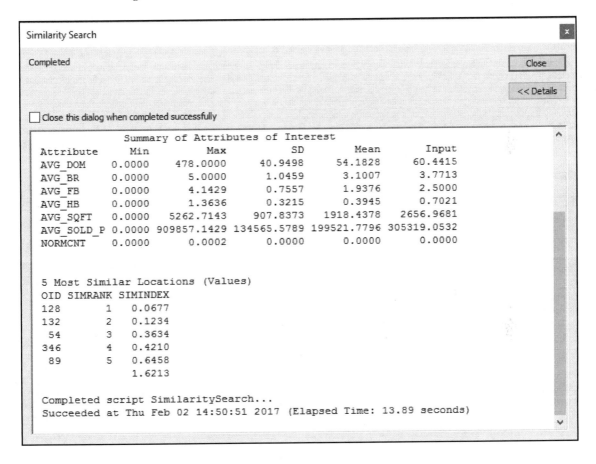

7. The map includes a new layer called `ZillowNeighorhoods_SA_Similar` (or something similar based on the name you gave to the output feature class) that is symbolized according to the similarity index as shown in the following screenshot. The Stone Oak neighborhood is symbolized by a red dot. In order, the neighborhoods identified as most similar to Stone Oak include Hills and Dales, Hunters Creek, Countryside San Pedro, Vista Del Norte, and Encino Park. These five neighborhoods represent potential locations for a new office location where the market area is similar to the existing Stone Oak location. This analysis could be expanded to include additional potential locations by re-running the tool and selecting a higher number of results:

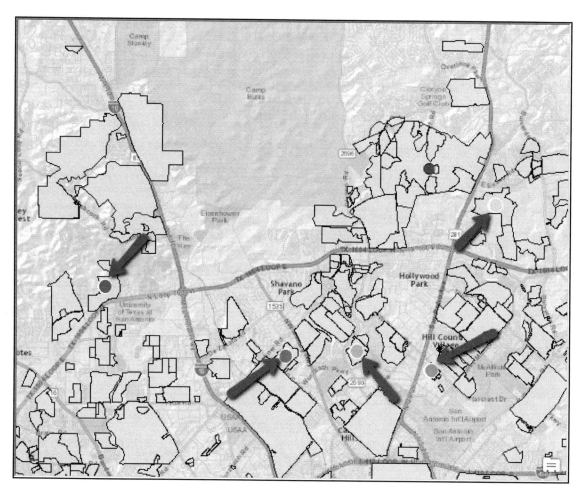

8. Remove the `ZillowNeighborhoods_SA selection` layer from the ArcMap **table of contents** pane.

9. Remove any selections by navigating to **Selection | Clear Selected Features**.

10. Save the map document.

The Grouping Analysis tool

The **Grouping Analysis** tool groups features based on feature attributes as well as optional spatial/temporal constraints. The output of this tool is the creation of distinct groups of data where the features that are part of the group are as similar as possible and between groups are as dissimilar as possible. Including this tool in the analysis of similar neighborhoods is an extension of what you learned by running the **Similarity Search** tool:

1. The `ZillowNeighborhoods_SA` layer can be used in the grouping analysis. The **Grouping Analysis** tool requires a unique identifier field as one of the input parameters. This layer doesn't have a field that can be used as a unique identifier, so open the attribute table, add a field called `OID_` that is of the `Long` data type, and populate the contents of this field using the contents of the `FID` field.

2. The input feature class for the **Grouping Analysis** tool needs to be projected since it requires some distance calculations. Find the **Project** tool found in the **Data Management** toolbox, project the `ZillowNeighborhoods_SA` shapefile to a new shapefile called `ZillowNeighborhoods_SA_Prj.shp`, and place it in the `C:\GeospatialTraining\SpatialStats\Data\RealEstate\ZillowNeighborhoods-TX` folder. The output coordinate system should be `NAD_1983_UTM_Zone_14N`.

3. You can remove the `ZillowNeighborhoods_SA` layer from **ArcMap** as it will no longer be needed.

4. Open the **Grouping Analysis** tool found in the **Spatial Statistics Tools** toolbox and define the following parameters:
   - **Input Features**: `ZillowNeighborhoods_SA_Prj`
   - **Unique ID Field**: `OID_`
   - **Output Feature Class**: In the default geodatabase (`Default.gdb`), create an output feature class called `ZillowNeighborhoods_Group`
   - **Number of Groups**: 4
   - **Analysis Fields**: `Avg_DOM, Avg_BR, Avg_FB, Avg_HB, Avg_SqFt, Avg_Sold_P, NormCnt`
   - **Spatial Constraints**: `NO_SPATIAL_CONSTRAINT`
   - **Initialization Method**: `FIND_SEED_LOCATIONS`

- **Output Report File**:
  `C:\GeospatialTraining\SpatialStats\RE_GroupingAnalysis.pdf`

  For all other parameters, use the default values provided.

5. Click on the **OK** button to execute the tool.
6. The **Grouping Analysis** tool will create several outputs such as the summary statistics written to the progress dialog, an output report, and a new feature class that will be added to the ArcMap **Table Of Contents** pane.
7. The output map should appear as shown in the following screenshot and is color coded by group. Remember that your output may not appear exactly as that shown here; your groups may appear slightly different than what you see in the following screenshot:

8. Open the `RE_GroupingAnalysis.pdf` file to take a look at the output box plots for a better understanding of the variables that were included in the analysis. We can make general observations about each of these groups, including the following:

   - **Group 1 (blue group)**: This generally has below global median values for all variables.
   - **Group 2 (red group)**: This has significantly above global median values for almost all variables.
   - **Group 3 (green group)**: This has preceding global media values for almost all variables.
   - **Group 4 (orange group)**: Features assigned to this group had null values for all features. There weren't any sales in these neighborhoods, so they should be removed from the analysis since we have no data in this case.

   The current office location in Stone Oak falls within the green group. Because the client would like to concentrate their marketing efforts on similar neighborhoods, we can provide a list of the neighborhoods identified in green to use in their marketing efforts. This could also supplement our analysis of potential locations for new office locations.

9. Open the attribute table for the `ZillowNeighborhoods_Group` layer. The `SS_GROUP` field contains the group number. Use the **Select by Attributes...** tool to select records where `SS_GROUP` is equal to 3.

10. Export the selected set of features to a new shapefile called `Zillow_Neighborhoods_Group3` and place it in the `ZillowNeighborhoods-TX` folder. Lone Star Realty could use the boundaries of this layer in a direct marketing campaign by obtaining lists of addresses within each neighborhood and then sending direct mail or directing other marketing techniques to these areas. We'll use the `Zillow_Neighborhoods_Group3` layer in a later section of this chapter.

11. For now, you can turn off the visibility of the layers created during the similarity search and grouping analysis.

12. Save the map document.

Finding areas of high real estate sales activity

In this section of the study, we'll identify neighborhoods with high and low sales activity. This will include hot spot maps for both real estate activity in general as well as sales in our target range of $250,000 to $400,000. We'll also use the **Cluster and Outlier Analysis** tool to identify any potentially hidden, or outlier, neighborhoods where sales activity is significantly higher than surrounding neighborhoods that are experiencing low sales activity and vice versa.

Running the Hot Spot Analysis tool

We'll use the **Hot Spot Analysis** tool to generate two hot spot maps: one for all sales in the metropolitan area and another for sales within a range of $250,000 to $400,000:

1. If necessary, open ArcMap with the `SanAntonioRealEstate` map document.
2. Open the **Hot Spot Analysis** tool.
3. The `ZillowNeighborhoods_SA_Prj` layer has a `NormCnt` field that was created in the *Data preparation* section of this chapter. This field was calculated by dividing the contents of the `Count_` field (the total number of residential sales by neighborhood) by the `AREA` field. Select the `ZillowNeighborhoods_SA_Prj` layer as **Input Feature Class**, and `NormCnt` as **Input Field** along with the other parameters you see in the following screenshot. Remember that the output location and name can be of your choice, but it is easier to create it in the default geodatabase (`Default.gdb`). For the **Conceptualization of Spatial Relationships** parameter, select `FIXED_DISTANCE` but leave the **Distance Band** parameter empty to let the tool define an appropriate distance:

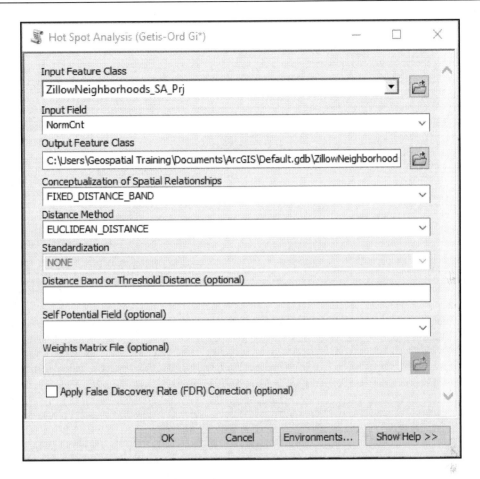

4. Click on **OK** to execute the tool.

5. The output feature class, displayed in the following screenshot, is the result of our initial hot spot analysis of all residential sales across the Zillow neighborhoods. The hottest areas according to this analysis are on the first northwest and northeast sides of the study area. However, for this particular study, we want to refine the analysis of sales between $250,000 and $400,000, so we'll run the tool again with only sales that occurred in that range of sales price:

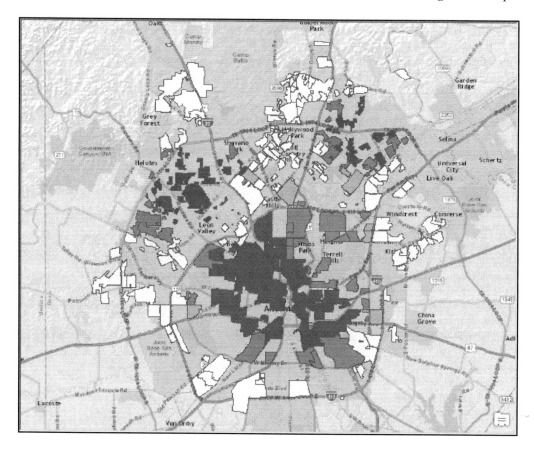

6. Use the **Select by Attributes...** tool to select features from the ResidentialSales layer where the Sold_Price field is between $250,000 and $400,000. This should result in the selection of 6,553 records.

7. Export the selected features to a new shapefile called ResidentialSales_TargetMarket.shp in the C:\GeospatialTraining\SpatialStats\Data\RealEstate folder. Add the layer to **ArcMap**.

8. Spatially join the `ResidentialSales_TargetMarket` layer to the `ZillowNeigborhoods_SA_Prj` layer to create a new layer called `ZillowNeigborhoods_SA_Prj_Target.shp` in the `ZillowNeighborhoods-TX` folder. A new `Count_1` field will be added to the `ZillowNeighborhoods_SA_Prj_Target` layer.

9. Run the **Hot Spot Analysis** tool with this new layer as the input feature class and `Count_1` as the input field. The output feature class should be called `Zillow_SA_Prj_TM`. You can define the location for this output feature class as the default geodatabase (`Default.gdb`). The rest of the input parameters should remain the same as the last run of this tool.

10. Click on **OK** to run the tool. The output should appear as shown in the following screenshot:

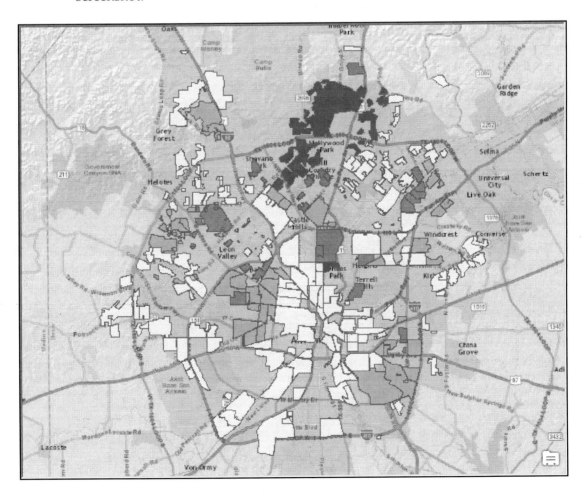

11. The result of the hot spot analysis (`Zillow_SA_Prj_TM`) with the target market ($250,000 to $400,000) data reveals some interesting patterns for Lone Star Realty. For this price range, the hot spots are primarily located in the north central location of the metropolitan area. The Stone Oak neighborhood, where Lone Star Realty's current office is located, is part of this hot spot, and some of the other neighborhoods identified as being in a hot spot might be good for the second office location.

12. Now we'll use the **Cluster and Outlier Analysis** tool to check whether we can identify any hidden, outlier neighborhoods within our target market. Here we define hidden neighborhoods as neighborhoods that are showing a positive sales volume but are surrounded by neighborhoods that are showing a negative sales volume. Open the **Cluster and Outlier Analysis** tool found in the **Spatial Statistics Tools** toolbox. Fill in the input parameters as shown in the following screenshot. You can define the name of the output feature class as `ZillowNeighborhood_SA_Prj_Outliers` in the default geodatabase (`Default.gdb`):

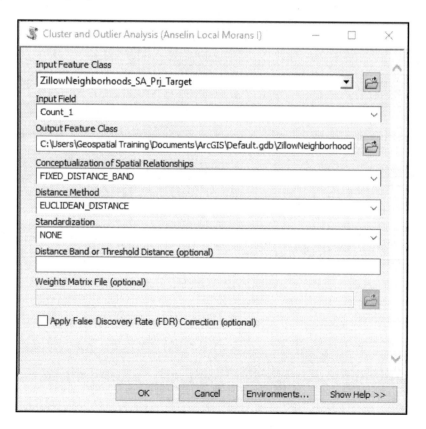

13. The output layer reveals some interesting information. Refer to the following screenshot. The neighborhoods in dark red are the areas that are experiencing high sales volume in our target market, whereas the neighborhoods surrounding this neighborhood are either experiencing low sales activity or no significant sales activity. In contrast, areas in blue are experiencing lower sales volume compared to their surrounding neighborhoods:

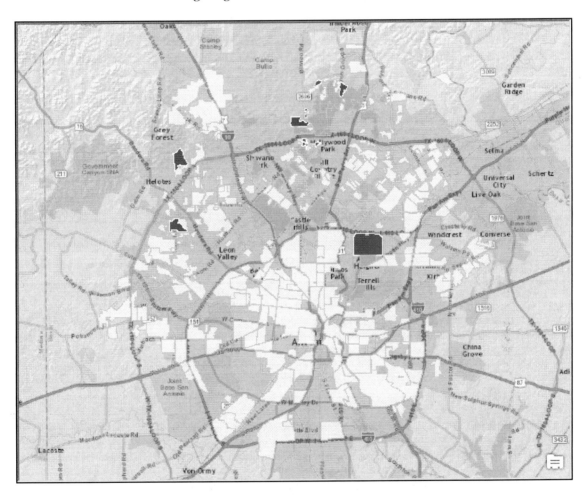

14. You can now remove a couple layers from your ArcMap **Table Of Contents** pane including the `ZillowNeighborhoods_SA_Prj_Target` and `ResidentialSales_TargetMarket` layers.

15. Save the map document.

    Based on our hot spot and cluster and outlier analysis, we have identified some important trends in the target market for Lone Star Realty, which is home sales in a range of $250,000 to $400,000. Most of the hot spots for this target market are in the same general area as the existing office location for Lone Star Realty. One of the aspects of this study is to help Lone Star Realty identify a neighborhood for potential expansion to a second office. Based on the information we now have as a result of this analysis, we can create a subset of neighborhoods that are identified as hot spots for the Lone Star Realty target market.

16. In this step, we'll subset some records from the `Zillow_SA_Prj_TM` layer that have been identified as hot spots for our target market sales range. Use the **Select by Attributes...** tool to create a new selection set from this layer where the `Gi_Bin` field contains the value 3. This should select all records that have been identified as hot spot - 99% confidence level (dark red). You can see the result of this operation in the following screenshot:

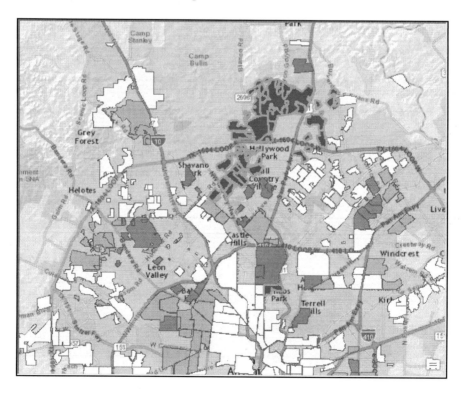

17. Next, select any features that were identified as low-high outliers (dark blue) in the `ZillowNeighborhood_SA_Prj_Outliers` layer. These are neighborhoods experiencing slower growth than would be expected based on the results of neighborhoods that surround them. To select these features, use the **Select by Attributes...** tool to select features where the `COType` field is equal to `LH`:

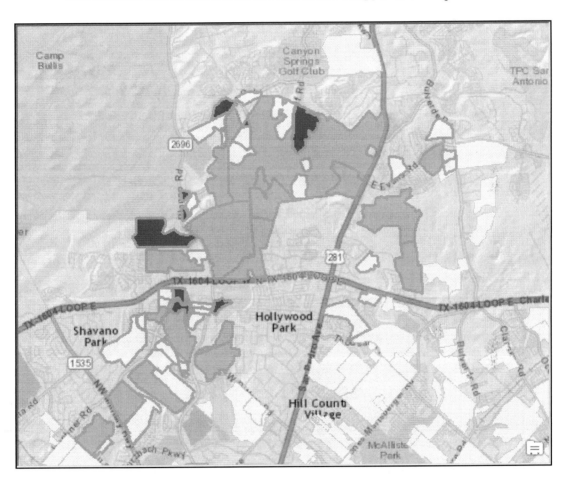

18. Now, use the **Select by Location...** tool to remove any selected features from the Zillow_SA_Prj_TM layer that are the same as any records selected in the ZillowNeighborhood_SA_Prj_Outliers layer. The following screenshot displays the parameters you should select when running this tool:

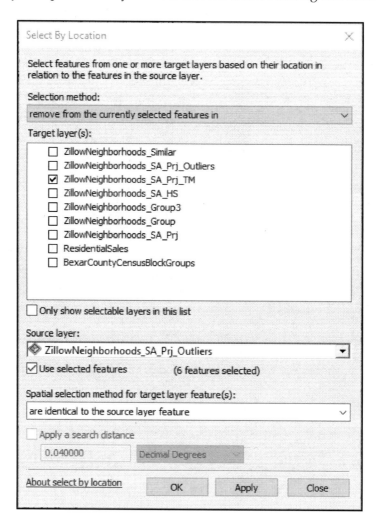

19. Next, create a new selection set on the
    `ZillowNeighborhood_SA_Prj_Outliers` layer where only features identified
    as high-low outliers are selected. These are features colored in dark red. You can
    use the **Select by Attributes...** tool to create this selection by selecting features
    where the `COType` field is equal to `HL`. You can see the result in the following
    screenshot:

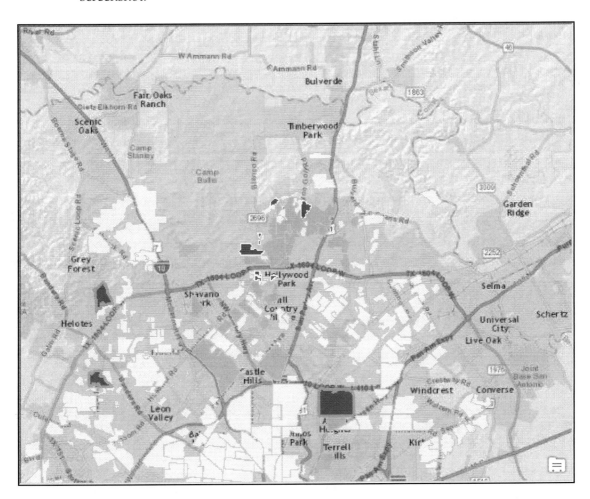

20. Finally, add the features that were identified in the last step to the existing selection set on the `Zillow_SA_Prj_TM` layer. Use the **Select by Location...** tool parameters shown in the following screenshot to accomplish this:

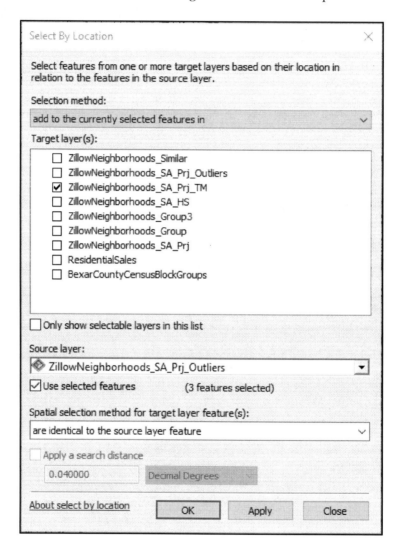

21. The final selection set for the `Zillow_SA_Prj_TM` layer should appear as shown in the following screenshot. This includes all neighborhoods marked as hot spots for our target market of $250,000 to $400,000 with any neighborhoods identified as low-high outliers (low sales volume neighborhoods surrounded by high sales volume neighborhoods) removed, and any neighborhoods identified as high-low outliers (high sales volume neighborhoods surrounded by low sales volume neighborhoods) added. Another way of saying this is that we are removing hidden, outlier neighborhoods where the pattern is unexpectedly low and adding hidden, outlier neighborhoods where the pattern is unexpectedly high:

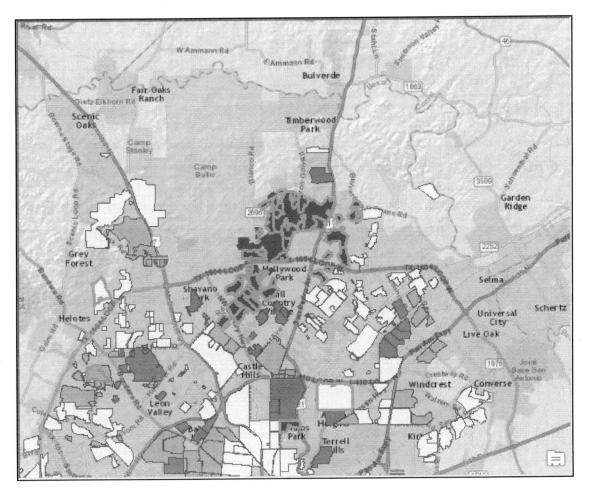

22. Finally, export the selected records from `Zillow_SA_Prj_TM` to a new shapefile called `PotentialNeighborhoodExpansion` and store it in the `C:\GeospatialTraining\SpatialStats\Data\RealEstate` folder. Add the layer to ArcMap and it should appear as follows:

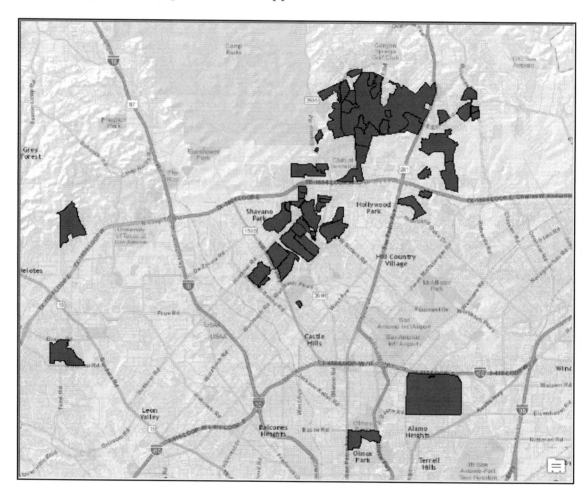

23. In the next step, we'll analyze the output of the analysis we have performed in this chapter to check whether we can make some final recommendations for Lone Star Realty.

Recommendations for the client

Lone Star Realty has asked assistance in providing some recommendations and analysis for their real estate practice. They are considering expansion plans to include the opening of a second office that would continue to focus on their target market of buyers and sellers in a price range of $250,000 to $400,000. To that end, our analysis has revealed some interesting information that we think is beneficial:

1. In ArcMap, turn on the `ZillowNeighborhoods_Similar` and `PotentialNeighborhoodExpansion` layers as shown in the following screenshot:

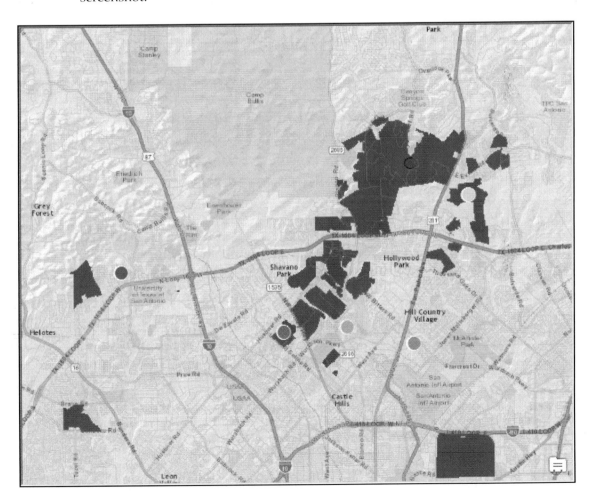

2. The current office is located in the far northern section of the metropolitan area and is well located for servicing real estate sales in their target market. It is surrounded by a number of neighborhoods that are experiencing high sales activity.

> Our similarity search for neighborhoods in San Antonio that have the same characteristics in terms of variables such as average sales price, number of bedrooms and baths, and number of days on market before a house sells has revealed several potential candidate locations with three of these potential locations located south of TX 1604 Loop. Our analysis of hot spot neighborhoods for this target market has also revealed a cluster of neighborhoods in the same general area. In our opinion, this area would make an excellent location for a potential second office location:

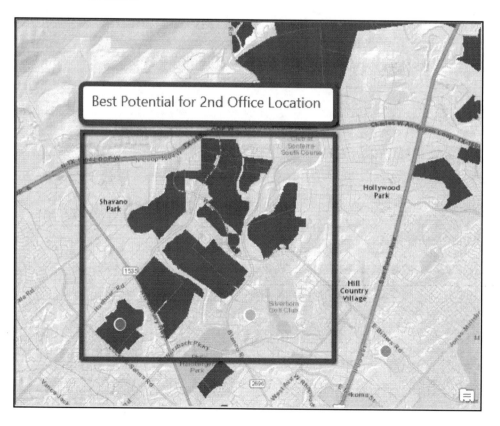

An alternative location in the **Encino Park** neighborhood, shown in the following screenshot, just east of **Highway 281** could also prove to be a good location for the second office. However, this location is near the first office and might not provide as much benefit as a second location further to the south:

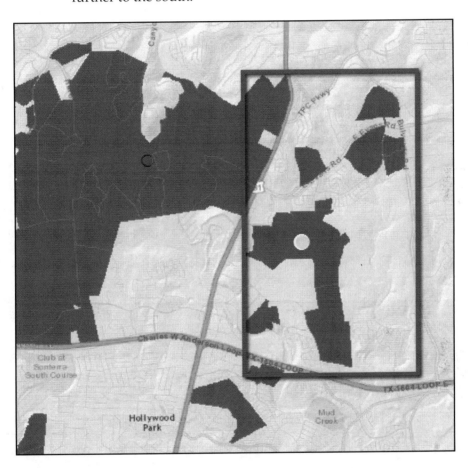

The results of our grouping analysis should also be beneficial for the marketing efforts of Lone Star Realty. Turn on the ZillowNeighborhoods_Group3 layer. You may also need to move it toward the top of the table of contents. This layer contains neighborhoods identified as being most similar to the current target market for Lone Star Realty. These neighborhoods, particularly those near their current office and potential second office, would be excellent targets for targeted marketing efforts:

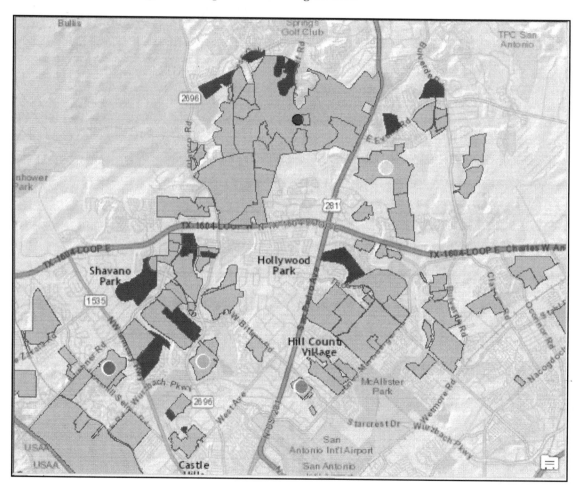

Summary

In this chapter, we used many of the tools found in the **Spatial Statistics Tools** toolbox to real estate sales in San Antonio, Texas. After some data preparation work, we used the **Similarity Search** and **Grouping Analysis** tools to determine neighborhoods that are most similar to the current office location of Lone Star Realty. We also used the **Hot Spot Analysis** and **Outlier and Cluster Analysis** tools to determine neighborhood hot spots and outliers for the Lone Star Realty target market of homes in the $250,000 to $400,000 range. Finally, we combined the results of our analysis to define an area that we believe would be an optimal location for a second office location.

Index

Made in the USA
Middletown, DE
02 May 2018